TEACHING Rhetorica
THEORY, PEDAGOGY, PRACTICE

Edited by
KATE RONALD AND JOY RITCHIE

Boynton/Cook
HEINEMANN
Portsmouth, NH

Boynton/Cook Publishers, Inc.
A subsidiary of Reed Elsevier Inc.
361 Hanover Street
Portsmouth, NH 03801–3912
www.boyntoncook.com

Offices and agents throughout the world

The editors and publisher wish to thank those who have generously given permission to reprint borrowed material:

Portions of "Documenting Violations: A Pedagogy of Rhetorical Witnessing and the Spectacle of Distant Suffering" by Wendy Hesford originally appeared in *Biography: An Interdisciplinary Quarterly* 27.1 (Winter 2004): 104–144. Copyright © 2004 by the Biographical Research Center. Used by permission.

Library of Congress Cataloging-in-Publication Data
Teaching rhetorica: theory, pedagogy, practice / edited by Kate Ronald
  and Joy Ritchie.
    p. cm.
  Includes bibliographical references.
  ISBN-13: 978-0-86709-589-0 (acid-free paper)
  ISBN-10: 0-86709-589-X (acid-free paper)
  1. English language—Rhetoric.   2. English language—Rhetoric—Study
and teaching.   3. Feminism and literature.   I. Ronald, Kate.
II. Ritchie, Joy S.
  PE1408.T368 2006
  808'.042071—dc22   2006023920

Editor: Charles I. Schuster
Production service: Lisa S. Garboski, bookworks
Production: Patricia I. Adams
Typesetter: TechBooks
Cover design: Jenny Jensen Greenleaf
Manufacturing: Steve Bernier

Printed in the United States of America on acid-free paper
10 09 08 07 06   VP   1 2 3 4 5

For Dennis Alcorn
and
George Ritchie

Contents

Acknowledgments   *vii*

About the Authors   *ix*

Introduction: Asking "So What?": Expansive Pedagogies
of Experience and Action
Kate Ronald and Joy Ritchie   1

1 Crimes of Writing and Reading
Andrea Lunsford and Lisa Ede   13

2 Coming Out: Or, How Adrienne Rich's Feminist Theory Complicates
Intersections of Rhetoric and Composition Studies, Cultural Studies, and
Writing Program Administration
Krista Ratcliffe   31

3 Shifting the Center of Gravity: The Rhetorics of Radical Feminist
Pedagogy, 1968–1975
Kathryn T. Flannery   48

4 "Each One, Pull One": Womanist Rhetoric and Black Feminist
Pedagogy in the Writing Classroom
Gwendolyn D. Pough   66

5 *Dissoi Logoi*: Women's Rhetoric and Classroom Practice
Beth Daniell   82

6 Documenting Violations: Rhetorical Witnessing and the Spectacle
of Distant Suffering as Pedagogy
Wendy S. Hesford   93

7 Objects, Memory, and Narrative: New Notes
Toward Materialist Rhetoric
Marguerite Helmers   114

8 Making Room for New Subjects: Feminist Interruptions
of Critical Pedagogy Rhetorics
Shari Stenberg   131

9 Taking Sides
Nancy Welch   147

10 Gender, Rhetorics, and Globalization: Rethinking the Spaces
and Locations of Women's Rhetorics in Our Field
Eileen E. Schell   160

Works Cited   *175*

Acknowledgments

The inspiration for this collection of essays came from the hundreds of students we have taught in courses on the rhetoric of women writers, in rhetorical theory, and in composition over the past decade as we've tried to answer a crucial question that the emerging canon of women's rhetoric posed for us every semester: What difference does this new body of work make to our teaching as well as to our scholarship? We are especially indebted to all our students who have helped enrich our pursuit of answers to that question. As readers may note, we include many of their voices and their insights in our introduction to this volume. Among the many students who have been most important to our work are Lisa Shaver, Cristy Beemer, Sarah Bowles, Jen Cello, Jay Damage, Elizabeth MacKay, and Shawn Rushford from Miami University, and Christine Stewart-Nunez, Whitney Douglas, Eric Turley, and Virginia Crisco from the University of Nebraska—Lincoln.

The Coalition of Scholars in the History of Rhetoric and the Biennial Conference on Feminism(s) and Rhetoric(s) also have provided us with stimulating and supportive forums in which to extend our thinking. We are also indebted to the insight of colleagues in our home departments and around the country who have challenged us through their scholarship and teaching. Many of them are authors of essays collected here, but others include Hepsie Roskelly, Kathy Boardman, Donna Qualley, Elizabeth Chiseri-Strater, Jeanne Williams, Jackie Jones Royster, Cheryl Glenn, Susan Jarratt, Lillian Bridwell Bowles, Brenda Jo Brueggeman, and Hildy Miller.

Most of all we are indebted to our editorial assistant, Cristy Beemer, for her tenacious, meticulous, and scholarly attention to details.

About the Authors

Beth Daniell has taught composition, composition theory, women's studies, rhetoric, and literacy studies at West Virginia University, Clemson University, and the University of Alabama. She has written *A Communion of Friendship: Literacy, Spiritual Practice* (2001, Southern Illinois UP) and coedited, with Peter Mortensen, *Women and Literacy: Local and Global Inquiries for a New Century* (to be published in 2006 by the NCTE/LEA Series on Literacy and Composition). Part of the Symposium on Rhetoric and Tradition, she continues examining reading and rhetorical practice. Beth is now Director of Composition at Kennesaw State University and is so happy to be back home in Atlanta that she only rarely cusses the traffic.

Lisa Ede is professor of English and director of the Center for Writing and Learning at Oregon State University. With Andrea Lunsford, she has published *Singular Texts/Plural Authors: Perspectives on Collaborative Writing* and *Selected Essays of Robert J. Connors*. Her most recent book is *Situating Composition: Composition Studies and the Politics of Location.*

Kathryn Thoms Flannery is professor of English and women's studies at the University of Pittsburgh and the author of *The Emperor's New Clothes: Literature, Literacy, and the Ideology of Style* and *Feminist Literacies: 1968–1975.* She currently serves as director of women's studies and enjoys teaching feminist poetry, feminist theory, and literacy studies.

Marguerite Helmers is professor of English at the University of Wisconsin—Oshkosh. She received a PhD in rhetoric and composition from the University of Wisconsin—Milwaukee. She is the author of *Writing Students* (1995), editor of *Intertexts: Reading Pedagogy in College Writing Classrooms* (2002), and coeditor with Charles Hill of *Defining Visual Rhetorics* (2004). She has contributed articles to the scholarly journals *College English*, the *Journal of Advanced Composition*, and the electronic journals *Enculturation* and *Kairos.* She has received several awards inside and outside the university: the James Berlin Outstanding Dissertation Award from the National Council of Teachers of English, the Distinguished Teaching Award at the University of Wisconsin—Oshkosh, and the Kimball Foundation Award for Excellence, and was a Fellow of the Center for Twentieth Century Studies in 1999–2000.

Wendy S. Hesford is an associate professor of English and director of the first-year writing program at the Ohio State University. She is the author of *Framing Identities: Autobiography and the Politics of Pedagogy* (University of Minnesota Press, 1999) and coeditor with Wendy Kozol of two collections:

Haunting Violations: Feminist Criticism and the Crisis of the "Real" (University of Illinois Press, 2001), and *Just Advocacy? Women's Human Rights, Transnational Feminisms, and the Politics of Representation* (Rutgers University Press, 2005). Her forthcoming books include a textbook with Brenda Brueggemann, *Rhetorical Visions: Reading and Writing in a Visual Culture* (Prentice Hall, 2007), and the single-authored book *Spectacular Rhetorics: Human Rights and the Trauma of Representation. Spectacular Rhetorics* will offer a rhetorical and cultural analysis of cinematic and literary representations of human rights violations against women and women's human rights activism in the late twentieth and early twenty-first centuries.

Andrea Lunsford is the Louise Hewlett Nixon Professor of English and Humanities and director of the Program in Writing and Rhetoric at Stanford University. She has designed and taught undergraduate and graduate courses in writing history and theory, rhetoric, literacy studies, and intellectual property and is the author or coauthor of fourteen books, including *The Everyday Writer; Essays on Classical Rhetoric and Modern Discourse; Singular Texts/Plural Authors: Perspectives on Collaborative Writing;* and *Reclaiming Rhetorica: Women in the History of Rhetoric,* as well as numerous chapters and articles. Her most recent book, with Lahoucine Ouzgane, is *Exploring Borderlands: Composition and Postcolonial Studies.*

Gwendolyn D. Pough is associate professor of women's studies, writing, and rhetoric at Syracuse University. She is the author of various essays and articles on black feminism and black rhetorical traditions. Her book, *Check It While I Wreck It: Black Womanhood, Hip-Hop Culture and the Public Sphere,* was published by Northeastern University Press. She writes fiction under the pen name Gwyneth Bolton. Her published novels are *I'm Gonna Make You Love Me* (Genesis Press, March 2006) and *If Only You Knew* (Harlequin Books, July 2006)

Krista Ratcliffe is an associate professor of English at Marquette University in Milwaukee, Wisconsin, where she directs the First-Year English program and teaches undergraduate and graduate courses in rhetoric and composition theory, writing, autobiography, and women's literature. She has served as president of NCTE's College Forum and as president of the Coalition of Women Scholars in the History of Rhetoric. Her research focuses on intersections of rhetorical theory, feminist theory, and composition pedagogy. Her publications include *Anglo-American Feminist Challenges to the Rhetorical Tradition: Virginia Woolf, Mary Daly, Adrienne Rich* (SIUP, 1996), *Who's Having This Baby* with Helen Sterk, Carla Hay, Alice Kehoe, and Leona VandeVusse (Michigan State UP, 2002), and *Rhetorical Listening: Identification, Gender, Whiteness* (SIUP 2005); her articles and reviews have appeared in edited collections as well as in *CCC, JAC, Rhetoric Review,* and *College English.*

Joy Ritchie is Professor of English and Women's Studies and Chair of the Department of English at the University of Nebraska—Lincoln. When she can, she teaches graduate and undergraduate classes in writing and rhetoric, English Education, and Women's Studies. Her publications include *Teacher Narrative as Critical Inquiry: Rewriting the Script*, co-authored with David Wilson (Teachers College, 2000) and *Available Means: An Anthology of Women's Rhetoric(s)* (Pittsburgh, 2001).

Kate Ronald is the Roger and Joyce L. Howe Professor of English at Miami University, where she teaches graduate and undergraduate courses in composition and rhetoric and directs the Howe Writing Initiative in the School of Business. Her recent publications include *Reason to Believe: Romanticism, Pragmatism, and the Teaching of Writing*, co-authored with Hephzibah Roskelly (SUNY, 1998), and *Available Means: An Anthology of Women's Rhetoric(s)* (Pittsburgh, 2001),

Shari Stenberg is assistant professor and Director of Composition at Creighton University in Omaha, Nebraska, where she teaches courses in writing, composition theory, pedagogy, and literacy. Her book *Professing and Pedagogy: Learning the Teaching of English* was published by NCTE (2005), and her work has also appeared in *College English, Composition Studies, JBW* and *sympokē*.

Eileen E. Schell is associate professor of writing and rhetoric and a faculty affiliate in women's studies at Syracuse University, where she teaches undergraduate and graduate courses in writing and rhetoric and undergraduate courses and community writing workshops on memoir, autobiography, and place-based writing. She is the author of *Gypsy Academics and Mother-Teachers: Gender, Contingent Labor, and Writing Instruction* (Heinemann, 1998) and coeditor with Patricia Lambert Stock of *Moving a Mountain: Transforming the Role of Contingent Faculty in Composition Studies and Higher Education* (NCTE, 2000), which won the 2003 Conference on College Composition and Communication Best Book Award. Her coauthored book *Rural Literacies* with Kim Donehower and Charlotte Hogg is forthcoming from Southern Illinois University Press (2007). She is currently researching and writing *The Rhetorics of the Farm Crisis: Globalization, Sustainability, and the Future of the Family Farm*, which analyzes the public rhetorics surrounding the loss of small family farms in the United States.

Nancy Welch teaches classes in writing, rhetoric, and women's studies at the University of Vermont. She is the author of *Getting Restless: Rethinking Revision in Writing Instruction* and a short-story collection, *The Road from Prosperity*. Her latest book, *Living Room: Teaching Public Writing in a Post-Publicity Era*, is forthcoming from Boynton/Cook.

Introduction

Asking "So What?": Expansive Pedagogies of Experience and Action

Kate Ronald
Joy Ritchie

This collection grows directly from our study and teaching of historical and contemporary women rhetors over the past twelve years. Since we first designed a course on women's rhetorics we have always asked our students what difference their study of women's rhetorical practice makes to their own. In this collection we asked our contributors the same question. And, as so often happens when you ask a question in the classroom, answers were surprising, and surprising answers often teach teachers more than they expected. Here's what Angie, one of our students, wrote at the end of an undergraduate class, The Rhetoric of Women Writers, when we asked her how she might define her learning:

> It's the end of the semester, and I still can't define the rhetorics of women writers. But this is not a problem—I think that part of the usefulness of the term lies just in its problematic nature. . . . Just posing the question of a rhetoric of women writers seems to imply a feminist recognition of imbalance. . . . In this way I think the concept is indeed a useful one—it challenges us to ask the questions to explore why we even ask the question in the first place. Approaching the rhetorics of women writers we are challenged to question our own definitions and assumptions, our boundaries and limits, but we are also encouraged to look beyond definition and boundary. Rhetoric comes to crisis at the intersection of reality and language. At root the rhetorics of women writers seems paradoxical: an attempt to institutionalize and define a polymorphous practice that continually defies institutions and definitions. I think that one of the most valuable lessons I've learned from this class is the necessity of action, of involvement.

Teaching Rhetorica explores the "problematic and polymorphous" nature of women's rhetoric and takes up our students' challenge to action, inviting our contributors to extend and translate the renaissance of recent scholarship on women's rhetorics into their experiences as teachers, both inside and outside the classroom.

The essays in *Teaching Rhetorica* take what we see as the next step in the recovery of women's rhetorics and the resulting redefinition of *rhetoric* that has accompanied this revival. Just as the renaissance of research in women's rhetorics has expanded our conceptions of traditional sites, methods, and subjects of scholarship, this research, we believe, should also lead to expanded and changed sites, methods, and subjects of pedagogy. We asked the scholars and teachers in this volume to consider the following: What difference does this emerging canon of women's rhetorics make to our teaching of writing and rhetoric? How is the recovery of women's rhetorics translating into revised, reexamined theories, practices, and pedagogies of writing, rhetoric, and discourse—and into revised understandings of ourselves as teachers? In other words, how are scholars teaching *Rhetorica*, and what is *Rhetorica* teaching them? How is this new and expanding body of rhetoric changing conceptions of theory, pedagogy, and professional practice?

Our title, *Teaching Rhetorica: Theory, Pedagogy, Practice* is a shameless play on Andrea Lunsford's landmark collection, *Reclaiming Rhetorica* (1995), the first scholarly analysis of women's rhetorics. Lunsford and Lisa Ede lead off our new collection—ten years later—with a catalog of all the exciting work that's been done in "regendering" the rhetorical tradition over the last ten years. Their overview documents the central place that scholarship in women's rhetorics has assumed in our discipline, and listing all this work in one place provides clear evidence that *Rhetorica* is, in fact, well on her way to being reclaimed. We believe that now, ten years since *Reclaiming Rhetorica* was published, when the Coalition of Women Scholars in the History of Rhetoric and the Biennial Feminism(s) and Rhetorics Conference are recognized as important sites for vibrant multidisciplinary intellectual exchange, it is useful to ask ourselves what *Rhetorica* is teaching us; in other words, what difference has this renaissance made in the field?

We turn increasingly to women rhetors as we regularly teach undergraduate and graduate courses in this specialty, rhetorical theory and history, in women's literature and also as we teach first-year composition and theories of writing and rhetoric to undergraduates and teachers. We have made this shift because of the very challenges that Angie writes about and because of the possibilities women's rhetorics offer for encompassing previously unexamined perspectives. [See Ritchie and Ronald, "Riding Long Coattails" (1998), and Ronald and Ritchie, "Pedagogy and Public Engagement" (2005).] We are directing dissertations and research projects in historical and contemporary women's rhetorics, including scholarship on the rhetorics of early modern European women leaders, on the public rhetoric of early American women's magazines, on the creation of rhetorical spaces in nineteenth-century suffragist rhetoric in Nebraska, on early women rhetoricians' contributions to pedagogical rhetoric, on the rhetoric of the Million Mom March for gun control, and on the history of the figure of *Rhetorica* herself, just to name a few. As we talk with our students (and with one another) about these projects, we find ourselves repeatedly asking, "so what?" Or, perhaps more politely, "That's so interesting. But what will this research tell us beyond 'that's interesting'?" In our undergraduate classrooms we ask the question even more politely, encouraging students to think about how their reading of rhetoric by women translates into rhetorical strategies and stances that they can use in their own contexts.

By focusing on consequences here we don't mean to underplay the importance of recovering rhetoric that has been silenced or devalued or of continuing the work of "regendering" rhetorical traditions, but we do mean to push our students, ourselves, and the contributors to and readers of this collection to ask difficult questions about the implications of research into women's current and historical rhetoric and women's rhetorical practices. We ask that pragmatic so what? question globally by considering how rhetoric and composition will use this new area of study. How will this work make a difference in contexts beyond and alongside scholarship? Locally, we insist on exploring what difference reclaiming the emerging canon of women's rhetorics makes to our teaching of writing and rhetoric. We did not begin this project with a preconceived answer in mind, although we assumed that our contributors might be thinking along these same lines about connections between recovery and pedagogy. Just as our students so often do, and just as the best scholarship regularly does, the contributors surprised us—delightfully. In addition to giving direct answers to the question, What difference does women's rhetorics make to our teaching? these scholar/teachers expand the entire concept of rhetorical theory and practice, leading us to more complex and divergent notions of feminist rhetorical theory as well as feminist pedagogy. The essays in this collection do not seek to establish a new canon of women's rhetorics nor do they draw on a monolithic rhetorical or feminist theoretical position. In fact, at times they take contradictory positions on "standard" feminist scholarship; many are informed by theories that stand outside of or run parallel to feminist research and theory. The strength of these essays derives from one of the primary strengths of feminist theory—its fluidity, multiplicity, contingency, and polymorphous complexity.

The essays in *Teaching Rhetorica: Theory, Pedagogy, Practice* offer expansive definitions of what might constitute "women's rhetorics" based in broad rhetorical contexts, from the rhetorics of performance artists on the national stage to the material rhetoric of ordinary women's "altars" at home. These essays suggest wide-ranging considerations of who might take her place in the changing and emerging canon of this new field—from established rhetors like Adrienne Rich and Alice Walker to second-wave feminist activists and contemporary documentary filmmakers. And they model expansive applications of how *Rhetorica* teaches and therefore might be taught—from ways that Adrienne Rich can inform administering a composition program to ways that women who never set foot in a classroom can teach teachers. In other words, we believe that this collection, not surprisingly after all, represents an important next step in our attempts to "use" women's rhetorics productively. As with all good classrooms and good courses, we found the activity of compiling this collection left us with more questions than answers; however, thanks to these thoughtful essays, we think we have provocative new questions, expanded definitions, and exciting sites for more research and teaching.

Rhetorica as an Expansive Practice

In her groundbreaking book, *Anglo-American Challenges to the Rhetorical Traditions* (1996), Krista Ratcliffe provides an important model for beginning to answer our so what? question about the consequences of studying women's rhetorics. As she describes her method of rereading, extrapolating, and reconceptualizing the rhetorics of Virginia Woolf, Mary Daly, and Adrienne Rich, she says: "I offer these extrapolated theories as my reading of three women's texts, readings that inform my rhetoric and composition studies every time I sit down to write or walk into a classroom" (Ratcliffe 1996, 6). To engage in this rhetorical analysis, she says we need to learn to "read, write, talk, listen, and think like a teacher," to realize the "interconnectedness of theory and praxis, not as a transparent exchange but as a complex intersection that informs not just [the] first semester of teaching but the rest of all our teaching lives" (142). Ratcliffe "takes" Woolf, Rich, and Daly not only into every classroom but also, as she illustrates in her essay, "Coming Out" in *Teaching Rhetorica*, into every meeting and administrative decision. In other words, she shows us the expansive sites in which *Rhetorica* "teaches" us about theory, pedagogy, and action. All the authors in this collection have similarly reflected on women's rhetorics and the ways those rhetorics reshape their thinking about teaching writing, literature, pedagogy, or instruction in nonacademic settings. In other words, the following essays show the expansive uses to which we've all put women's rhetorics in the complex interplay among our scholarship, teaching, material experience, and action.

Teaching Rhetorica, then, defines pedagogy broadly, as part of the experience of its authors and the consequences of their reading, thinking, and acting in communities of other scholars, teachers, and citizens. The authors of these essays do not confine pedagogy to the classroom but insist that we are teaching all the time—in administering writing programs and in directing graduate work, and in every committee and faculty meeting. Shari Stenberg and Krista Ratcliffe use their studies of women's rhetorical theory to redefine the ethics of program administration and leadership, and critical pedagogy itself. Andrea Lunsford and Lisa Ede draw on the rhetoric of performance artists Kathy Acker, Anna Deveare Smith, and other transgressive rhetors to extend our conceptions of authorship and to reconsider the consequences of discursive risk-taking in the classroom. Gwendolyn Pough rereads womanist rhetoric and black feminist pedagogy to posit new possibilities for critical pedagogical approaches to conflict and to reconsider teacher and student subjectivity and authority. Wendy Hesford analyzes the pedagogical implications of visual media, expanding rhetorical categories to account for witnessing and trauma. Pedagogy extends beyond the classroom and the academy as well: Beth Daniell, Nancy Welch, Marguerite Helmers, Eileen Schell, and Kathryn Flannery explore the pedagogical implications of their research, which is grounded in their active participation with women's groups and activist organizations and in material cultures of women. This collection treats pedagogy as the experience of "practice"—in expanded contexts—and as a direct result of studying women's rhetorics.

The essays in *Teaching Rhetorica* suggest that rhetoric and composition should look again at the predilection of our discipline to consider the so what? question to be regressive and antitheoretical. We are acutely aware of Lynn Worsham's concerns about the "will to pedagogy" as we attempt to consider the implications of women's rhetorics for our teaching (1991, 96). In "Writing Against Writing: The Predicament of Ecriture Feminine," Worsham questioned what she saw as our field's desire to turn every theory into a teaching strategy. She worried over the "pedagogical imperative" that she thought threatened to uncomplicate, water down, or regulate new theories and rhetorics, particularly French feminist thought (1991, 96). We share her concerns about making easy connections between women's rhetorics and teaching strategies; however, we remain convinced, given our own teaching of rhetoric by women, that this emerging canon both demands and deserves a rethinking of writing and rhetorical pedagogy and, as Worsham says, the "ideological investments" those represent (84). Moreover, as essays by Lunsford and Ede, Flannery, Ratcliffe, Stenberg, and Pough demonstrate, the so what? question leads us back to just the critical project Worsham foregrounds: the way rhetoric can be used to exclude, domesticate, and marginalize or to open up discursive possibilities.

Lillian Bridwell Bowles and others have examined the "alternative" rhetorical possibilities to dominant discourses that women writers offer students and teachers. But "alternative discourses" end up as just that—alternative, marginal, lower in the hierarchy (Bridwell Bowles 1992). Unlike the classical tradition that Kathleen Welch (1990) claims has had such adaptability to composition, women's rhetorical practices and theories have not been integrated into our curriculum and pedagogies or into our own discourses of leadership and administration. Despite the current energetic conversations about this newly reclaimed body of women's rhetorics and its significant contributions to regendering an understanding of rhetorical history and theory, there's been little documentation or theorizing about its effect on teaching writing and rhetoric or running composition programs. We're not simply interested in how we *add* these women rhetors to our courses, how we stir them into the canon we already teach or use them as texts for classes. We believe instead that they provide a catalyst for examining how their presence might affect the kinds of classroom structures, projects, and goals we might create. Beyond that, as Nancy Welch, Wendy Hesford, Beth Daniell, and Eileen Schell suggest, they extend the parameters of rhetorical sites into the local community, to social and cultural sites not traditionally considered rhetorical, and to global contexts far beyond the walls of academic institutions.

Rhetorica as Expansive Experience

Whitney, a graduate student in one of our recent classes, wrote:

> All semester we have considered how women rhetors theorize from lived experience, and we have questioned the limitations of experience. Reading Audre Lorde on the uses of the "erotic" and the uses of "anger" has shown me the rhetorical power that can come from working from places I would normally reject because they are "nonrational," dangerous, or taboo. . . . I think of one of my students who wrote about experiencing racism when she was in second grade. In her narrative, she mentioned it nonchalantly, coming to terms with years of racist remarks by saying that it was okay because people "just don't understand." I wonder how having an example of a voice like Lorde's on the uses of anger might change the way she could render her experience. Had she understood anger as an interpretive rhetorical strategy, might it have changed the story she told?

Whitney is examining the consequences of women's rhetorics for herself and for the students in her first-year writing classes. Like the authors in *Teaching Rhetorica*, she investigates her own experiences of reading and teaching, practicing what Ann Berthoff (1984) calls "thinking about thinking" in order to examine the expanded rhetorical possibilities that emerge from the expanded contexts, experiences, and topoi on which women rhetors draw.

When we assembled the work of women rhetors for *Available Means* (2001) we included writing by women who had mastered the rhetorical tradition and employed it to subversive ends, such as Margaret Fell, Sor Juana Inez de la Cruz, and Anna Julia Cooper; we also included writers like Virginia Woolf, Adrienne Rich, Audre Lorde, Patricia Williams and others who quite obviously articulate important alternative sources of knowledge, as well as principles for writing and speaking, writers who employ new styles and forms in order to break out of a rhetorical tradition that, they believe, reinscribes women in powerless and silent positions and limits women's ways of acting in the world. But we also included writing that comes from the "wrong places," writing that defies traditional criteria and categories, especially concerning ethos that draws on new topoi, and writing that employs the "dangerous moves" that Lunsford describes in *Reclaiming Rhetorica* (1995, 6). We wanted to prompt scholars, teachers, and students to look to other rhetors who are more transgressive, who cause us and our students to reexamine our assumptions about rhetorical propriety, to stretch the heuristic possibilities of rhetoric for constructing and deconstructing knowledge and power.

One of the women rhetors who has taught us and our students about the expansive possibilities of rhetoric—expanding epistemologies, contexts, sites, and topoi—for action is Dorothy Allison, especially in *Two or Three Things I Know for Sure* (1995). We examine that work here because it leads us to think differently about the relationships among experience, rhetorical theory, and pedagogical practice, to consider what difference those often surprising connections make.

Allison's *Two or Three Things I Know for Sure* is overtly a memoir about coming to terms with a history of abuse, incest, and hopelessness among the working-class poor white women in a South Carolina family. But it is also, we have found, a powerful piece of rhetorical theory that emerges out of lived experience. One of our colleagues has challenged the assumption that Allison offers anything radically different from Aristotle, Augustine, or Burke—that in fact there are strong resemblances—and that it's difficult to find any text that falls outside the range of possibilities offered by traditional rhetorical theory. To some extent this may be true. But we argue that Allison provides us with an expanded definition of what Susan Jarratt says many women rhetors understand: the double role of language as both "political and figurative" activity (1998, 9). Asserting the right to speak from the "wrong side of the track" is both political and figurative, challenging existing power relations about who is entitled to speak and be heard among social classes and genders, challenging conceptions of writer/author relationships, and presenting expanded definitions of ethos and expanded epistemologies. Allison stretches definitions of rhetorical contexts by transgressing the boundaries between public and private, and addresses what is not present in traditional rhetorics—the materiality and diversity of embodied, gendered, sexual lives. In doing so Allison provides her readers—our students and us as teachers—with a theoretical tool with which we also can act rhetorically.

The book, which Allison also performs, begins: "Let me tell you a story," and she does tell stories about being raped by her stepfather when she was five years old, about being "horrified" by the women she loved most in her life, about the women in her family who ran away, and about those who stayed (1995, 1). She ran. And sprinkled throughout the book, among the stories, are the "two or three things" Allison has learned "for sure."

> Two or three things I know for sure, and one of them is what it means to have
> no loved version of your life but the one you make. (3)

Here Allison is speculating about epistemology—always a foundation of rhetorical theory. She explores how truth is constructed in language, how language is invented and arranged, not in order to create something artistic or beautiful, or even primarily to persuade or communicate information, but in order to keep from dying, to make a version of her life that she can live. In her stories Allison is talking about—and giving direction for—what one can do with words. Language is fluid and dynamic, operating differently from one context to another—not a particularly new idea. We already know that language conceals, reveals, insulates, cuts through, betrays, and surprises. Allison asserts that she can and must control reality through her stories/language while reminding us of her powerlessness, her struggle to understand her abusive history through the veil of language that made it so hard for her to find ways to think, much less to speak, about what happened to her. This is a strategic method for how, first, to speak at all, especially when one is not authorized to do so about subjects that transgress traditional rules about public and private contexts. But it is a model for how to use language to survive and change one's reality.

Allison says in the middle of the book:

> Let me tell you a story. I tell stories to prove I was meant to survive, knowing it is not true. My stories are no parables, no *Reader's Digest* Unforgettable Characters, no women's movement polemics, no Queer Nation broadsides. I am not here to make anyone happy. What I am here for is to claim my life, my mama's death, our losses and triumphs, to name them for myself. I am here to claim everything I know, and there are only two or three things I know for sure. (1995, 52)

One of the basic tenets of traditional rhetoric is the attention to audience. One of the grounds for dismissing women's writing has traditionally been that it ignores audience, that it's merely therapeutic, or private, or primarily an assertion of the right to speak and nothing more. Allison's claim that she is writing for herself, not to make anyone happy, might seem to put her in this category. But she is creating a unique relationship with her readers. She's not quite telling the truth about what she's attempting. These stories, which she has performed live, enact a complicated, convoluted relationship between speaker and audience. Not only does the book present itself as a nontraditional form to imitate and admire, it also provides readers with a method for unfolding and holding on to the paradoxical relationships between fiction and fact, silence and speaking, certainty and doubt, cultural norms and taboos.

Allison illustrates dramatically that women's rhetorical contexts, situations, and exigencies demand different rhetorical strategies. She explodes traditional conceptions of reasoning and evidence. Her own attempts at persuasion emerge from the context of a nightmare, where all the "evidence" pointed to her destruction: the man raped her, and he was big, and her mother knew what he was doing all along and didn't save her. How is it possible to reason with that? More specifically, Allison must shatter traditional conventions about invention, evidence, and methods of appeal: getting right in our face, the rhetorical topoi she explores take her readers to places we simply don't want to go, situations too painful to consider or situations—like lesbian sexuality—that dominant heterosexual norms don't accept. She flouts any advice about analyzing the audience's "needs" or sensitivities. The rules about finding the issues, laying them out logically and civilly and weighing evidence, simply don't work in this context; there's no enthymeme to explain her confusion between love and violence. She cannot call upon her own ethos as a method of appeal because she's not conventionally appealing—she's white trash and lesbian and angry. And her pathos calls up none of the warm feelings of sympathy or catharsis that conventional advice says can be so effective. So Allison mobilizes alternative means to persuade.

Allison's assertion at the end of this passage that her stories aim to "change the world" also suggests that her rhetoric isn't solipsistic. Like so much of women's writing, Allison's book is urgent, steeped in her immediate context, emerging from her need to act for her own and other women's survival. Is this urgency the reason that it is easy to dismiss the theoretical substance of writers like Allison? Or is it that we have overlooked or dismissed the theoretical substance of works like Allison's that seem so personal, local, and particular—so urgent, unruly, and lacking in the cool, distanced propriety of argument?

Perhaps our colleague is correct in arguing that Allison's provisionality, fluidity, and contextuality aren't anything new. But the embodied, intimately contextualized nature of these rhetorical practices does, we believe, suggest a different way that rhetorical theory works: by asserting possibilities of a different ethos—one that is not tempered, distant, cool, or objective; one that lends specificity to material differences, from a different, gendered, othered perspective that insists on the inextricable links between experience and rhetoric, language and action. In other words, as we've taught and studied *Two or Three Things I Know for Sure,* we have come to see Allison not only as part of *Rhetorica* to be taught but also as *Rhetorica* teaching—as a theory and a pedagogy that we and our students can practice. Her work, like so much of the work discussed in the essays collected here, expands and enlarges the grounds on which we study and teach.

Rhetorica Teaches Expansive Action

In a first-year composition class, after reading Helene Cixous' "Sorties" (1975/1986) and Audre Lorde's "Transformation of Silence into Language and Action" (1984), Jordan wrote about how he might "use" his learning for his own rhetorical action:

> While Lorde establishes the need for a discourse community of women that can break the silences, Cixous claims that women have no such community at all and are venturing into uncharted territory by speaking .... In simpler terms, there is no system that accepts and recognizes women rhetoricians. Yet, Cixous says, "One can begin to speak." . . . One can learn a few things from analyzing these two pieces together. First and foremost, that simple statement: "one can begin to speak." A discourse community will form to replace an absence, and others will follow.

Although Jordan's optimism about the ease of communities' forming and creating new sites for speaking may be naive, this imperative to action and the

belief that rhetoric can create change has dramatized for us and especially for
our students that *Rhetorica* is never "mere rhetoric." As they study women
rhetors from Christine de Pizan to Gloria Anzaldua and from Margaret Fell to
Patricia Williams, students often begin to see the possibilities for using lan-
guage/rhetoric to interpret, take action, and construct new realities, as Jordan
seems to do in his writing about Cixous.

   Jordan's analysis points to another way in which studying women's
rhetorics expands possibilities for rhetorical action. The rhetorical move Jordan makes is one that women's rhetoric seems to inspire in our students and in
scholar/teachers. Like the authors who have contributed to *Teaching Rhetorica*, he engages here in the kind of transgressive juxtaposition of scholarly
positions that traditional rhetoric (academic argument) often disallows.
Although he may be doing so naively, Jordan brings together the radical materialist feminist rhetoric of Lorde with the radical feminist psychoanalytical
rhetoric of Cixous to engage in the kind of critical thinking that can create new
possibilities for action and change.

   We offer our own juxtaposition here by adding Toni Morrison's Nobel
Lecture (1993/1999) to our previous discussion of Dorothy Allison as an
example of the potential *Rhetorica* holds for expansive action, for locating
meaning in consequence and action. Morrison engages in what Susan Jarratt
describes as the "double play" of rhetoric (Jarratt 1998, 9), taking on the political and the figurative dimensions of a debased, unethical version of rhetoric
that she critiques and seeks to change:

> The systematic looting of language can be recognized by the tendency of its
> users to forgo its nuanced, complex, mid-wifery properties, replacing them
> with menace and subjugation. Oppressive language does more than represent
> violence; it is violence; does more than represent the limits of knowledge; it
> limits knowledge. . .it must be rejected, altered, and exposed. (Morrison 1999,
> 15–16)

Morrison's subject in this lecture is writing/narrative, but the old blind wise
woman who is its speaker also acts as a teacher to the children who present her
with the riddle of a bird in their hands, asking her if it is dead or alive. As a
writer, she interprets the bird as language, and the riddle as the "problem" of
language as living or dead. She and the children, together, work to "expose"
and "alter" language that is merely "artful" or "self-congratulatory." Morrison's answer to "obscuring state language or the faux language of mindless
media," to the "calcified language of the academy or the commodity-driven
language of science," lies in her own self-conscious practice as a writer (1999,
16). She and the children arrive at a conception of language, or "word-work,"
as "sublime because it is generative" (22). But the old woman defines that sub-
limity through use: she rejects, alters, and exposes intellectual history that
requires "rationalizations for and representations of dominance—lethal
discourses of exclusion blocking access to cognition for both the excluder and

the excluded" (21). She (and the children) argue for "unmolested language [that] surges toward knowledge, not its destruction" (22), imagining (and illustrating) a "history connected to experience" (25). Moreover, she acts throughout the essay as a teacher, alternately taking on and then observing the old woman's role as guide to the children.

We see in Morrison's Nobel Lecture the same symbiotic relationship between theorist/practioner and history/experience that the authors in *Teaching Rhetorica* investigate. Using their own experiences as scholars, program administrators, teachers, and activists, they, like Morrison, explore how their experience, and the experience of "others," translates into rhetorical theory and what difference that exploration makes to their pedagogical and public actions.

Asking so what? is a pragmatic move on our part, not a practical one. As the authors in this collection have taught us, it's far less important to glean a unified set of readings, teaching methods, assignments, or course outlines from our study of women's rhetorics and from scholars' work gathered in *Teaching Rhetorica* than to think expansively about how this new field of women's rhetorics changes our conception of theory/practice and rhetoric/composition. Our impulse to take this pragmatic stance arises directly from what our experience tells us are the central uses of women's rhetoric: it challenges dominant epistemologies, asserts new topoi/contexts from which to argue, places material experience—especially that of women, women of color, sexual minorities, and other nonmainstream groups—at the center of knowledge formation, and it reconnects language/rhetoric to action and change.

Pragmatism tells us that meaning resides in consequence, in the effect of an idea. William James defines the pragmatic attitude as "looking away from first things, principles, 'categories,' supposed necessities; and of looking toward last things, fruits, consequences, facts" (1975, 32). In reading and teaching *Rhetorica* we observe that women often refuse "first things, principles, and established categories." Christine de Pizan, Margaret Fell, and the Grimke sisters do not accept a biblical principle that categorized women as the source of evil, inherently inferior, and unequipped for education, public speaking, and civic participation. Ida B. Wells, Alice Walker, and Patricia Williams challenge traditional rhetorical principles of logic and evidence. Gloria Anzaldua, like Dorothy Allison, exposes and alters conventional precepts of rhetorical arrangement and style. For many of the women rhetors we teach, knowledge arises from experience rather than from tradition; further, many call on knowledge that arises from traditions and rituals outside or underneath dominant Western, white, or male epistemologies. Knowledge, then, is judged according to the standard Adrienne Rich sets forth: "When where, and under what conditions has the statement been true?" (1986, 214). The "meaning" of rhetoric, and its "fruits," therefore changes when we take into account the experiences and facts of women rhetors' lives and writing.

This collection uses that pragmatic definition of meaning to suggest that a responsible reading of women's rhetorics should lead to more "fruits and facts," to possibilities for action and to changed practices, for our students and for us as teachers and scholars, especially if this renaissance of recovery is to make a difference to our professional, pedagogical, and public lives. One of the principal impulses of women rhetors is to inspire action, to seek specific consequences. In her analysis of African American women rhetors in *Traces of a Stream*, Jackie Jones Royster says, "they offer us prime examples of the will and capacity to use literate resources in order to participate in public arenas, and also of the desire to generate, and not just participate in, sociopolitical action. Among African American women there is . . . evidence of an ancient and dusky commitment to language and action" (2000, 25). As Royster also points out, African American women rhetors redefine the relationships among audience, writers, and message, replacing traditional appeals to logic, emotion, and character with a focus on context, the ethos of material experience, and an insistence on rhetorical action (32).

As Royster insists, then, research needs to be "acted upon" (280). And that's a pragmatic assumption. The authors here take up that call by exploring what differences their work in women's rhetorics have made to their action, how what they have learned from women's rhetorics has translated into concrete consequences in their classrooms and for scholarly and public communities. Ann Berthoff, one rhetorician who seems to us forgotten in this renaissance of women's rhetorical theory, explains the pragmatic attitude as "thinking about our thinking." She provides a frame for reading these essays by insisting that that "how your theory works and what it changes will best tell you what your theory is" (1987, xxiii). Each of the essays here attempts the difficult task of exploring what rhetorical theory by women might mean, what that theory might change in our teaching of writing and rhetoric, or how it might cause us to rethink our positions as teachers, scholars, and administrators, and citizens.

But more to the point, the rhetorical women we teach and study, including the subjects (and the authors) of these essays, have purposefully sought to keep the context, the immediacy of experience and action, attached to meaning rather than to create an abstract set of prescriptions disconnected from the contexts or stripped of the exigencies of everyday life. They always asked, so what? So should we. Further, these essays both learn from and teach the expansiveness of *Rhetorica*. Perhaps we should not be surprised by these authors' wide-ranging answers to our so what? question. What the essays in *Teaching Rhetorica* demonstrate is another feminist (and pragmatic) assumption: that the whole of experience must be accounted for to arrive at meaning, and that meaning is always fluid, always contextual, always open to the community's changing scrutiny. As James put it, "truth happens to an idea; it becomes true, is made true, by events" (1907, 97). What we planned for in proposing this collection is another event in the making of women's rhetorics. What we hope *Theory, Pedagogy, Practice* will offer to readers is that sense of the expansive possibilities of *Teaching Rhetorica*.

1

Crimes of Writing and Reading

Andrea Lunsford
Lisa Ede

Since the publication in 1989 of Karlyn Kohrs Campbell's two-volume *Man Can Not Speak for Her*, scholars of rhetoric and writing have done much to reclaim and describe women's contributions to rhetorical history and practice. Such work has necessarily entailed a challenge to the scope and definition of the rhetorical tradition, and to traditional understandings of historiography. The following chronology indicates the significance and breadth of this work:

1990

Kathleen Welch. *The Contemporary Reception of Classical Rhetoric*

Lisa Ede and Andrea Lunsford. *Singular Texts/Plural Authors: Perspectives on Collaborative Writing*

1991

Karen Foss and Sonja Foss, Eds. *Women Speak: The Eloquence of Women's Lives*

Susan Jarratt. *Rereading the Sophists: Classical Rhetoric Refigured*

C. Jan Swearingen. *Rhetoric and Irony: Western Literacy and Western Lies*

1995

Shirley Wilson Logan, Ed. *With Pen and Voice: A Critical Anthology of Nineteenth-Century African-American Women*

Catherine Hobbs, Ed. *Nineteenth-Century Women Learn to Write*

Andrea Lunsford, Ed. *Reclaiming Rhetorica: Women in the History of Rhetoric*

Krista Ratcliffe. *Anglo-American Feminist Challenges to the Rhetorical Traditions: Virginia Woolf, Mary Daly, Adrienne Rich*

1996

JoAnn Campbell, Ed. *Toward a Feminist Rhetoric: The Writing of Gertrude Buck*

1997

Gere, Anne. *Intimate Practices: Literacy and Cultural Work in U.S. Women's Clubs, 1880–1920*

Cheryl Glenn. *Rhetoric Retold: Regendering the Tradition from Antiquity Through the Renaissance*

Jacqueline Royster, Ed. *Southern Horrors and Other Writings: The Anti-lynching Campaign of Ida B. Wells, 1892–1900*

1998

Carol Mattingly. *Well-Tempered Women: Nineteenth-Century Temperance Rhetoric*

1999

Shirley Wilson Logan. *"We Are Coming": The Persuasive Discourse of Nineteenth-Century Black Women*

Molly Meijer Wertheimer, Ed. *Listening to Their Voices: The Rhetorical Activities of Historical Women*

Christine Mason Sutherland and Rebecca Sutcliffe, Eds. *The Changing Tradition: Women in the History of Rhetoric*

Karen Foss, Sonja Foss, and Cyndi Griffin, Eds. *Feminist Rhetorical Theories*

Susan Kates. *Activist Rhetorics and American Higher Education: 1885–1937*

Christine Nguyen Fredrick. *Feminist Rhetoric in Cyberspace*

2000

Jacqueline Jones Royster. *Traces of a Stream: Literacy and Social Change Among African American Women*

2001

Michelle Bailiff. *Seduction, Sophistry, and the Woman with the Rhetorical Figure*

Joy Ritchie and Kate Ronald, Eds. *Available Means: An Anthology of Women's Rhetoric(s)*

Kami Day and Michele Eodice. *(First Person)2: A Study of Co-authoring in the Academy*

2002

Jane Donawerth, Ed. *Rhetorical Theory by Women Before 1900*

Nan Johnson. *Gender and Rhetorical Space in American Life: 1866–1910*

Elizabeth A. Flynn. *Feminism Beyond Modernism*

Carol Mattingly. *Appropriating Dress: Women's Rhetorical Style in Nineteenth-Century America.*

2003

M. Jacqui Alexander, Lisa Albrecht, Sharon Day, and Mab Segrest, Eds. *Sing, Whisper, Shout, Pray: Feminist Visions for a Just World*

Beth Daniell. *A Communion of Friendship: Literacy, Spiritual Practice, and Women in Recovery*

Gesa E. Kirsch, Faye Spencer Maor, Lance Massey, Lee Mickoson-Massey, and Mary P. Sheridan-Rabideau, Eds. *Feminism and Composition: A Critical Sourcebook*

Roxanne Mountford. *The Gendered Pulpit: Preaching in American Protestant Spaces*

Susan Zaeske. *Signatures of Citizenship: Petitioning, Antislavery, and Women's Political Identity*

2004

Joyce Blackwell. *No Peace Without Freedom: Race and the Women's International League for Peace and Freedom, 1915–75*

Katherine Chandler and Melissa Goldthwaite. *Surveying the Literary Landscapes of Terry Tempest Williams*

Lisa Ede. *Situating Composition: Composition Studies and the Politics of Location*

Cheryl Glenn. *Unspoken: the Rhetoric of Silence*

Karyn Hollis. *Liberating Voices: Writing at Bryn Mawr Summer School for Women Workers*

Gwendolyn Pough. *Check It While I Wreck It: Black Womanhood, Hip-Hop Culture, and the Public Sphere*

Sarah Robbins. *Managing Literacy, Mothering America: Women's Narratives on Reading and Writing in the Nineteenth Century*

Wendy Sharer. *Voice and Vote: Women's Organizations and Political Literacy 1915–30*

2005

Lindal Buchanan. *Regendering Delivery: The Fifth Canon and Antebellum Women Rhetors*

Krista Ratcliffe. *Rhetorical Listening: Identification, Gender, Whiteness.*

Jacqueline Rhodes. *Radical Feminism, Writing, and Critical Agency: From Manifesto to Modem*

In the introduction, Kate Ronald and Joy Ritchie acknowledge this impressive body of work and go on to raise a number of thought-provoking questions about our field's ongoing efforts to document and inquire into women's rhetorical practices. We need to continue to build on this work, Ronald and Ritchie argue—and we need to do so on multiple levels. What challenges to conventional understandings of history and theory, they ask, do women's rhetorical practices represent? What are the potential consequences of recent efforts to reclaim and redefine women's rhetorical practices for the actual *teaching* of writing?

As we worked on this chapter, we found that these questions reverberated for us in powerful ways. Most generally, they reminded us that as important as it has been to reclaim women's contributions to rhetorical history and practice, these contributions will not automatically have consequences for the day-to-day teaching of writing. Hence the need for this collection. The questions that Ronald and Ritchie pose also encouraged us to bring together two lines of inquiry with which we have for some time been engaged. As teachers of writing and writing program administrators, we have long recognized the need to subject our pedagogical practices to ongoing critique—to never assume that we have (at last) determined the best way to understand and teach writing. We have not necessarily linked this effort, however, to our historical and textual inquiry into women's discursive theories and practices. The opportunity to place these two strands of our work in dialogue has stimulated much productive thought.

As teachers of writing, for instance, we have been aware that the institutional, cultural, political, and economic contexts in which we work hold the potential to co-opt, subvert, or in other ways discipline our teaching. We recognize, as well, that the ideologies that most strongly inform our assumptions and practices are not necessarily shared by our students—and thus conflict is an important element of the rhetorical situation of our classrooms.

Reading and thinking about the discursive practices of Marguerite Porete, Anne Hutchinson, Geneva Smitherman, Kathy Acker, and Anna Deveare Smith—some of the women we will consider in this chapter—reminds us that we cannot know how students will experience various rhetorics. We regularly invite students, for example, to experiment with discursive practices that in one way or another transgress conventional academic norms: we do so when we invite students to write collaboratively or to compose texts that experiment or "play" with language. Placing this pedagogical invitation in the context of crimes of writing and reading reminds us that whereas some students will experience our invitation as a stimulating opportunity to experiment with new and interesting ways of enacting writing, others will consider this same invitation a threatening and unwanted solicitation to crime.

Later in this chapter, we will have more to say about the insights we have gained as teachers as a result of considering both our and our students' discursive practices from the perspective of crimes of writing and reading. We turn now, however, to a discussion of these crimes—one that is wide-ranging not only in its historical breadth but also in the diversity of examples we discuss. We are not the first, of course, to observe that women's practices of reading and writing have all too often been represented as "crimes" that posed such serious threats to the rhetorical status quo that, for many women throughout history, the mere desire to learn to write and read becomes a suspicious and even criminal act. In sketching in this history, we will point to specific women who insist on persuing "improper" discursive behaviors and reflect on the ways in which our engagement with their texts and practices has influenced both our theoretical understandings and pedagogical enactments. As we do so, we will attend to the specific historical conditions in which people write and read. Such a focus can, we believe, cast additional light on the tensions among readers' and writers' desires and those cultural, political, social, economic, and rhetorical assumptions and practices that can work to limit or even criminalize them.

Our interest in crimes of reading and writing grew most immediately out of our own experiences as coauthors who, especially when we began collaborating, felt "othered" by our desire to write together. (In reviews for tenure and promotion, for instance, both our chairs and departmental and college committees made it clear that they did not know how to "count," or in other ways assess our collaborative scholarly work, and hence they did not value it.) Our earliest explorations of the extent to which coauthoring is not only devalued but proscribed—especially by those in the humanities—focused on the discursive practices of the many writers in the workplace who are called on to work collaboratively on both the production of knowledge and of texts. Early on in our research, we realized that simply documenting the practices of these writers would do little to dislodge deeply held assumptions about the nature of authorship and of intellectual property—or of transgressions against these assumptions—so our efforts expanded to encompass historical and theoretical efforts to rethink what it means to be an "author" or to have an "original" idea.

This work eventually led to the publication in 1990 of *Singular Texts/Plural Authors: Perspectives on Collaborative Writing* and to a series of essays and conference presentations on collaboration and intellectual property, especially as they relate to women's discursive practices. Along the way, we became increasingly interested in identifying and studying the work of women who—sometimes consciously, sometimes unconsciously—have written texts that others view as either deviant or criminal. (This range stretches from the eccentric, as in the case of Sojourner Truth, to the actionable, as our discussion of Kathy Acker will demonstrate.) As we did so, we often had to remind ourselves that the very definition of a "crime" of writing is historically situated. In the Middle Ages, for instance, perhaps the worst crime of writing for either a man or a woman was blasphemy, since at that time it was God who could be said to "own" language and its power. In more secular periods, such as the Elizabethan period in Great Britain, sovereign states held that power—and sedition was the prime crime of writing. For the last three hundred years, anything that threatened the hegemony of the originary author (whether an individual person or a corporate entity) or author construct was likely to be viewed as a violation of copyright law, and thus as a crime.

Once we took the focus even momentarily off singular authorship, a whole range of practices came into view, practices that challenge the authorial tradition or are in other ways transgressive—from medieval women mystics' collaborative writing with scribes (or with God, for that matter, who "authored" their visions); to Renaissance women translators who smuggled their own subversive ideas into prefaces to the translated or "proper" material; to the conversational rhetoric women such as Margaret Fuller practiced as a mode of resistance to the linearity so favored at the time; to the many contemporary women who have insisted on pursuing practices of writing that challenge the norm.

Crimes of Writing

Among such contemporary writers whose acts have been criminalized, few are more visibly transgressive than Kathy Acker. Susan Stewart concludes her study *Crimes of Writing* with a brief discussion of Acker's *Don Quixote: Which Was a Dream.* "Here," says Stewart, "it is important not to consider this [book] a matter of rewriting or revision, for there is no attempt to translate, update, or improve upon the fabric of history other than to parody such a gesture of renovation" (1991, 286). Here, in short, is a book that will "plagiarize" to forge whatever "identity" it might arrive at. In Acker's work, Stewart notes in a concluding understatement: "all the relations between attribution, authority, theory and practice, primary and secondary texts, intention . . . become exaggerated" (288).

And that's putting it mildly. Acker, born—according to various "official" sources, in 1943, 1945, 1947, or 1948—and raised in New York City, attended a private girls' school before her parents disowned her. In subsequent years, she continued her education both on the streets and at other schools, eventually studying for (but not completing) a PhD in English literature at New York University. From her first novel, *Politics* (1972), to her final novel, *Pussy, King of the Pirates* (1996), Acker produced a significant body of work that went, as she herself might have said, well beyond experimentalism. Combining high theory and low street talk, dreams of friendship and scenes of sadomasochistic cruelty, Acker rewrites the so-called works of others, collapsing genres, time periods, genders, and selves in a series of dizzying texts that have been called everything from "literary trash compactors" (LeClair 1986, 10) to "prose assemblages" (McCaffery 1996, 14) to texts of great "outlaw intelligence" (Olsen 1994, np).

What accounts for these descriptions? We can fairly easily chart the characteristics of Acker's work that seem most threatening, that may account for her being labeled an outlaw, a criminal, or the term she herself preferred, a "pirate." Identity in Acker's works, for example, and especially *sexual* identity, is completely fluid. As a result, any traditional sense of "intentionality" or "voice," and hence of authorial power or agency, is absent. One way that Acker consistently challenged notions of agency was through her rejection of or play with personal pronouns. She seldom uses first person, for instance, as this opening to the second part of *Don Quixote: Which Was a Dream* demonstrates: "Being dead, Don Quixote could no longer speak. Being born into and part of a male world, she had no speech of her own. All she could do was read male texts which weren't hers" (1984, 39). Likewise, in her essay "Humility," a description of the ordeal she went through when Harold Robbins and his attorneys charged her with plagiarism and her "feminist" publisher did little to help (even though Acker carefully refuted each of the charges brought against her), she consistently drops out the pronouns: "In Paris decided that it's stupid to live in fear . . . . Still trying to explain . . . the deconstructionist needs to use the actual other texts" (1990, 128). Such striking omission of personal pronouns is part of Acker's insistent rejection of traditional authority, an insistence that resulted in many charges against her, including that of plagiarism.

Indeed, in her terms, Acker could not keep from plagiarizing. *Don Quixote: Which Was a Dream*, for example, mixes such real-life events as an abortion with passages from and references to not only Cervantes and the Cid, but to Borges (whose "Pierre Menard, Author of the Quixote" pairs well with Acker's text), de Sade, Machiavelli, Milton, Shakespeare, *Wuthering Heights, Waiting for Godot*, and the work of many literary and feminist theorists. Her *Great Expectations*, another "piratical" text, operates on a similar trajectory. In these and other novels, Acker acts out her theory that language cannot be owned—particularly not by coherent, organic "individuals."

The use of extreme violence, pornography, and explicit sexual material—another hallmark of Acker's work that led to censure—is related to her effort to resist what she sees as the degradation brought on the world by global capitalism and commodification, including the commodification represented by the author construct. Though many (including us) find aspects of her work shocking, she insisted that "I'm really not interested in shocking people in the usual sense but the idea of shock as a form of teaching . . . I want to show them that their perceptual habits are distorted, too rigidified" (McCaffery 1996, 16). Thus in her life and in her work, Acker attempted to define a space outside the patriarchal laws of discourse and society she believed have trapped most artists and, she acknowledged over and over, *all* women—including those who identify themselves as radical feminist theorists. (In his dissertation study, John Logie devotes a chapter to a reading of Acker and Cixous that does much, we think, to contribute to an understanding of Acker's own brand of feminism). To do so, Acker used the "criminal" techniques described earlier to wrench genres and languages completely out of context, to remake them through and with one another, to both deconstruct and construct. In interviews, she talked in detail about her exploration of deconstruction and her use of deconstructive methods as well as her eventual rejection of these techniques as finally too limited and limiting. Throughout her life, Acker searched for a way to reject and escape the confines of genre, which she saw as related to, indeed created by, hegemonic and patriarchal practices.

Acker's willingness to challenge the conventional assumptions and forms of Western authorship—to deny the myth of individual genius and originality and to engage in the crimes we have just described—is shared by another contemporary writer we find fascinating. Anna Deveare Smith, playwright, actress, and author and sole performer of such plays as *Fires in the Mirror: Crown Heights, Brooklyn, and Other Identities* and *Twilight Los Angeles, 1992* is in a number of ways less scandalous than Acker, both in terms of her intentions and in terms of the nature and consequences of the texts she writes and performs. But Smith's work, like Acker's, though valued by many, has nevertheless at times been viewed as a crime of writing.

Some background about Smith's project may be helpful in exploring this reaction. For almost twenty years, Smith has been engaged in an extended project titled *On the Road: A Search for an American Character* ("Theater in Search of the American Character" n.d.). Whether she is writing and performing a play about the Crown Heights riots or the civil unrest and destruction that engulfed Los Angeles in the wake of the initial Rodney King verdict, Smith deliberately and self-consciously constructs dramas solely from the words of others, thus flouting the prevailing assumption that as a playwright she must create character and plot from the "smithy" of her own individual imagination. As author, Smith (depending on your perspective) thus collaborates with—or appropriates and thus "steals"—the words of those she interviews. There are additional ways in which Smith's plays depend on collaboration with others. In *Twilight Los Angeles*, for instance, Smith worked with four individuals of various races who functioned as dramaturges and thus assisted her in the preparation of the play. In the introduction to the print version of *Twilight Los Angeles*, Smith calls attention to the importance of their role, noting that "these dramaturges brought their own real-world experiences with race to bear on the work. They reacted to *Twilight* at every stage of its development" (A. Smith 1994, xxii).

The scope and ambition of Smith's project are substantial. As part of her work for *Twilight Los Angeles*, for instance, Smith interviewed more than two hundred individuals, from relatively anonymous persons, such as the wife of a Korean store owner injured in the riots, to such well-known figures as Maxine Waters, Cornell West, and Daryl Gates. In this project, as in others, once the interviews were completed Smith listened to the tapes over and over—and over and over. Her goal, as she has explained, is to listen carefully not only to her interviewees' words but to the rhythms, the tics and tremors of their language, and thus to arrive at the essence of their characters.

In performance, and using minimal props and costume changes, Smith attempts as fully as possible to embody the individuals whose words she speaks. In so doing, Smith operates out of a sophisticated Bakhtinian understanding of the relationship between language and subjectivity. In speaking about her work, for instance, Smith says:

My sense is that the American character lives not in one place or the other but in the gaps between the places, and in our struggle to be together in our differences. It lives not in what has been fully articulated but in what is in the process of being articulated, not in the smooth-sounding words but in the very moment that the smooth-sounding words fail us. It is alive right now. We might not like what we see, but in order to change it, we have to see it clearly." (Stepanek n.d.)

In describing her work, Smith acknowledges the ethical complexity of her effort. "'Acting isn't nice,' she has said . . . . 'It's giving but it's also stealing'" (Lloyd 1998). Although Smith has not been accused of stealing the words of others, as Acker was in her dustup with Harold Robbins, questions of originality have nevertheless played a role in the reception of her writing. For though in recent years Smith has encountered a good deal of success—in 1996 she was awarded a "genius award" of $280,000 from the MacArthur Foundation, an Obie Award, and the Ford Foundations's first artist in residency, and she also served as the founding director of the Institute on the Arts and Civic Dialogue, a Harvard University institute devoted to socially conscious art— she has nevertheless paid a price for her reliance on the words of others (Lloyd 1998). An article on Smith in the 1994 volume of the *Current Biography Year-book* details, for instance, the decision of the Pulitzer Prize committee, which "after having listed *Fires in the Mirror* as a finalist for the award, disqualified *Twilight: Los Angeles, 1992* from consideration, reasoning that the text, because it had been taken from interviews, was not original and that other actors could not perform the play, since its authenticity lay in Smith's having conducted the interviews" ("Anna Deavere Smith" 1994, 547).

Yet Acker and Smith—in different ways and for different reasons—have succeeded in challenging powerful and deep-seated understandings about the nature of authorship and creativity, even if they have been punished or disciplined for doing so. We believe that scholars and teachers of writing need to pay very close attention to such challenges, exploring their causes as well as the uses to which they are put. As we do so, we need to take care to avoid oversimplifications and easy oppositions. As the examples of Acker and Smith illustrate, despite the ongoing critique of the sovereign subject and *his* ownership of text, the gap between theoretical critique and change at the level of praxis is broader and deeper than many have wished to acknowledge. Thus, although we are eager to recognize the power of Acker and Smith's transgressions, it would be a mistake to think of them as unidimensional exemplars of resistance or as easily comparable.

In looking at Acker and Smith's lives and works, for example, one might be tempted to contrast them in various ways—according to race, for instance, or to the differing receptions of their work. These certainly are not insignificant issues, but they are almost certainly more complex than they at first appear. In comparison with Smith's work, for example, Acker's oeuvre has been more thoroughly and consistently marginalized in significant and ongoing ways. (As readers may be aware, Smith also appeared as a regular character in the popular

TV series *West Wing*.) For though Kathy Acker certainly succeeded in publishing a significant body of work—a selected bibliography included in Larry McCaffrey's interview with Acker lists fourteen books of fiction, as well as other publications—many were published in nonmainstream presses, such as the Empty Elevator Shaft Press and Diana's BiMonthly Press. Even Grove Press's publication of her later works did not bring her into the mainstream—or into favor with many feminist critics. Acker's marginality interests us a great deal, since some of it at least is the direct result of Acker's own choices. She was, after all, a white woman who had the benefit of private and advanced higher education; her privileged position in terms of class and race needs to be factored into any understanding of how marginalization works in her case, since this privilege allowed her some freedom to take the risks, to commit writerly crimes, and to choose to deeply distrust the mainstream.

Anna Deavere Smith's case is, we find, equally complex. Acclaimed in 1993 when she was named *Glamour Magazine's* Woman of the Year for "putting race center stage" (qtd. in N. Martin 1994), Smith responded by emphasizing that her goal was not to shift anything to the center. Rather, she said, her goal was to be "present," to be "available," to be "a witness to the changes taking place in American culture" (N. Martin 1994). In calling attention to this fact, we are by no means disvaluing the potentially radical nature and consequences of Smith's work but rather noting differences between Smith's stated intentions and the way in which her work is most often characterized.

In broadest terms, if Acker's work continues to be represented as that of the bad girl of postpunk sensibility and often dismissed on those grounds, Smith's work is often figured in heroic terms, as "theatre's antidote to social irrelevance" (Lloyd 1998). Clearly, both Smith's production and the public text of her dramas have been broadly accepted and disseminated. (*Fires in the Mirror*, for instance, was broadcast on PBS's Great Performances, and *Twilight Los Angeles* was much in the news during the tenth anniversary of the Los Angeles riots.) Whether she is being profiled in *The New Yorker* (Lahr 1993) or hailed by *Newsweek* as "the most exciting individual in American theatre" (Kroll 1993), the *newness* and *uniqueness* of the effort—and the transformation she brings about via her individual acting skills—are consistently emphasized.

As writers such as Jacqueline Jones Royster, bell hooks, Victor Villanueva, Gloria Anzaldúa, and others have taught us, those whom our society constitutes as *other* may in our contemporary world find themselves allowed (as they might not have been in the past) to speak and to write. But it is a rare day when they are genuinely *heard*.[1] Our inquiry into the work and lives of Kathy Acker and Anna Deavere Smith confirms this understanding. For whether they are being reviled or adored, Acker and Smith both exemplify and demonstrate very strong challenges to traditional concepts of voice and singular authorship. Yet, in many ways, their work has not been *heard* in these terms, a fact we find to be strikingly ironic. In fact, most commentators continue to describe both Acker and Smith as "unique" and "original" voices and to comment on their individual accomplishments, in effect disregarding (refusing to hear) the persistent challenges both writers make to these very terms. Whether this irony reflects the unerring ability of late-capitalist individualism to co-opt acts of resistance or whether it reflects a kind of profound ambiguity and tension within Smith's and Acker's work (or perhaps some of both?) is not at all clear to us at this point.

Crimes of Reading

What *is* clear is that we can learn important lessons by examining such complex cases and by setting them in a broader communicative context that considers not only writing but reading. When we first began work on crimes of writing, it seemed to us that reading has been a much safer activity for women than writing has been. On reflection, however, we recognized that unsanctioned ways of reading have also been marked as misinterpretations, thefts, even felonies or immoral behaviors. This understanding reminded us that although reading often does not result in a material product, it—like writing— is an act of meaning-construction. It reminded us, in other words, that just as inquiry into acts of writing crimes can provide unique insights into some of the most commonsensical, and thus ideologically invisible, assumptions about what it means to write "properly," so too with reading crimes.

As we began exploring crimes of reading, we noted that these acts seemed more pervasive, but also less recognizably dangerous, than crimes of writing. In the midst of our research on this topic, however, we read Azar Nafisi's *Reading Lolita in Tehran*, a gripping memoir that describes, among other things, an underground (and highly dangerous) class on English and American literature that Nafisi taught in her home for two years after resigning from Tehran University in protest of its fundamentalist practices. In a society where the legal age for marriage at that time was nine, the punishment for female adultery was stoning, and a woman could be punished if a few strands of her hair fell out of her veil, gathering a group of young women together to read banned literature—and to spend a few hours free of their veils and chadors—was dangerous indeed. Yet Nafisi took this risk to maintain her intellectual and emotional life and to help other women resist some of the most severe restrictions of Muslim fundamentalism.

Reading Lolita in Tehran is for us a powerful reminder of just how dangerous—how criminal—acts of reading can be. Obviously, the nature of this danger can vary depending on culture and time period. In some cases, all that is at risk is a reader's social and cultural standing: there are reasons, after all, why a contemporary academic with a secret passion for popular romance novels might slip her current reading away in a drawer before welcoming her distinguished colleagues to a party. (Janice Radway's *Reading the Romance: Women, Patriarchy, and Popular Literature* is a fascinating ethnographic study of a group of women readers of such novels.) As Laura Smythe's work on Marguerite Porete demonstrates, however, reading can be not only dangerous but also a crime: Porete, a French beguine, was burned at the stake for heresy in 1310 on the evidence of her only book, *A Mirror for Simple Souls*. As Smythe notes, contemporary accounts and the *process-verbal* of Marguerite's trial strongly suggest that her greatest crime was not the writing of her text but her persistence in making copies of it available for reading, and that her condemnation and murder could well have been precipitated by her accusers' deliberate misreading of her text.

Other examples of dangerous reading acts are not hard to summon up. Think of Abelard and Heloise, for example, whose textual partnership and collaboration led to pleasure and eventually to sexual union, not to mention to disastrous consequences for both. In a recently completed dissertation, Kimberly Benedict explores the relationships between medieval women mystics and their scribes, relationships that sometimes highlight the sensuality of reading and recording, the ways in which sexuality and textuality could, and sometimes did, interact. Such acts of reading God's messages could be particularly dangerous, for the mystic receiver of those messages as well as for the transcriber of them.

Similar crimes of reading abound in early European America. Janice Knight, for example, explores the antinomian controversy, looking closely at how women's claims to interpretive or readerly authority were debated, and deplored. Of such claims, Anne Hutchinson's was surely strongest, eliciting charges of conspiracy, heresy, and spiritual harlotry. When Hutchinson continued to claim that her readings of the Bible came from God and were thus indisputable, John Winthrop called her heretical opinions "brats hatched from her leprous mind," and she was brought to civil trial and eventually banished— all for her insistently prophetic acts of reading.

In her keynote address at the conference "The Emergence of the Female Reader, 1500–1800" held at Oregon State University in May, 2001, Janice Radway contrasted conventional schooled reading practices, which call for reading as transfer, delivery, and assessment, with what she characterized as "promiscuous practices of reading," practices that make it difficult to tell where the author begins and ends and where the reader takes up, where interpretation can morph into poaching or stealing, as happens, for instance, when *Star Trek* fans claim the right to read new meanings into episodes by casting Mr. Spock and Captain Kirk as lovers or when online groups of *X-Files* fans rewrite episodes and, indeed, write new episodes in which Scully and Mulder's relationship is far from platonic. Radway has coined the term "interpersonation" to designate such transgressive practices of reading and writing. As an earlier example of such interpersonation, we might recall the Brontë children, whose reading of their own private language, world, and writings has been labeled pathological by many critics, even as the power of this reading for Charlotte and Emily, especially, has been acknowledged.

We might also consider the fears created when, in nineteenth-century America, new reading materials became available to the general public. As Cathy Davidson has shown in her analysis of novels written early in the Republic, these materials challenged elite authority, because new forms of popular literature (the newspaper, the romantic novel, and so on), unlike traditional poetry, could be read by anyone who possessed even modest literacy skills.[2] Whereas some saw an enlarged reading public as a positive sign of political and social change, others feared that these new readers, especially readers marked as marginal by gender, race, or class, would corrupt conventional standards of reading taste. Without a new group of women readers who relished the transgression of traditional taste by preferring sentimental to "serious" literature, the "mobs of scribbling women" derided by Hawthorne could not have been successful.

Who was right? Those like Hawthorne who upheld conventional "high" standards of reading and literature, or the new and transgressive readers of popular novels? We raise this question not to attempt an answer (and black-and-white questions like this one don't usually lend themselves to answers anyway, but only to heated debate) but rather to emphasize the importance of how reading practices, whether transgressive or conventional, are evaluated or valued. Certainly, it is tempting to identify marginalized readers and then to praise their implicit resistance to conventional elite cultural texts, to cheer on those who challenge the disciplinary tendencies of traditional reading in clearly transgressive ways. As Trysh Travis points out in "Divine Secrets of the Cultural Studies Sisterhood: Women Reading Rebecca Wells" (2003), it has become commonplace in cultural studies to identify and privilege narratives that resist hegemonic practices. Such practices, in Travis's view, too often obscure real material connections between readers and the texts they choose to read.

In one of her own attempts to look hard at specific historical conditions, Travis considers the phenomenon of the *Divine Secrets of the Ya-Ya Sisterhood*, which achieved national prominence in the United States and spawned many Ya-Ya Sisterhood clubs, not as a result of public relations efforts by major presses but rather through word of mouth from readers and independent bookstores. Initially drawn to the Ya-Ya Sisterhood phenomenon, which seemed to represent a potentially effective naming and claiming of women's experiences, Travis ultimately developed reservations. Her study of the publishing history of the Ya-Ya Sisterhood, as well as personal interviews with relevant individuals in the publishing industry and online discussions with members of Ya-Ya clubs, suggest that *The Divine Secrets of the Ya-Ya Sisterhood* is more about commercial shaping of readerly desires than the enabling of women's actual desires. Although Travis applauds the benefits that grow out of a book that encourages women to meet for regular conversation, she also argues that critics should not interpret the Ya-Ya Sisterhood phenomenon as a challenge to existing discursive authority. In short, the more Travis studied the purportedly transgressive acts of the Ya-Ya Sisterhood readers, the more she saw that these acts are already scripted in the text and in claims for it. Rather than contesting existing authority, then, these readers seem at least potentially caught up in the workings of an ever more efficient, subtle, and complex cultural industry, one that continues to discipline readers.

Other studies that focus on "specific historical conditions in which people make and read books," such as Jacqueline Jones Royster's *Traces of a Stream: Literacy and Social Change Among African American Women* (2000) and Anne Ruggles Gere's *Intimate Practices: Literacy and Cultural Work in U.S. Women's Clubs 1880–1920* (1997), cast additional light on the tensions between readers' desires and those of institutions intent on creating—or restricting—markets for particular texts and ways of reading them. Gere's *Intimate Practices*, for instance, considers (among other topics) the ways in which male professors of English (there were no other professors of English in American colleges at that time) from 1880 to 1920 figured women's acts of critical reading—acts that often took place in women's clubs throughout the United States—as inconsequential and amateur, reserving "real" reading for themselves. The women who met together on a regular basis to discuss their responses to various texts were hardly criminals, but their responses were nevertheless trivialized and disvalued by the male academic establishment.

In *Traces of a Stream*, Jacqueline Jones Royster tells an equally compelling story that links transgressive reading and writing practices. In this study, which brings together "what we know now about literacy with what we know now about African American women," Royster focuses on "the material conditions and the activities of African American women" (2000, ix; x). In the introduction to her study, Royster characterizes her effort as "A Call for Other Ways of Reading" (3), and reading figures prominently in her analysis. Like Gere, Royster focuses particularly on the club woman movement—in her case the rise of the Black Club women's movement. As she does so, Royster consistently emphasizes the ways that African American women's insistent efforts to read texts that would otherwise be denied to them have led to the writing of their own texts—and to social change as well.

As Gere's and Royster's studies evidence, the forces of control and discipline are ever at work in our culture. Particularly in the lived experience of the historical moment, it can be difficult to ascertain whether a particular literate act constitutes a (resistant) crime or a (co-opted) accommodation. In any literate act—whether of reading or writing—there will always be a tension between control and discipline, between self-expression and (variously bounded) acts of communication with others. This tension is especially apparent today in the debates within feminism and in rhetoric/composition over the nature and consequences of the growing use of such alternative discourses as personal criticism and multivoiced texts. Some feminists, for instance, find the use of the personal to be a liberating and productive practice; for others, it represents a self-indulgent solipsism. Likewise, some in rhetoric and composition advocate the teaching of alternative discourses, whereas others project dire warnings about the consequences of doing so. In these debates we see the forces of control and discipline predictably hard at work.

In fact, it's possible to trace the forces surrounding this particular debate all the way back to the many struggles over use of vernacular languages in the West, and certainly to the beginnings of the American experience. In this regard, the African American struggle for language rights has been particularly intense and long lasting. In her contribution to the double fiftieth anniversary issue of *CCC*, "CCCC's Role in the Struggle for Language Rights" (1999), Geneva Smitherman chronicles this struggle and argues that scholars in rhetoric and composition need to know this history and to continue to learn its lessons. We have learned a great deal from Smitherman, beginning with our reading of *Talkin' and Testifyin'* in 1977, and we have been very much aware of the transgressive nature of her writing practices. In fact, the reception of her work—especially early on—suggests that the very forces of control and discipline we have examined in this essay have worked to marginalize her writing and reading practices.

In this regard, it's telling that *Talkin' and Testifyin'* (1977) was published at virtually the same time that Mina Shaughnessy's *Errors and Expectations* (1977) appeared—yet at the time it was Shaughnessy's text that attracted the lion's share of attention and accolades. In our view, both Smitherman's forceful and (for some) controversial argument and her transgressive writing practices (especially her masterful code switching) contributed to the easiness with which audiences turned away from her text and toward Shaughnessy's. In recent years, Smitherman's work has received more attention: she was honored, for instance, in 2001 with the CCCC Exemplar Award. But we believe the significance of her ongoing project continues to be deflected by the forces that regulate academic and public discourses.

Discursive Crimes and the Teaching of Writing

How does this discussion of struggles over vernacular Englishes and the ways in which they influence the reception of writers' texts relate to the issues that teachers of writing—and the students in our classes—face when we decide whether particular discursive acts constitute "proper" (lawful) or "improper" (criminal) discourse? Our answer to this question is perhaps predictable, given our engagement with rhetoric and its traditions, for we believe that questions such as the one we pose here can be answered only by a rhetorically sensitive and situated analysis. Feminists, for example, can justifiably disagree about Acker's work. Does her writing, in its dependence on sexual violence, strike a blow for liberation or further enslave and degrade women? Does her work represent an "alternative" discourse that we should value and teach, or does it represent a crime, a violation of literary, social, and cultural norms that we should abjure? Do her practices hold potential theoretical implications for or constitute an implicit alternative to the traditional rhetoric of authorship and intellectual property, or are they simple examples of the crime of plagiarism? Teaching Acker's work demands attention to such questions as well as a full exploration of their implications for students and their lives.

What is true of Acker's texts is, of course, potentially true for any student text as well. A student writing a personal narrative or experimenting with alternative discourse strategies in a first-year writing class may indeed experience the writing of such texts as an act of productive resistance to the hegemonic assumptions and practices of the academy. But there is no guarantee that such will be the case. The student may just as likely feel that writing such essays means nothing more or less than meeting yet another academic requirement and may associate truly resistant writing with hip-hop, email, blogs, instant messaging, fanzines, and other self-sponsored writing and reading. (A Christian student attending a secular university might, for instance, find participating in a weekly Bible study group more transgressive in that particular context than reading a secular text.) Other students may feel that personally grounded writing assignments represent an unwarranted invasion of their privacy; they might prefer to respond to assignments that emphasize the conventions of academic discourse.

The divergent experiences and understandings we have just described are a reminder that although teachers can and must plan our writing classes—and can and must intervene in our students' writing processes via such activities as creating syllabi, making assignments, and evaluating essays—we cannot control the results of these activities for students' learning. We cannot, in other words, guarantee that an assignment that we hope will function as an invitation to a productive "crime" of writing and reading will be experienced in this way. Think, for instance, of the resistance that many students express when teachers ask them to engage published texts in highly critical ways. To the extent that students' previous education and culture have encouraged them to view texts as authoritative and/or as the neutral transmitters of established knowledge, this invitation to critical inquiry may strike students as a textual "crime." Our observations here may strike readers as unnecessarily pessimistic, and in one sense they are. We do believe that teachers cannot predict or control what students learn in our classes; but we also believe that teachers can think and act in creative ways about both the decisions we need to make as teachers and the decisions students need to make as writers. When we recognize that assignments we present to students as invitations to innovative, critical, and perhaps even experimental writing and reading may strike students as crimes to be avoided if at all possible; for instance, we can better understand why students can be so reluctant to take risks in both their writing and reading and why they can be so critical of others (whether published or student writers) who do so.

When we think of discursive risk-taking as potentially criminal, we can understand why even experienced writers and readers can find it difficult to challenge the conventions of the academy. In this regard, one of us recalls a particularly difficult conversation with a graduate student whose thesis she was directing. This graduate student, a feminist, wanted to write a thesis that was grounded not only in scholarly work but also in her own experience. Doing so, she argued, was itself a feminist act, and yet this graduate student found it extraordinarily difficult to write her thesis. When asked about this difficulty, she spoke at length about the power that the single word *thesis* exerted on her. "Every time I start to write something related to my own experience," she said, "I think of the word 'thesis'—and of the theses I've read in the library—and I think that what I'm trying to do is wrong, impossible, inappropriate. A thesis is supposed to have a thesis, which means it needs to be objective, neutral, and traditionally scholarly. How can I do that and also relate my ideas to my personal experience?"

If a graduate student who has both studied and enacted feminist theory and practice can find that her desire to write a resistant text is disciplined by the fear that she is undertaking a criminal act, imagine how powerful such understandings can be for less experienced, less confident, less self-conscious students. When teachers recognize the power that the academy holds to discipline students and to convince them that some kinds of acts represent crimes of writing and reading, we can use this understanding as we make decisions about syllabi and assignments. Teachers who want to encourage students to take risks that may strike students as crimes of writing or reading, for instance, may make these assignments low-risk activities in terms of the role they play in students' final course grades. Or they may build in strategic elements of choice in major assignments so that students can find an appropriate comfort level as they experiment with new discursive practices.

Teachers may also find it helpful to talk with students about issues related to crimes of reading and writing. Like many colleagues, for instance, we regularly raise issues of power and authority as they are related to acts of reading and writing. "Why does Annie Dillard get to have comma splices in her writing, but you don't?" we might ask. In discussions of such resistant texts as Anzaldúa's *Borderlands* (1987), we try to create opportunities for students to reflect on the risks—and benefits—inherent in such writing practices. More generally, we attempt explicitly to theorize our pedagogical practices and to share this theorizing with students. If we assign an activity that students may experience as criminal, dangerous, or offensive (such as asking students to articulate and then interrogate their racialized and gendered reading practices), we explicitly discuss those aspects of the assignment that students may consciously or unconsciously view as unlawful or miscreant.

Although we believe that the perspective on crimes of writing and reading that we have articulated here can help teachers make important day-to-day decisions in their classrooms, we conclude this essay by commenting on several important challenges that remain—challenges that are grounded in potential gaps and differences among the assumptions, values, and practices of teachers and students. As feminist teachers, for instance, we want to encourage our students to take risks and to challenge conventional understandings of gender and patriarchy. In our experience, our goals often differ from those of our students. How hard do we push students in encouraging them to take risks in their thinking, reading, and writing? Recognizing the key role that affect plays in student learning, how can we distinguish between an assignment that will provide an opportunity for students' growth and one that will seem so criminal that students will, in effect, shut down—meeting the letter of the assignment perhaps, but not its spirit.

Another difficult question involves the extent to which teachers should bring alternative discourses, which by their very nature represent potential crimes of reading and writing, into the classroom. From one perspective, doing so seems reasonable. If we as teachers find alternative discourses powerful, why not teach students to write such discourses? Yet if we do so, are we implicitly "disciplining" the challenge that these texts represent to hegemonic academic practices by turning them into schooled assignments? And what about students' own desires? As we noted earlier, many students already enact resistant writing practices. What are we telling students if we ignore these practices and focus on those we favor?

Questions such as these remind us that there is much that remains unclear and contested about both crimes of writing and reading and feminist practices in rhetoric and composition. As readers are aware, feminists often disagree about basic issues in feminist theory and practice. Similarly, there is much room for disagreement about crimes of writing and reading. Though we believe that certain discursive practices (such as Azar Nafisi's 2003 heretical and dangerous reading of Vladimir Nabokov and F. Scott Fitzgerald in Tehran) clearly constitute crimes of writing and reading, the answer to the question, what represents a (resistant) crime versus an accommodation to or variation of conventional practices is hardly obvious. Consider in this regard Oprah Winfrey's book club, which she reintroduced in 2003. From one perspective, this book club can be seen as a potential act of resistance to the corporatized and masculinized world of publishing. It can also be viewed, however, as an accommodation to, or even a capitalization of, this same world.

In closing, we return to a question that we posed at the start of our essay: What are the potential consequences of recent efforts to reclaim and redefine women's rhetorical practices for the actual *teaching* of writing? As our analysis suggests, these consequences have less to do with advocating for particular pedagogical practices and more to do with general understandings of what is at stake when we teach writing. They remind us, as we pointed out earlier, that as teachers we cannot control the results of our pedagogical practices for students' learning. Thus, although we continue to invite students to write collaboratively or to compose texts that experiment or play with language, we do so knowing that depending on their own interests and situations students may experience these invitations in quite diverse ways. Given this diversity, it becomes all the more important for teachers to inquire into both our and our students' rhetorically and materially grounded situations. The results of this inquiry will always be tentative and uncertain: rhetoric is, after all, the search for the best available means of persuasion in a particular situation—whether that situation involves writing an argument or teaching a class.

Notes

1. We have learned a great deal from Krista Ratcliffe's important work on how to listen rhetorically, an act that makes it possible for others to be heard.

2. See the discussion of this topic in Charles Paine's *The Resistant Writer: Rhetoric as Immunity, 1850 to the Present* (1999, 66). The Davidson reference is to *Revolution and the Word: The Rise of the Novel in America* (1986).

2

Coming Out

Or, How Adrienne Rich's Feminist Theory Complicates Intersections of Rhetoric and Composition Studies, Cultural Studies, and Writing Program Administration

Krista Ratcliffe

As a feminist scholar in rhetoric and composition studies and as a writing program administrator (WPA), I feel compelled to question our field's intersections
with cultural studies—not because I deem such intersections unproductive but,
rather, because when I listen to contemporary cultural studies panels on gender
or read contemporary cultural studies articles about gender, I frequently ask
myself: "Is this information new? Haven't I heard it before?" Call me retro (or
just old and crotchety), but my answer is often: "YES, I have heard this information before . . . in feminist theory . . . although something feels amiss here."
What feels amiss to me in some cultural studies work on gender is the silent
presence of feminism. Whenever this silent presence troubles me, I flash back to
a bell hooks' claim: "I am excited about cultural studies . . . as a critical political
intervention . . . [But there is] the danger of cultural studies appropriating issues
of race, gender, and sexual practice, and then continuing to hurt and wound in
the politics of domination" (Hall 1992, 294). This charge is serious, yet it invites
not so much a definitive response as a continual vigilance.[1]

But what form should such vigilance take? The answer to this question
depends on the desired outcome. If the desired outcome is to affirm the status
quo (in which feminism functions as a silent presence within cultural studies
work on gender), then vigilance simply implies that feminist scholar/teachers
should ignore this silent presence. If the desired outcome is to challenge the
status quo and increase a feminist literacy among colleagues and students,
then vigilance implies that feminist scholar/teachers should articulate this
silent presence in scholarship and pedagogy. If the desired outcome is to convert colleagues and students to feminist ideology, then vigilance implies that
feminist scholar/teachers should proselytize colleagues and students. Although

each option has its allure at different moments, as a scholar and WPA, I am particularly interested in the second one, the promotion among colleagues and students of a feminist literacy (i.e., an understanding of feminist issues, stakes, tactics, and politics). For personal and institutional reasons, as a WPA I cannot deny the feminist grounding of my scholarship and administrative practices (option one), nor can I realistically expect to convert all my colleagues and students to feminism (option three); but I can offer opportunities for colleagues and students to gain a feminist literacy (option two) by initiating conversations that not only correct misimpressions of feminism but also articulate the silent presence of feminism within cultural studies work on gender.

As a scholar and WPA, I want to initiate such conversations by asking hard questions about the intersections of feminism and cultural studies in rhetoric and composition studies, especially as they pertain to writing program administration. For the purposes of this article, two questions concern me. The first provides the grounds for my thinking: that is, have contemporary cultural studies projects on gender gained more popularity in our field than feminist projects? This question implies more than a simple popularity contest; it implies a question of method. For although cultural studies projects may employ gender as one of many analytic lenses for critiquing culture, feminist projects employ gender as a primary but not solitary analytic lens for promoting feminist politics. If I am correct in believing that cultural studies projects have gained greater popularity than feminist ones, then a related question emerges: that is, what is the significance of gender's ascendancy over feminism? This question of significance implies more than a "who's on top" contest; it implies a question of political effects.

One response to the question of political effects is offered by Rosemary Hennessy, who explains the negative consequences of prioritizing gender over feminism in this way: "[s]ubstituting the social category 'gender' or the identity 'woman' for the set of discourses constituted by feminism mutes the interestedness and the potential collective power posed by feminism as a critique of the systemic inequities wrought by capitalist patriarchy" (1992, 12). I agree. But the question of gender versus feminism may be more complicated than constructing a binary opposition of the two and deeming feminism the better choice. Indeed, Adrienne Rich's feminist theory offers rhetoric and composition studies a way to bridge Hennessy's binary opposition by juxtaposing a contemporary cultural studies focus on gender (and other cultural categories) with a feminist politics. Such a move may be imagined topologically by positing Rich's feminist theory as a metonym (i.e., juxtaposed alongside cultural studies), not as a synecdoche (i.e., subsumed or silently present within it).

People sometimes ask why I still focus on Rich instead of more current theorists, such as psychoanalytic and postmodern feminists.[2] My answer is that Rich's texts still speak to me—with clarity, with dignity, with ethics, with wisdom. She is no more irrelevant today in rhetoric and composition studies than is Aristotle, for like Aristotle's thought, Rich's theory may be adapted to time and place. Moreover, just as Aristotle's theory provides one historical grounding for contemporary rhetoric and composition studies, Rich provides one historical grounding for contemporary cultural studies work on gender, for Rich's theory pioneered feminist cultural studies projects when many early cultural studies scholars were still focusing mostly on class. So, in this article I hope to facilitate a metonymic coming out of Rich's theory in rhetoric and composition studies alongside cultural studies work on gender, my goal being to foster a feminist literacy in colleagues and students.

To demonstrate the potential synergy between Rich's theory and cultural studies work on gender, I turn to an analytic method offered by cultural studies scholars Lawrence Grossberg, Cary Nelson, and Paula Treichler in their edited collection *Cultural Studies* (1992). They argue that cultural studies is particularly engaging because its domains, methodologies, and intellectual legacies are constantly blurred and open for debate (1). To demonstrate that Rich's feminist theory integrates a cultural studies focus on gender (and other cultural categories, such as race) with a feminist politics, I borrow these three categories (domains, methodologies, and intellectual legacies) and add a fourth (pedagogical legacies).

Domain: Rich's Theory of Subject Position and Agency via a Politics of Location

Rich's feminist theory contributes to rhetoric and composition studies because it maps gendered rhetorical terrain that too often remains unmapped in traditional rhetorical theories (Ratcliffe 1996, 108–19). For example, her politics of location provides feminist definitions of subject position and agency. These two concepts are critical for rhetoric and composition studies, for as Jacqueline Jones Royster demonstrates throughout "When the First Voice You Hear Is Not Your Own," every rhetorical theory and every rhetorical situation assumes an understanding of both subject position (i.e., who is speaking—and from what personal/cultural positions?) and agency (i.e., what makes such speaking possible?). But to be fully understood, Rich's concepts of subject position and agency must be contextualized within her feminist theory.

Rich defines feminism in "The Anti-Feminist Woman" as "an imaginative identification with all women (and with the ghostly woman in all men)," further arguing that "the feminist must, because she can, extend this act of the imagination as far as possible" (1979, 71). Grounded in psychical and cultural identifications, this definition is not essentialist and does not exclude men; grounded in the imagination, it does presume a space for agency (albeit limited) within our identifications. In "Disobedience and Women's Studies" Rich claims that feminism provides "a political and spiritual base from which . . . to examine rather than . . . hide . . . racism" and other negating socializations (1986, 84). This definition extends feminism's focus beyond a single cultural category (gender) and posits it as a politicized woman-centered lens through which the intersections of gender and other cultural categories (race, age, nationality, class, etc.) may be recognized, critiqued, and acted on. From this base of gender-as-it-intersects-with-other-cultural-categories, Rich builds her related concepts of subject position and agency.

Rich defines subject position in terms of a politics of location. This location invokes both the general category of (ghostly) Woman and the particularity of each person's experiences, located in specific times and places. In other words, at any particular time and place, all people are socialized by similar gender codes, yet each person may identify with this socialization in particular ways. Rich exemplifies her concept of subject position by examining her own locations: "I need to understand how a place on the map is also a place in history within which as a woman, a Jew, a lesbian, a feminist I am created and trying to create" (1986, 212). By juxtaposing the names she accords herself (woman, Jew, lesbian, feminist), Rich recognizes the discourses and experiences that inform her own subject position and its attendant agency.

Rich defines *agency* as the choices available to a person within his/her politics of location. She exemplifies this definition by again examining her own locations and then by demonstrating how the names she accords herself (woman, Jew, lesbian, feminist) function as synecdoches, or parts of her identity (1986, 212). When taken together, these names do not create a totalizing identity for Rich but rather make visible the spaces and slippages among the names, and it is within these spaces and slippages that Rich recognizes her socialization. With this recognition comes the potential to critique and to act on her socialization; in other words, with this recognition comes the potential for agency.

Of course, conscious agency is always limited by the unconscious and by the material conditions of particular locations. For example in her 1982 "Split at the Root," Rich recognizes one such limitation to her agency: "I would have liked, in this essay, to bring together the meanings of anti-Semitism and racism as I have experienced them and as I believe they intersect in the world beyond my life. But I'm not able to do this yet" (1986, 122). Rich is able to find the agency for "moving into accountability" when she closes her essay with a self-declared ethics:

> I know that in the rest of my life, the next half century or so, every aspect of my identity will have to be engaged. The middle-class white girl taught to trade obedience for privilege. The Jewish lesbian raised to be a heterosexual gentile. The woman who first heard oppression named and analyzed in the Black Civil Rights movement. The woman with three sons, the feminist who hates male violence. The woman limping with a cane, the woman who has stopped bleeding are also accountable. The poet who knows that beautiful language can lie, that the oppressor's language sometimes sounds beautiful. The woman trying, as part of her resistance, to clean up her act. (1986, 123)

As Rich demonstrates, a person's subject position as well as the agency afforded by that position is constantly changing. What remains constant is the constant change along with the ethical imperative for accountability.

Given these interrelated concepts of subject position and agency, Rich's politics of location emerges as more than simply a born or lived cultural position; it is also a space of imaginative identifications and complex ethical choices. It admits its situatedness, its multivocality, its ethical contradictions, and its vested interests. It refuses the easy label of "essentialist identity politics" by positing gender categories (note the plural) that blur, overlap, circle back on themselves, and change from moment to moment, text to text, body to body, identification to identification.

In addition to helping readers and writers identify their own subject positions and find agency in the spaces and slippages of their own locations, Rich's politics of location also offers the possibility of identifying subject positions and finding agency in intersubjective spaces and slippages between/among people. As such, Rich's rhetoric emphasizes not only ethics but politics in its more traditional sense of polis. Whereas feminist politics assume agency and successful communication, these possibilities are not givens in Rich's theory. They entail conscious effort, hard work, occasional danger. For example, in her epistolary essay "Dearest Arturo," she defines their friendship as the intersections of many social categories: "We're both different generations, cultures, genders; we're both gay, both disabled, both writers" (1993, 22). These intersections not only define Rich and Arturo, informing the logics within which they function, but also make visible the (im)possibilities of interpersonal and intercultural communications. Rich is very aware of this phenomenon; twice in her letter she asks Arturo: "Does this make sense to you?" (1993, 23; 27). Her attempts to make sense to Arturo presume that agency and successful communication can emerge not just from identifications in which differences are bridged (thank you, Kenneth Burke) but also from identifications in which differences are recognized and respected.

In the wake of poststructuralism, subject position and agency have been hotly debated concepts in feminist circles, not so much in relation to whether they exist but rather where and how. Like Joan Hartman and Ellen Messer-Davidow in *(En)Gendering Knowledge*, Rich defines agency in terms of capability, not intentionality, and the extent to which people and systems are "mutually constitutive" (Hartman and Davidow 1991, 13). Consequently, Rich's agency does not assume the autonomous will of liberal humanism that can single-mindedly overcome structural oppression with a conscious decision; neither does it assume the lexical subjectivity of radical poststructuralism that reduces humans only to discursive positions. Rather, it is predicated on a woman's (un)conscious participation in constructing her own life and history via the limits and possibilities of her politics of location. This participation is exemplified by Rich's persona in "Love Poem XV": "If I cling to circumstances I could feel / not responsible. Only she who says / she did not choose is the loser in the end" (1975, 11–15). Note that Rich posits victory not as the successful execution of the choice but as the process of making the choice itself.

Finally, Rich reminds us that questions of subject position and agency beg questions of power. She notes that power is a troublesome concept for women and feminists: "It has been long associated for us with the use of force, with rape, with the stockpiling of weapons, with the ruthless accrual of wealth and the hoarding of resources, with the power that acts only in its own interest, despising and exploiting the powerless—including women and children" (1986, 5). Because women cannot hide from the existence and effects of patriarchal power, she argues that women must reimagine agency as power effected through our politics of location, not as power bestowed upon us by others (1986, 5). And just as importantly, women must own the power afforded us by our locations—and use it.

In terms of language, however, women have struggled to find and accept such agency and power, as Rich notes in "When We Dead Awaken": "I think it has been a peculiar confusion to the girl or woman who tries to write because she is peculiarly susceptible to language. She goes to poetry or fiction looking for *her* way of being in the world . . . and over and over in the 'words' masculine persuasive force' she comes up against something that negates everything she is about" (1979, 39). Yet, again, it is in the gaps and slippages of this gendered negation that a woman (or anyone in a disempowered position) may find her own agency—and power—to assert her voice and attempt to resist oppressive logics and cultural structures.

In sum, Rich's feminist theory offers rhetoric and composition studies complex concepts of subject position and agency via a politics of location. These concepts recognize that identity is shaped by subjective and intersubjective identifications and that agency is available within and among the spaces and slippages of these identifications. In this way, Rich's theory articulates a gender analysis indebted to cultural studies, one that foregrounds a feminist politics that works toward a more just society, especially but not solely for women.

Method: Rich's Re-vision

Rich's method of re-vision contributes to rhetoric and composition studies because it offers a strategy for feminist invention that enables readers and writers to question the status quo and imagine/enact, when necessary, feminist alternatives. Not content simply to define a subject position and proclaim that agency exists, Rich posits a method for exercising agency, that is, re-vision. Rich defines re-vision as "seeing again," as diving into the wreck of women's history, myths, and lives to uncover erasures and, ultimately, to construct a more just society (1979, 35). She delineates the process of re-vision as follows:

> To question everything. To remember what it has been forbidden even to mention. To come together telling our stories, to look afresh at, and then to describe for ourselves . . . To do this kind of work takes a capacity for constant active presence, a naturalist's attention to minute phenomena, for reading between

the lines, watching closely for symbolic arrangements, decoding difficult and complex messages left for us by women of the past. It is work, in short, that is opposed by, and stands in opposition to, the entire twentieth-century white male capitalist culture. (1979, 13–14)

Readers of Rich's poetry and prose will recognize this process as one she practices in all her texts. Such "seeing again" enables her to recognize and critique socialization while affording her the options to reaffirm, resist, and/or revise that socialization.

Like Nancy Sommers' concept of revision in "Between the Drafts," Rich's use of that term possesses the potential to affect all of life (1986, 5). Re-vision affects the personal when we use it to search for personal identity, the cultural when we use it to negotiate structural injustices (1979, 35), and the discursive when we use it to reread lives, systems, and texts (1979, 39). Moreover, the personal, the cultural, and the textual are not three distinct categories but rather are intersectional, bound together by language that possesses a material and metaphoric dimension. The material dimension posits the immanence of language:

Language is as real, as tangible in our lives as streets, pipelines, telephone switchboards, microwaves, radioactivity, cloning laboratories, nuclear power stations. We might hypothetically possess ourselves of every technological resource on the North American continent, but as long as our language is inadequate, our vision remains formless, our thinking and feeling are still running in old cycles, our process may be "revolutionary" but not transformative. (1979, 247–48)

For language to facilitate transformative agency, the material dimension must be supplemented by a metaphoric one. Because metaphors generate comparisons between unlike things, they inevitably presume differences, but these differences are often mystified by metaphor's focus on similarities. Rich, however, emphasizes differences, believing they can expose within dominant discourses the spaces and slippages that enable agency.

Rich best defines metaphor by how she employs it throughout her poetry and prose.[3] Her most famous example is the title of her well-known poem "Diving into the Wreck," which challenges readers to plunge into history, myths, and their own lives, looking for the lost treasure of women's erased contributions. This metaphor of the wreck stands in stark contrast to the dominant metaphors of cultural studies analyses. As James Berlin and Michael Vivion readily admit, the dominant metaphors of cultural studies are Marxist and poststructuralist (to which I would add masculinist). For example, when class becomes the dominant cut across the social and gender becomes just another category, when society becomes "digital," and when teachers become "cultural warriors," such critics must re-vision these metaphors if they are not to limit or erase feminist concerns (Berlin and Vivion 1992, xiv).

Rich's re-vision may be read as a form of autoethnography that results in a feminist literacy—and sometimes in a commitment to feminist politics. Rich's re-vision also provides a historical grounding for current cultural studies work on gender. For example, in her 1990 article "Post-Marxism and Cultural Studies," Angela McCrobbie calls for a "new" method of cultural studies resistance—specifically, "a new paradigm for conceptualizing identity-in-culture, an ethnographic approach which takes as its starting point the relational interactive quality of everyday life and which brings a renewed rigor to this kind of work by integrating into it a keen sense of history and contingency" (1992, 730). To me, McCrobbie's call echoes the silent presence of Rich's feminism, for Rich's feminist theory has been performing McCrobbie's call since at least 1972. My point is not to dismiss McCrobbie's article; indeed, it is important to rhetoric and composition studies because it links ethnography to cultural studies. Nor is my point to establish Rich as the origin of feminist theory; her work rests on the shoulders of centuries of feminists who preceded her. My point is that Rich's theory is important to rhetoric and composition studies because it provides a feminist model of autoethnography.

If we consider Rich's re-vision as an autoethnographic move and allow it to inform rhetoric and composition scholarship and pedagogy, we may arrive at a pedagogy similar to what Jim Berlin describes in "Poststructuralism, Cultural Studies, and the Composition Classroom" (1992), in which he explains how he established a writing program at Purdue University based on analyzing language as a discursive map of cultural codes (gender, race, class, etc.). Yet, if we place Rich's theory alongside Berlin's, we may function from a slightly different ideological base—one that does not necessarily make good little feminists out of all our colleagues and students but that offers them a feminist literacy, not simply gender, as another category of analysis. Feminist literacy may cause feminist issues, stakes, tactics, and politics to register on people's radar and perhaps even become a daily part of their academic and public sphere debates, much as women's suffrage and equal pay have done.

Intellectual Legacy

Rich's feminist theory offers myriad intellectual legacies for rhetoric and composition studies; here, however, I focus on only three. The first is a clearly articulated feminist theory of language. As the previous two sections demonstrate, Rich's feminist theory posits language as a powerful force in subject formation and its attendant agency. Yet, her theory recognizes that language is not all-powerful, that it "cannot do everything" (1973, 71–2). As Elspeth Probyn reminds us in "The Culture of Everyday Life," "there are also questions of actual, real dangers to people, to women who walk on the street" (Fiske 1992, 171). Even if it is through language that we articulate people and streets, a word is not a body and cannot always stop a bullet. Thus, Rich's language theory exposes how the textual intersects, but is not identical with, the personal and the cultural.

The second intellectual legacy is a feminist tactic for analyzing not only how gender intersects with other cultural categories, such as class, race, age, nationality, etc., but also how the personal intersects with the cultural and textual. For example, Rich describes how as a young (age) girl (gender) growing up in the South (region) in the United States (nationality), she was encouraged to learn manners (class) that obfuscated racist thinking (race):

> I still try to claim I wasn't brought up to hate. But hate isn't the half of it. I grew up in the vast encircling presumption of whiteness—that primary quality of being which knows itself, its passions, only against an otherness that has to be dehumanized. I grew up in white silence that was utterly obsessional. Race was the theme whatever the topic.
>
> In the case of my kin the word sprayed on the overpass [Niggers] was unspeakable, part of a taboo vocabulary. That word was the language of "rednecks." My parents said "colored," "Negro," more often "They," even sometimes, in French. Such language could dissociate itself from lynching, from violence, from such a thing as hatred. (1993, 181)

The (personal) lessons of white silence echo and enable the (cultural) white silence in response to the (textual) inscribing of racist language on the overpass. Such personal lessons teach Rich that language enables white speakers to dissociate from the racial markings of their own bodies, parlors, schools, churches, and public restrooms. This dissociation fosters denial—personal, cultural, and textual. And according to Rich's theory, this denial is a form of violence; it explains Martin Luther King Jr.'s claim that the real hindrance to the civil rights movement was not the ultraconservative white hate groups but rather the hesitation of white moderates (King 1963/1999, 417).

The third intellectual legacy that Rich's theory offers rhetoric and composition studies is a tactic for resisting denial, which emerges via an intertextual reading of feminist theory. For example, to counter the fact that Anglo-American feminisms have too long been predicated on a narrow, whitewashed vision of the world (1986, x), Rich proposes in "North American Tunnel Vision" that the central concepts of African American and Native American feminisms be integrated with Anglo-American ones. Such concepts include nonessentialized identity politics, simultaneous oppressions, ideology grounded in concrete experience, and a refusal to be bribed into silence or inaction in return for a room of one's own (1986, 165). Rich's purpose is not to appropriate these other theories nor to whitewash such reconsiderations but, rather, to articulate her location as a white woman and to resist the blindnesses associated with this location (and she reminds us that all locations have blindnesses). In "Notes toward a Politics of Location" she offers a simple yet effective starting point for such resistance: "When we talk about we, we should ask ourselves 'who is *we*?'" (1986, 231).

These three intellectual legacies offer a feminist literacy, which challenges us to question commonly accepted patterns of thinking, feeling, and acting and then to reaffirm, resist, and/or revise them. In sum, Rich's intellectual legacies provide us ways of being within the world within language, both in terms of scholarship and pedagogy.

Pedagogical Legacies:
Rich and Writing Program Administration

Rich's feminist theory provides rhetoric and composition studies myriad possibilities for pedagogy. But before these possibilities are discussed, the problems inherent in theory/pedagogy intersections should be examined. The slash between theory and pedagogy in the previous sentence does not signify a seamless transaction but rather a complicated gap. For theory does not smoothly translate into pedagogy any more than pedagogy easily generates theories. Indeed, before a theory can be performed in a classroom, it must be interpreted by an instructor, whose politics of location not only helps her see pedagogical possibilities within a theory but also blinds her to other possibilities. During this interpretive process, a theory is conflated with an instructor's other identifications and disidentifications; hence, what an instructor imagines as a theory enacted in his classroom is actually his own version of that theory translated into the classroom in a particular way. That "way" is influenced as much by the instructor, the students, the institution, and the historical moment as it is by the theory itself. That explains why 100 different teachers might do 100 different things with Rich's concept of a politics of location.

That a pedagogical "application" of a theory cannot be replicated by all instructors via the scientific method does not negate theory's import for pedagogy.[4] Rather, it clarifies how much work an instructor must do to become a pedagogue. Theory is not a cookie cutter to be laid on an instructor, a classroom, or a writing program; it is not a template to be slavishly and acontextually followed. If it were, just think how much easier teaching (and WPA administration) would be. Rather, theory is a space for questioning and planning, for explaining what has happened and predicting what may. As such, Rich's feminist theory offers WPAs concepts, metaphors, and writerly/readerly tactics that may inform their decision making when designing a writing program or training TAs to teach within it.

To exemplify how Rich's theory may (not) inform a WPA's work, I offer my own WPA experiences at Marquette University, a Jesuit PhD-granting university in Milwaukee, Wisconsin. In January 2002 I began redesigning Marquette's First-Year English (FYE) program, which consists of a two-semester writing course. The redesigned program had to meet the rhetoric criteria of the university's new core curriculum and be ready for implementation when I became WPA in August 2002.

During the redesigning process, my first thought was of the students: I wanted them to appreciate the "common core curriculum" experience that Marquette promises; I wanted them to understand the power of language, literacy, and rhetoric that Rich champions, and I wanted them to write well as students and as citizens. But what did they want? To find out, I talked with students in undergraduate classes who asked for, among other things, challenging reading, practical writing assignments, and very little busy work. I also heeded results of alumni surveys, which claimed that for our graduates the writing norm in the working world is collaborative.

My second thought was of instructors: I wanted them to have a program structure that provided solid pedagogical support yet enough space in which to perform their own teaching identities, based on their own politics of location, even as they simultaneously performed identities as graduate students or part-time instructors at other institutions. But what did they want? To find out, I informally chatted with instructors and formally attended a meeting of the Association of English Graduate Students to determine their thinking about Marquette students and about teaching composition. They wanted, among other things, intellectually engaging work, pedagogical support, and some freedom within the program structure.

My third thought was of the English department in which I work: I wanted to respect the mission of the department and uphold its tradition of supporting its graduate program via the FYE program. But what did the department want? To find out, I spoke with the chair and reflected on conversations with colleagues, specifically the outgoing FYE Director, Virginia Chappell, and the director of the writing center, Paula Gillespie.

My fourth thought was of the institution: I wanted to respect Marquette University's Jesuit principles of "caring for the whole person," of "creating men and women for others," and of according rhetoric a prominent place in its core curriculum. But what did people within the institution want? To find out, I consulted with colleagues outside of English. My goal was not to offer FYE as a service course (although I think WPAs are a bit naive when we deny that function) but rather to generate a dialogue about writing. As a result of these conversations, the FYE English committee was reconfigured that fall to include not just English department faculty but also one member from each college other than Arts and Sciences.

My fifth thought was of myself. What did I want? Well, mostly I wanted answers to these questions: (1) what program design did I believe in? (I knew that the design would somehow have to integrate literacy and rhetoric and Rich's re-vision); (2) what program could I train TAs to teach? (I knew that I could not narrowly design a course that only I wanted to teach); (3) what program could I defend to administrators and parents who might call? (I knew forcing a feminist politics on students would backfire); and (4) how could Rich's feminist theory help me reconcile competing needs of students, instructors, the English Department, the university, and myself? The answer to the last question is complicated—and local, as all politics are—and still in process. But perhaps the best way to address the question is to critique the program that I designed and the pedagogical support system that I established. Here is the FYE program description that I designed:

> Critical Literacy is the ability to recognize, analyze, employ and, when necessary, interrupt discourse conventions (e.g., accepted topics, genres, and styles) within particular discourse communities (e.g., home, work, church, school). For example, an academic history essay requires different writing conventions than does an academic chemistry report, and both require different writing conventions than does a letter to the editor or a business report. With these ideas in mind, the First-Year English Program at Marquette University is designed to help students learn both general conventions of good writing and context-specific conventions so that students may present their ideas and beliefs most effectively. According to Quintilian, this ability to analyze and employ language effectively in a variety of situations is called facilitas.
>
> To foster Critical Literacy via facilitas, the First-Year English Program offers a two-course writing sequence. English 001 focuses on Academic Literacy, introducing students to the critical thinking, reading, and writing skills that are grounded in western logic and expected from well-rounded university students. English 002 focuses on Public Sphere Literacy, introducing students to the critical thinking, reading, writing, speaking, and listening skills expected of informed public citizens.
>
> Each unit in English 001 and English 002 contains the following elements: literacy, rhetoric, and writing goals; sequenced reading and writing activities that focus on local, national, and/or global issues; collaborative activities; ungraded short writings that work toward the final written project; and, of course, a final written project. English 002 has additional public speaking instruction and oral presentations. At the end of each semester, students have the opportunity to revise one paper for a new grade and to submit a comprehensive portfolio of their writings, along with a letter of reflection.
>
> The goal of Marquette University's First-Year English Program, with its emphasis on critical literacy in academic and public spheres, is to offer students ways of understanding the world and acting within their communities, via language, for the greater good of all. (Ratcliffe 2002b)[5]

No mention of Rich's feminist theory of rhetoric appears in this description, but unlike cultural studies work on gender that seems unaware of previous feminist theory, my design was informed by Rich's theory. For example, although the focus on critical literacy echoes a contemporary cultural studies approach embraced by many of our faculty and graduate students, this focus also echoes Rich's linkage of the personal, the textual, and the cultural in that students are taught to express their values and beliefs for a variety of audiences in a variety of genres. Although the program goals of critical literacy (e.g., recognizing, analyzing, employing, and interrupting discursive conventions) echo contemporary cultural studies pedagogies, they also echo Rich in encouraging women to recognize and, when necessary, to resist and/or revise the personal, the textual, and the cultural. Although the rhetoric focus echoes my mid-1980's graduate school training with Ed Corbett and Andrea Lunsford, it also reflects Rich's articulation about the importance of language in our gendered socializations. Although the focus on ideas and beliefs emerges from the Jesuit notion of educating the whole person, it also emerges from Rich's insistence that we recognize how the term *person* is gendered and raced and classed—in Jesuit and other traditions. And although the focus on "the greater good of all" reflects the Jesuit impetus for social justice, it also reflects Rich's feminist politics, in which she makes certain to specify that the term "all" includes women.

Likewise, Rich's feminist theory echoes in my unit designs for the two-semester FYE course. English 001 (now subtitled Academic Literacy) asks students to write in a variety of genres (e.g., poetry, narratives, freewriting, summary, critical responses) as short writings and then to write thesis-support essays as their final products. This focus allows students to explore different ways of expressing themselves; it also allows students to learn how to adapt such expressions into academic prose. This emphasis helps students learn to articulate and refine their own writing processes as well as to find effective voices within the academy. With these writing goals in mind, English 001 offers the following inquiry-based units:

Unit One: Academic Exposition

Unit Two: Academic Analyses

Unit Three: Academic Critique

Unit Four: Academic Argument

Unit Five: Academic Reflection and Essay Exams

The unit on academic exposition juxtaposes academic writing with personal literacy narratives and asks students to explain the import of literacy; this focus echoes Rich's process of writing about her own experiences as a way of understanding cultural issues. The unit on academic analyses asks students to research authoritative sources on topics of their choice and to insert their own voices into the conversation; this focus echoes Rich's belief that hiding one's voice behind abstract prose can be a dysfunctional silence. The unit on academic critique asks students to employ an academic theory as a springboard for questioning and evaluating a pop culture phenomenon; this focus echoes Rich's claims that theory must be tied to material culture and that material culture is ripe for feminist critique. The unit on academic argument asks students to make rhetorical functions of language visible and to argue about the effects of language on people and cultures; this focus echoes Rich's assertion that language both socializes people and provides a means for reaffirming, resisting, and/or revising such socialization. The unit on academic reflection is a tradition within Marquette's FYE program that asks students to revise one essay and to write a letter reflecting on their own writing for the semester; in the best cases, this assignment provides an opportunity for Rich's re-vision.

English 002 (now subtitled Public Sphere Literacy) asks students to write in a variety of genres as short writings and as their final products. Like English 001, it encourages students to explore different ways of expressing themselves; unlike English 001, it allows students to learn how to adapt their expressions into different public sphere genres, such as letters to the editor and business memos. This focus helps students learn to keep articulating and refining their own writing processes as well as to keep searching for effective voices within the public sphere. With these writing goals in mind, English 002 offers the following inquiry-based units.

Unit One: Media Literacy

Unit Two: Narrative Literacy

Unit Three: Civic Literacy

Unit Four: Workplace Literacy

Unit Five: Reflection

The unit on media literacy asks students to write a thesis-support essay critiquing rhetorical, narrative, and cultural coding in advertising texts so that students can learn how academic habits of mind may be used to analyze public sphere issues; this focus echoes Rich's exhortation to expose for re-vision cultural images of women. The unit on narrative literacy asks students to write a thesis-support essay critiquing the narrative, cultural, and ethical dimensions of competing narratives, for example, different versions of Cinderella; this focus echoes Rich's method of "diving into the wreck" of women's history and narratives so as to determine what is erased or misrepresented, to articulate the historical/cultural grounding of the narratives, and to grapple with the ethical dilemmas posed by the narratives. The unit on civic literacy asks students to write a creative nonfiction piece on a compelling cultural issue and persuasively address it to a public audience, rather like a *Newsweek* "My Turn" column; this focus echoes Rich's written essays, which posit her personal narratives as the grounds for writing in order to persuade a public audience about cultural issues such as women's education or white silence. The unit on workplace literacy asks students to adopt a problem/solution trope and write memos, letters, and informal reports about a problem at school, on the job, in a volunteer group, and the like; although this focus, to be honest, is influenced less by Rich than by my institutional pressures, it echoes Rich's notion that women should learn to assert their voices in public forums.

Although Rich's influence pervades my design of the FYE program, the program fosters in instructors and students not necessarily a feminist politics but rather a feminist literacy, that is, an understanding of some feminist issues, stakes, tactics, and politics. Within this program structure, FYE instructors may choose whether or not to perform a feminist pedagogy. By feminist pedagogy, I mean "the situated knowing-being-doing-learning" that presumes gender as the primary but not sole lens of analysis and that emerges via pedagogical tactics and course content, "which are driven by teachers' (un)conscious feminist assumptions, influenced by students' particular subjectivities, circumscribed by institutional values, and affected by particular historical moments and cultural locations" (Ratcliffe 1996, 153).

For example, in the unit on academic argument in English 001, all instructors may assign Aileen Pace Nielson's "Sexism in English: A 1990's Update" and Geneva Smitherman's "White English in Blackface" (1973) along with articles by James Baldwin, Victor Villanueva, and George Orwell. Whether the assignment results in a feminist pedagogy depends on the instructor's politics of location as well as on how the instructor frames the discussions, assignments, and class dynamics. A feminist teacher may inadvertently conduct a nonfeminist lesson plan just as a nonfeminist teacher may inadvertently teach feminist issues. And teachers may consciously teach with or against the grain of a text. Likewise, students may consciously read with or against the grain of the text, although instructors need to remember that the power dynamics of the classroom privilege the teacher's perspective. In sum, when engaging these texts via reading and writing, instructors may choose whether or not to adopt a feminist politics and pedagogy; regardless of that choice, however, instructors and students may develop a feminist literacy about language. Is this my ideal goal? No. Is it a realistic one, given my politics of location? Yes.

So how may instructors choose to develop a feminist pedagogy? Well, I have provided multiple pedagogical supports. First, I designed a custom reader, *Critical Literacies*, to be used in our program. Unit introductions offer issues that encourage discussion from feminist perspectives; for example, the media literacy introduction offers a discussion of *Sports Illustrated* and *Sports Illustrated Women*; and unit readings include some feminist selections. Second, I designed a FYE Blackboard site where instructors may access unit summaries, sample calendars, sample policy statements, sample lesson plans, handouts, and pertinent Web links; they also may post their own. I also make available on Blackboard definitions of terms for each unit as well as my own reflections about the thinking that drove my unit design. These Blackboard materials have proved incredibly popular, not just because they are convenient but because FYE instructors know that they can choose whether or not to use my materials. Instructors in our program are required to use the assigned textbooks and to meet each unit's writing and speaking goals, but how instructors meet these goals is, again, their choice. When instructors employ the Blackboard materials, the assistant director (always a PhD student) and I encourage them not simply to download a lesson plan and walk into class but to rethink the lesson plan in terms of their own pedagogy and politics of location—and then to post that lesson plan to Blackboard.

Two questions haunted me as I redesigned Marquette's FYE program and again as I wrote this essay. The first was easily answered; the second, less so. The first question was, "Should I demand that TAs forward Rich's feminist agenda?" And my answer was a definite "no." Dictating a particular feminist pedagogy at the programmatic level works against the very goal of a feminist literacy that I am hoping to foster in instructors and students; moreover, such dictation robs instructors of the freedom to choose their pedagogy based on their own politics of location, a choice that is central to Rich's feminist theory. Indeed, forcing a feminist pedagogy on an instructor who is skeptical of feminism (if it can even be done) spells disaster for students, instructors, and program morale. So I decided to design a program that encourages a feminist literacy yet also makes feminist pedagogies possible. The second question was, should I foreground Rich more? As I initially designed the program, my answer was "no." I was apprehensive (yes, I admit it) that some TAs might be put off by an emphasis on feminism and on Rich in particular.

Am I pleased with my choices—and my silences? Yes and no. Writing this essay has reaffirmed my decision to create a structure wherein instructors may perform their own pedagogies, feminist or not, while attaining a feminist literacy. Writing this essay has also helped me realize that scholarship provides a more equitable forum than writing program administration for persuading instructors to adopt a feminist pedagogy. Readers may decide whether or not to continue reading; FYE instructors do not share the luxury of tuning out their "boss." But writing this essay has also encouraged me to "out" Rich more in Marquette's TA orientation, practicum, and staff meetings as well as in the reflections that I share with the staff. Although I have obviously mentioned Rich, I have not credited her enough. Indeed, I plan to make a copy of this article available to all FYE instructors. This move will (I hope) model for instructors ways that theory may inform a program design and model for skeptics of feminism the importance of choice, which of course is always constrained to some degree by personal, cultural, and textual concerns. In sum, as a WPA I cannot offer anyone a paint-by-number formula for feminist pedagogy; I can, however, show how Rich's feminist theory pertains to rhetoric and composition studies, and I can encourage WPAs and teachers of writing (myself included) to out Rich more, celebrating her pedagogical legacies by promoting a feminist literacy that possesses the potential for feminist politics.

Notes

1. I would like to thank the anonymous reviewer of this manuscript for his/her editing suggestions.

2. For definitions of multiple feminist theories, see Tong's *Feminist Thought: A More Comprehensive Introduction* (1998).

3. For more discussion on Rich's theory of re-vision and language function, see Ratcliffe, *Anglo-American Feminist Challenges* (1996, 113–19).

4. When I talked about theory/pedagogy connections in the previous paragraph, I purposely used the verb *enacted* rather than *applied*. The *application* metaphor mystifies the complicated relationship between theory and practice. Often when I hear people talking about "applying theory to the classroom," they speak as if they are simply slapping on a new coat of paint rather than ingesting a theory to see how their (dis)identifications with it inform their own thinking and praxis.

5. This description also appears in *Critical Literacies*, the custom reader that I designed specifically for our program.

3

Shifting the Center of Gravity

The Rhetorics of Radical Feminist Pedagogy, 1968–1975

Kathryn T. Flannery

> knowledge is the first step toward gaining power to control our
> lives.
>
> —*Big Mama Rag* (May 1974)

> Throughout the United States women are forming their own law firms and
> legal clinics, establishing their own business companies, running their own
> printing presses, publishing their own magazines and newspapers, starting
> their own credit unions, banks, anti-rape squads, art galleries, and schools,
> hospitals, non-sexist playgroups and child care centers, bands, theater
> groups, restaurants, literary magazines and scholarly journals…. These pro-
> jects express a rejection of the values of existing institutional structures
> and . . . represent an active attempt to reshape culture through changing values
> and consciousness.
>
> *The New Woman's Survival Catalog* (1973)

> Female liberation has no dues, no national officers, no "official" publica-
> tions, nor any party platform. If you would like to start a female liberation
> group, by all means DO IT! Order some literature that seems to speak to you
> and your situation, then get together with women around you—your neigh-
> bors, your co-workers, & (or) classmates, to share reactions to this material.
>
> *PM 3: The Women's Movement, Where It's At* (1971)

In June 1971, at a conference to consider alternatives for the future of higher
education, Joseph Williamson concluded his talk with the assertion that
"teaching strategies for radical change" would have to be devised "outside the

universities as they exist" (43). He discussed three elements necessary for such change: *teaching methodologies* "which attempt . . . to democratize the classroom and break open the patterns of passivity and intimidation which characterize so much of education in the university"; *radical content* designed to introduce "material into the classroom . . . to raise the consciousness of students" through "courses in United States imperialism, Black Studies, the role of women in society, the recovery of a radical 'tradition' from Socrates to John Brown and W.E.B. Dubois"; and finally, the *context* "in which radical education takes place" (Williamson 1971, 40). Because academics had failed to pay sufficient attention to this last element, Williamson contends, they had "deluded" themselves about their "effectiveness as radicals in the teaching profession" (41). New methodologies and new contents might give students "some breathing space within the old structures" but that by itself would not be enough. Without changing the old structures—those "systems of order and legitimation"—changes in classroom practices offered no more than the "illusion of being radical" (41).

Among those sites outside the university most likely to yield viable alternatives, conference participants identified particular feminist counterinstitutions as models for radical change. Whereas much of the larger radical movement—that loosely conjoined amalgam of New Left, students' rights, antiwar, and Black Power groups—could feel "alien, sectarian, [and] harsh," making it difficult to imagine how to integrate in oneself the multiple roles of teacher, political activist and person, the women's liberation movement seemed to promise something other, "with its connection of the personal and the political and its innovative organizational methods" (Garver 1971, 25). As radical women's groups made visible their struggles to create democratic structures—"to build new liberated forms" as an *off our backs* editorial put it—they also served as laboratories for the development of richer, more humane, and politically effective pedagogical practices ("Dear Sisters" 1970; Huse 1971, 47). But what in particular were the feminist methodologies and contents that conference participants would have seen as offering such promise? And as importantly, in what sense could one say that pedagogies defined in the context of feminist *counter*institutions were portable, that they could survive translation into the university setting with some degree of radical energy remaining?[1] An analysis of these counterinstitutional practices demonstrates the seriousness of Williamson's cautionary statement. He provides a check against a nostalgic reclaiming of past practices under the assumption that they can function equally well whatever the context. The usefulness of historical work, as I see it, is not in finding in any simple applications for the present so much as it is in complicating our understanding of current practice through a disruption of familiar genealogies.

Some recent genealogical work in feminist pedagogy might lead one to expect consciousness raising to be the primary pedagogy we inherit from second-wave feminism, with an accompanying pedagogical rhetoric that

hinges on ethos defined in terms of authorial self-positioning and the authority of individual experience.[2] But I have found this expectation too limited. On
the one hand, not all feminists found consciousness raising sufficient to do
the educative work of a radical movement. On the other hand, even those
women who did find consciousness raising a viable pedagogy did not agree
on a single method or process. Further, early women's studies courses within
the academy did not wholeheartedly embrace consciousness raising nor
treat it as the Ur-pedagogy.[3] As I have worked to reconstruct what Adrienne
Rich called the "women's university-without-walls" through a reading of the
remarkable print production of radical feminism during this period, I have
found a greater range of pedagogies improvised by ordinary women from the
means and materials at hand (see Flannery 2005). As part of their pedagogical
efforts, radical feminists were appropriating forms of rhetoric that were
already available in the culture, especially the rhetorical practices familiar in
New Left, Black Power, and countercultural movements, but they were putting
those practices to new or other uses. What is especially striking to me about
feminist print production in the period is the extent to which women were
deploying a wide range of rhetorical practices in the service of a larger epistemological—and therefore, pedagogical—project. At its core, radical feminists
called into question traditional understandings of "woman," not to replace one
unitary concept with another, but to fracture traditional and repressive ways of
knowing. With remarkable exuberance (and a fair dose of anger) they saw the
project of creating new knowledge as necessarily collective: for women to
resist inherited understandings—to "keep others from foisting off their truths
onto us—or speaking for us" as the *Lavender Woman* collective put it—they
had to learn together what had been withheld, what had been distorted, what
had been ignored, and what had to be made anew or made from scratch (Brody
1985, 12). And, they had to teach themselves *how* to go about gathering, evaluating, and crafting knowledge to be useful. But because they understood that
the very rhetorical forms that they had available to them traditionally had been
used against them—and that literacy itself had been deployed as a class-, race,
and gender-marked weapon—they had to figure out how to realign those
forms, how in some cases to reclaim tainted practices for radical use.

In her 1975 essay "Toward a Woman-Centered University," Rich cele-
brated the exciting resurgence of women's intellectual work that she saw all
around her, calling it a feminist renaissance. In an effort to rewrite history,
women were "questioning and reexploring the past" and in the process
"demanding a humanization of intellectual interests and public measures in
the present" (1979, 126). This work was taking place primarily outside the
academy in "unofficial, self-created groups":

> It could be said that a women's university-without-walls exists already in
> America, in the shape of women reading and writing with a new purpose-
> fulness, and [in] the growth of feminist bookstores, presses, bibliographic

services, women's centers, medical clinics, libraries, art galleries, and work-shops, all with a truly educational mission. (1979, 126)

Rich saw in this loosely connected network of pedagogical spaces the poten-tial to put pressure on the traditional university. Although universities had "gradually and reluctantly" admitted women, the system of higher education was structured simply to absorb their presence by using "exceptional women" to justify the status quo and thus to blunt the possibilities of change. "It would be naive," Rich contended, "to imagine that the university can of itself be a vanguard for change" (1979,127). Rather, it is "probable that the unrecog-nized, unofficial university-without-walls . . . will prove a far more important agent in reshaping the foundations on which human life is now organized" (127). Rich does not discount the value of the university altogether: it can be a place where "people find each other and begin to hear each other," and it can be a source of "certain kinds of power" (127). But to be more than that, Rich urged that women in universities shift the "center of gravity," to make univer-sities places where women can recreate themselves after "centuries of intellectual and spiritual blockading" (128). Like Williamson, Rich directs attention to the women working outside or on the edge of the academy to find models for gravity-shifting pedagogies.

In mimeographed flyers, newsletters, newspapers, journals, and pam-phlets, radical feminists worked out a complex sense of their educational mis-sion. Their rhetoric is marked by self-conscious struggles to open up what would count as legitimate knowledge; to figure out what forms that knowledge should take to be most useful to women politically, socially, and personally; and to devise ways to better engage women in the construction of new knowl-edge. A striking feature of much of this work is the extent to which feminists sought to break down what were perceived to be the traditional boundaries between expert and novice, teacher and learner, writer and reader, rhetor and audience. On the assumption that "liberation is not handed down from above," radical feminist writers tended to present themselves as fellow seekers, as fel-low learners, and most important, as akin in capability to their readers, in contrast to what was perceived to be the hierarchical rhetoric not only of traditional educational institutions but of the male-dominated Left (McAfee and Wood 1969, 18). Although part of the rhetorical purpose in this outpouring of print was certainly to share knowledge, to make knowledge available for further use, an equally important purpose was to persuade women through exhorta-tion, demonstration, and example that they were capable of judging the rela-tive value and utility of all kinds of knowledge and that they could be—indeed, needed to be—knowledge producers themselves. Even as writers expressed a wariness of expertise and "professionalism"—a negative code word often appearing in conjunction with "education privilege" or "race privilege" to denote the way an "educated elite" seeks to "corner the market on knowledge and communication"—they were at the same time recognizing the importance of women developing vital skills and knowledges and of producing useful and effective work in order to be a force for change (*Ain't I a Woman* 1970, 2). Writers asserted, sometimes quite heatedly, the legitimacy of their literate practices and of particular notions of feminism, and yet at the same they often resisted codification at the level of language and at the level of ideology—resisting, that is, a one-right-way approach to either feminism or feminist discourse.

The epistemological assertion of such rhetoric is in part that legitimate knowledge can come from all kinds of women. Although it has become commonplace in histories of the mid-twentieth-century resurgence of feminism to presume that women's liberation was a white, middle-class, and straight movement, radical feminist print production makes clear that a broader range of women were in fact building the women's university-without-walls.[4] At least for a short time, as bell hooks has noted, women were attempting through writing to create spaces for contact across difference, to counteract the cultural and economic isolation that had historically kept women apart (hooks 1984, 6). At least for a short time, radical publications attempted to draw on the writing of and to engage with a wide audience that was not exclusively white, middle class, straight, college educated, and adult. Significantly, as hooks explains, the scope of this radical project was not sustained. That it was not sustained makes it all the more important to return to this moment of political volatility to consider what enabled a radical and diverse feminist pedagogical rhetoric to flourish for a short time outside the academy.

This was a moment in time when more women than ever had access to education, even though full critical literacy was not in fact available to all, and when so many ordinary women, across a spectrum of difference, were breaking into print in order to question dominant pedagogical and epistemological assumptions and practices and build toward a revolutionary future. Feminist publications provided a forum for such questioning and served as key pedagogical resources for building a mass movement. The explicit assumption in much of this print production was that if women were going to radically transform society, they would have to be more than uncritical consumers of knowledge generated elsewhere. Thus, a key feature of radical feminist rhetoric was the construction of readers not only as capable knowers but also as responsible for their own learning. They were thus expected to become actively involved, individually and collectively—as producers of knowledge, as writers, and as part of a pedagogical network sharing what they knew and knew how to do. In the hundreds of feminist periodicals that sprang up across the country, editorial collectives sought to create a dynamic rather than consumerist relationship with their readers.[5] Editorials explicitly positioned the reader as a necessary part of the collaborative, creative enterprise. They made clear that it was not enough for readers to remain *merely* readers. Not only for the success of a given periodical, but for the success of the feminist movement, readers would need to learn how to become writers and thus activist cocreators. In this sense, writing was itself seen as a radical act.

Words alone might not be enough—as editorials made clear—but actively participating in the creation of feminist knowledge was a vital part of the revolutionary movement. In their inaugural editorial, the *off our backs* collective addressed their "Dear Sisters," inviting readers to help build a "movement so that we may be freed from myth and prejudice" (1970, 2). This would require that the movement claim "as its own its long ignored and suppressed history" and that it build "new liberated forms" (2). "In order to succeed," however, the newspaper—but also, presumably, the movement of which the newspaper is a part—needs the readers "to use this paper to relate what [they] are doing and what [they] are thinking"—that is, readers need to contribute in writing their news and their ideas (2). Similarly, the New Orleans' *Distaff* offered itself as a "monthly feminist forum" for the "realization of women's initiative, insights, and talents—a media for women to be heard" (in Grimstad and Rennie 1973, 29). Iowa City's *Ain't I a Woman* collective envisioned expanding to include "all sisters in the mid-west," recognizing that that would require "new structures that do not allow people to fall into leader/follower, boss/worker, powerful/powerless roles" (1970, 2). Detroit's *Womankind: A Newspaper for Women* sought "to share creative inspiration and information with other women" with the assumption that this would indeed be a two-way process: "we ask you to participate with well-written reportage, . . . fiction, . . . poetry, . . . photography and graphics [and] essays from cross-cultural points of view" ("Women for a Better Society n.d., 1). That so many women took such invitations seriously is evident not only in the numbers of periodicals full to overflowing with women's work but also in the number of editorials that apologize for late issues by citing the overwhelming number of submissions, or that worry about having harmed those whose work has been rejected because of limited space, or that discontinue accepting poetry (by far the most popular form for readers) because there was simply no more room ("Letter to Our Contributors" np; see also *Big Mama Rag* 4:6).

The editorial invitation to the reader to become active cocreator was reiterated by contributing writers who had themselves responded to the call. Louise Gross and Phyllis MacEwan's "On Day Care" (1970) is fairly representative. The paper was first published in Baltimore's *Women: A Journal of Liberation* in 1970 and was shortly thereafter reprinted by the New England Free Press in pamphlet form with a few typescript additions. Nowhere in the article do the writers indicate their personal investment in their topic, in the sense that they might have personally struggled to find adequate day care for their children or that they had direct experience organizing and running a center. Rather, they offer a relatively formal, idea-driven argument, using the first-person plural sparingly to refer to themselves as authors and occasionally to encompass a larger, collective "we"—as in "as adults *we* can place these events into categories" (Gross and MacEwan 1970; emphasis added). But, significantly, they introduce their argument by seeking to engage the reader actively in the project at hand. They first offer their own work as a starting place, pointing out, as do many writers, that their knowledge is necessarily limited and requires others to develop it further:

> We consider this paper to be an introduction to the problems of existing day care centers and the possibilities of future centers. Although we have pointed out some specific areas for radicalizing a day care center, we certainly have not developed a comprehensive model describing what an ideal day care program would look like. (Gross and MacEwan 1970)

Like many other radical feminist rhetors, Gross and MacEwan present the work of women's liberation as necessarily collaborative and urge their readers to join in the effort: "We hope to develop this paper into a more thorough pamphlet and we welcome groups that are presently organizing day care centers or teachers who are working in centers to send us their ideas and suggestions" (1970).

This kind of direct appeal does not appear again in the paper. Rather, the rest of the article rests on the suasive force of their ideas, moving from a brief history of childcare in the United State to a statement of need, to an analysis of the state of existing day care centers including a critical analysis of the "hidden curriculum" and the "teacher's ideology" (1970). In the final endnote and in the typescript additions to the Free Press pamphlet, however, they direct the reader once again to gaps in their discussion, suggesting places where others might want to contribute their knowledge:

> There are numerous implications of day care organizing which we have not included in this paper such as the questions of developing the day care center as a base for community political action.... And finally we have not discussed in this article the current mushrooming of profit-making, franchised day care centers which will be operated for profit—not for people. Capitalism knows no bounds! (Gross and MacEwan 1970, fn3)

This is a common rhetorical move in feminist publications—less, as I read it, a matter of apology for weakness than a way to alert readers to work that still needs to be done. As authors of another pamphlet put it, since their paper "was written in the midst of things it is neither perfect nor complete . . . [but] the major points are correct." Thus, they contend, "What we need [now] is a lot more debate and a lot more thoughtful activity" (Hopper n.d.). I read their pedagogy as idea driven, respecting the reader's ability to make use of information, to critically assess it, and build on it. The rhetoric does not depend on the personal in the sense of revealing details of an individual's private life but hinges instead on identifying elements of women's lives that have historically been cordoned off from the political realm, what has been treated as "merely" personal because it has to do with "private life."

Gross and McEwan offer their work as a starting place. Indeed, out of the exuberance of first discovery, much of the rhetoric of radical feminism celebrates a beginning—in the sense of a historic moment in time, a feminist renaissance, but more importantly as an initiating action, a way to model *how* one can begin, how one can get started toward revolutionary change. Thus, in 1970, Pamela Allen traced the beginnings of the small-group process, to spark other beginnings, through a small, inexpensive booklet that circulated (and was cited) widely:

> I have written [this book] particularly for women *beginning* the small group experience and for women who are already in small groups but have not formulated a satisfying definition of themselves. Hopefully you will find the ideas stimulating, some of the concepts relevant to your needs. I hope that this will be the *beginning* of a dialogue between us. (5; emphasis added)

In the same year, Toni Cade Bambara published her anthology, *The Black Woman*, offered as a beginning that is both a stock taking and a polemical projection forward:

> If we women are to get basic, then surely the first job is to find out what liberation for ourselves means, what work it entails, what benefits it will yield. To do that, we might turn to various fields of study to extract material, data necessary to define that term in respect to ourselves. We note, however, all too quickly the lack of relevant material. . . . This then is a *beginning*—a collection of poems, stories, essays, formal, informal, reminiscent, that seem best to reflect the preoccupations of the contemporary Black woman in this country. (1970, 1, 11; emphasis added)

If the prototypical patriarchal and foundational beginning is expressed in the biblical formulation "in the beginning was the Word, and the Word was God," then the feminist originary gesture is most clearly antipatriarchal and antifoundationalist. These are beginnings that are provisional, open to revision, to restarts, and that require the hard work of a multitude of feminist hands. They function in this sense as pedagogical scaffolding, as ways to enable more women to learn how to do the work necessary for the new movement.

One of the more striking instances of this kind of revisionary rhetoric of beginning can be found in the pamphlet *Our Bodies Our Selves: A Course by and for Women* (1971) developed by the Boston Women's Health Course Collective. Denver's *Big Mama Rag* refers to the Boston Collective as one of a growing number of self-health groups nationwide that were "pounding away at the narrowness of U.S. medicine today by developing a larger body of knowledge with which to change what is poor but keeping the best parts of medical knowledge" ("Women Must Control" 1974, 11). In this area of the Women's Movement, as in others, the *Big Mama Rag* collective contends, "knowledge is the first step toward gaining power to control our lives" ("Women Must Control" 1974, 11). As the Boston Collective asserts, they are offering "more than an experiment in education"; they want their pamphlet "to be the beginning...of a revolution" (Boston Women's 1971, 24).

First printed by the Boston Free Press in stapled newsprint form, *Our Bodies Our Selves* quickly went through several printings, and over the years has continued to evolve to become a hefty commercially printed tome, recently celebrating its thirty-fifth anniversary. The work of the Boston Collective was cited in feminist periodicals across the country, sometimes criticized for its omissions and biases but also excerpted widely, listed in resource guides, and used as a model for creating other women's health collectives and self-health guides. From the outset, the collective emphasized the process of knowledge production. In the course introduction to the thirty-cent newsprint version, the collective reports how the book came into being from an initial desire to create a "laywoman's course on health." The group members spent a year researching, discussing, writing, and revising a series of papers on topics ranging from women's anatomy to the relationship between women's health and capitalism. After presenting the course to an expanded group of women, they enlarged the collective "to rewrite the papers so they could be printed and shared, not only with women in Boston, but with women across the country" (Boston Women's 1971, 1). They found through this process that other women wanted not only to learn but to "compare and combine our work and theirs" (1). Thus, they reported, after a year and much enthusiasm and hard individual and collective thinking and working, we're publishing these papers. *They are not final. They are not static.* They are meant to be used by our sisters to increase consciousness "about ourselves as women, *to build our movement, to begin to struggle* collectively for adequate health care, and in many other ways they can be useful to you" (Boston Women's 1971, 1; emphasis added).

Throughout the pamphlet, the writers present themselves as fellow learners who are excited to share what they have found, but also eager to learn from others. Drawing on "authoritative" sources—Blackwell's Scientific Publications' *Psychiatric Disorders of Obstetrics*, for example—as well as a range of other materials from first-person accounts, "popular" lay materials, literary sources, cultural critique, and exposés of faulty medical care, the writers evaluate the information they have found, assess the reliability of the sources they make use of, and share their thinking in progress. After a relatively straightforward outline of forms of birth control, for example, the writer of one of the papers acknowledges that the research she has summarized "is frightening and confusing" (Boston Women's 1971, 60). She offers no palliative conclusion, however, but recognizes that women do not want "contraceptives to become one more area in which we are intimidated and frightened into doing things we're not sure of or don't want to do" (60). The most reasonable response, then, is for women to educate themselves about alternatives so that they can understand their options and decide for themselves what is best (60). In a characteristic move, because the collective knows that "there is no universal definition of feminine behavior and character," they do not presume to say what is best for all women (25). They go so far as to conclude the pamphlet by quoting Herbert Marcuse's assertion that "health is a state defined by the elite"—that is by "white, upper class men." Because few people—not just women—have the "power to determine medical priorities," it is inevitable that medical research addresses health care concerns as defined by that elite, and health care providers fail to adequately meet the needs of nonelites (Marcuse qtd. in Boston Women's 1971, 134). A primary purpose of the pamphlet—and of the feminist self-health movement more generally—was thus to begin the process of education, to provide a greater range of tools, resources, and methods so women would be supported in their efforts to critically evaluate available knowledge and to define what would count as health "in a way that meets the needs of all our sisters and brothers—poor, black, brown, red, yellow and pink" (Boston Women's 1971, 134).

To this end, the Boston group was far more excited that their pamphlet generated collective interactions among women than that the papers served as foundational documents. The papers that make up the pamphlet "in and of themselves are not very important [but] . . . should be viewed as a tool which stimulates discussion and action, which allows for new ideas and for change" (Boston Women's 1971, 1). Such beginnings are thus not hallowed originary texts but catalytic actions intended to be transformative and transforming from the start. Although such rhetoric may not be so surprising in relation to health care—in the sense that we are accustomed to sloughing off old scientific information to make way for the "new and improved"—the assumption that laywomen could educate themselves to aid in their struggle to gain "control over the social options available" and "over the institutions of society that now define those options"—*that* was radical indeed (Ehrenreich and English 1977, 88).

The rhetoric of catalytic beginnings is evident in relation to the arts as well. If in the rhetoric of the arts establishment the "original" art object was assigned special status, radical feminist publications made it less likely that such work would be treated as rarefied objects to be reverenced because of the very proliferation of poetry, drama, fiction, and the visual arts made available through cheap newsprint or low-budget offset pamphlets and journals. At least part of the value of such work came in making very visible what ordinary women could do and, in that sense, serving as an invitation for others to try their hand at composing poems, stories, performance work, and visual art. In most cases the invitation was implicit, but occasionally a more explicit statement of pedagogical intent appeared. Feminist performance art often incorporated workshops into performances. The Washington, DC–based Earth Onion advertised their performances as performance/workshops because they wanted to avoid didacticism: "We don't try to be didactic . . . we don't feel we have answers to pass on! We want to present our honest, human responses, to develop our ability to do this, and to share what we learn with others" (1971, 2). As the theatre activist Anselma Dell'Olio put it, "the pitfalls of didacticism can be overcome and art emerge only when the playwright continually develops his [sic] thinking, rather than presenting the audience with a re-hash of old conclusions" (1970, 102). Feminist political art, to be something other than preaching or propaganda, required audience members to become cocreators. To this end, some performance groups incorporated into the performance an explanation or demonstration of the group's creative process, inviting audience members to join in, through writing, improvisation, and planning.

The San Francisco Women's Street Theatre provides a particularly striking example. They made available through the mail, for twenty-five cents, a script and directions for building and putting on a "cranky" performance (using a large paper movie on a scroll) with the expectation that others would write their own scripts and devise their own performances (1973, 317; see also *PM3* 1971). In terms very similar to those of the Women's Health Collective, they explain that they arrived at their script "after researching, writing, drawing, gathering instruments, rehearsing . . . for many months," but they too are less interested in offering a static text to be simply reproduced than in having others make active, creative use of what they have done: "Do not take us too literally; make additions, subtractions, or change the colors, the text, and any of the performing ideas as you want. IT'S YOURS TO PLAY WITH" (San Francisco 1973, 318). Indeed, they urge, "enjoy it as we have and WRITE YOUR OWN" (317). Without minimizing the intellectual and creative effort that went into their performance, the San Francisco group nonetheless seeks to reassure the reader that "if we can do it, you can too."

If part of the rhetoric of feminist publications is that readers/learners are capable of becoming writers/teachers, that they can contribute to a revolutionary beginning, a related aspect of the pedagogical dynamic is the foundational assumption that women are intellectually capable of handling a range of discourse without the intervention of conventionally defined authorities, that they can be their own authorities. In their editorial introducing *Notes from the Second Year*, a newsprint women's liberation anthology, Shulamith Firestone and Anne Koedt remark that they had been cautioned against presenting "ideas undiluted to the public" for fear that women would be scared off (1970, 2). But they chose to "give women more credit than that" because "women are smart enough to recognize their own interests" and they *"are tired of being talked down to"* (2; emphasis in the original). Women were thus understood to be capable of weighing for themselves the relative value of what they read. Radical feminist "content" could come from any number of sources, a speech by Fidel Castro, Frantz Fanon's *A Dying Colonialism*, first-hand accounts from female prisoners, a poem from the seventeenth-century nun Sor Juana Inez De La Cruz, Marx's *Capital*, historical documents, labor union pamphlets, the diary of a prostitute, Simone de Beauvoir's *The Second Sex*, biographies of Rosa Luxemburg and Harriet Tubman, C. Wright Mills' "Work and Social Structure," and so on and on (see Joan Jordan 1968). Disenfranchised knowledges (what women know about their own bodies, for example, that the medical establishment traditionally ignored) but also information from sources that were neither produced by nor intended for women (textbooks on obstetrics, for example) were all potential pedagogical "content." As one contemporary observer put it, as a "classic tactic of self-defense," women worked to combat a "larger more powerful opponent by using his strength against him"—that is, by sometimes making critical use of "official" and "authoritative sources" that were never intended to support women's independence (Grimstad and Rennie 1973, 32).

To judge from feminist print production, women were understood to have the intellectual and creative dexterity to find their way through a discursive carnival: no single form of discourse was understood to encompass all of womankind, nor was any single form understood to be sufficient to do the necessary work of radically reorienting human knowledge in the service of revolutionizing social structures. Within a single publication or across several publications one could find historical narratives; poetry; parody; mininovels; drama; testimonials; interviews; diaries; letters; how-to instructions for everything from gynecological self-exams to making muffins or fixing engines; arts reporting and media reviews; local, national, and international news reporting and analysis; advertisements; polemics; cartoons; children's stories; photographic essays; as well as a range of graphics from handmade prints and cutout patterns (for do-it-yourself art) to appropriated images from the past.

Few publications provided much textual apparatus to guide a reader through this mass of print either by identifying a writer's particular expertise or by locating a piece of writing in relation to some larger controlling concept of feminism. In this sense, such publications were antididactic, avoiding the look of either textbooks or ideological primers. Although an editorial collective might identify itself in terms of a particular ideological orientation—*Ain't I a Woman*, for example, as radical lesbian feminist—that designation rarely served as a wholly reliable heuristic for reading the contents of the publication. Most publications printed a range of perspectives within a loosely defined sense of radical feminism, but it would be difficult to say that any publication achieved (or aspired to) some ideological consistency. A cofounder of *off our backs*, Marilyn Webb recalls that "at the beginning . . . we didn't really have such things as correct ideological lines" (1980, 5). Some publications would identify a writer by noting movement affiliation. Thus, for example, on the back cover of the New England Free Press pamphlet reprint of "What is the Revolutionary Potential of Women's Liberation?" the coauthors are identified rather simply: "Kathy McAfee is a member of the N.Y. LEVIATHAN staff" and "Myrna Wood has been working with the women's liberation and antiwar movements in Toronto and Montreal" (McAfee and Wood 1969, 18). Or, in *Notes from the Third Year*, Florence Rush is identified as a member of OWL (Older Women's Liberation) and the New York Radical Feminists (Rush 1971, 18). Many writers did identify themselves within a text in terms of class, race, ethnicity, sexual orientation, educational or work status and in that sense claimed qualified or delimited expertise based on location or positionality. But just as many wrote anonymously, under a pseudonym (using only a given name or an assumed matrilineal), or identified themselves as a collective (see Flannery 2001). And a surprising number made little or no textual reference to themselves, some eschewing the first person (even the first-person plural) altogether. I was surprised, in fact, to find not a preponderance of first-person testimonials—though clearly there were many—but more writing that hinged on what might be called a relational rhetoric. That is, rather than an *I* in isolation used as guarantor of authority or legitimacy, much of the writing asserted or presumed a coalitional *we*. In this sense, the personal (that is always political) had to be invested in a given reading by the individual reader.

Often, no biographical information appeared either prefacing a piece of writing or within the text itself. Although some "headliners" appeared in radical feminist publications, of course, and many readers would have recognized the names of some women they had heard or heard about through their experiences in the movement, at demonstrations, at feminist bookstores, in consciousness-raising groups, and the like, the movement was so decentralized and the participation so widespread that the reader would have had to exercise a fair degree of interpretive independence. Additionally, at least for some readers, the fact that a feminist had acquired headliner status diminished rather than elevated her political credibility and rhetorical authority in the sense that "stars" were inconsistent with the egalitarian aims of the movement. For much of the work, then, especially early on, rhetorical authority rested on the force of ideas rather than some a priori notion of the writer's status or traditionally defined expertise or some notion of an ideologically consistent party line. Thus, to be a reader one would need to be actively engaged in a shifting dialogue within any given text, across texts, and in the interanimation between text and movement organizational work.

Various in method, eclectic in content, radical feminist pedagogy outside the academy was nonetheless consistent in challenging traditional, rigidified structures of authority. If the women's university-without-walls was intended in part to counter traditional structures of authority—for some, as a parallel but separate culture; for others, as a wedge to open up and transform those dominant structures—it did so in part by providing places for women to learn together how to exercise their creative and intellectual abilities and to assert their collective and individual authority. A key factor was that women were creating the structures, they were deciding what they wanted and needed to learn, and they were assessing the various products of their own labors. Even so, many radical women recognized the paradox at the heart of the women's university-without-walls: How could women create egalitarian, cocreative structures that would also enable the effective assertion of intellectual and political authority? Where could women learn how to productively assert authority and resist the imposition of authority if egalitarianism was to be defined in terms of the suppression of differences in expertise, talent, insight, knowledge, ability? How could women claim the necessary authority to resist dominant authority without falling into traditional hierarchies themselves? These tensions evident in the decentralized consortium of voluntarist, largely collectivist, and overtly political counterinstitutions would become all the more apparent when academics attempted to translate radical pedagogies from the "outside" into institutions of higher learning that traditionally had been designed to rank-order individual achievement in the service of objective knowledge.

A full accounting of nascent women's studies courses is beyond the scope of this essay, of course. Suffice it to say, no single feminist pedagogy was available for appropriation by the academy. Rather, early women's studies courses improvised both method and content from practices and materials available inside and outside the academy with the clear intention of reshaping institutions of higher learning so that they could be forces for social change. A series of pamphlets published by Pittsburgh's KNOW titled *Female Studies* serves as an important source of information about these early courses. The pamphlets include sample course materials from across the country, from various fields and disciplines, and from the elementary to the college level. Although course materials alone cannot tell us the whole story, they do offer a partial—and provocative—perspective. They suggest, for example, that even though many women recall consciousness-raising as the defining element in feminist pedagogy, the courses were more various in approach. Some form of collaborative work was fairly common, but rarely was it the primary method of instruction. Some instructors planned time outside of class explicitly for consciousness-raising, opening the groups to students and community members who were not enrolled in the courses themselves. Some reserved one class meeting a week or alternated class periods to make room for "rap sessions" or discussion groups and also to ensure that there would be time to address the course readings more systematically (see Munday 1975, 71; Roberts 1975, 98–101). Others treated consciousness-raising as itself a topic for discussion for a single class meeting, as a method of political organizing alongside other methods. And some courses seemed to make no use of small-group process. To the extent that instructors set the syllabus and assigned topics for discussion, and to the extent that small-group work was graded, collaborative work in the university courses was bound to differ significantly from the consciousness-raising groups outside the academy. Small groups were rarely free-form, and like many groups outside the academy, classroom groups tended to develop procedures to ensure fairness, to distribute responsibilities, and to further the curricular and content aims of the course. Whether or not a course incorporated consciousness-raising techniques, most instructors nonetheless signaled their desire to engage in what Joan Roberts calls "the process of mutual *learning*," with the understanding that such mutuality did not preclude the recognition of differences in knowledge and experience among students, and between the students and the teacher (1975, 94; emphasis in the original).

As is evident in the *Female Studies* materials, for all the focus on process, the particular pedagogical methods seem less important than the goal of "restructuring authority" (Roberts 1975, 94). This restructuring required a reciprocity of talent and knowledge between teacher and student: on the one hand, "women students go for help to women faculty whose training and awareness have *earned* them a reputation for authority, not from status, but from knowledge and experience"; on the other hand, "faculty have begun to recognize the tremendous talents and maturity of younger women students" (94). In this sense, it would be difficult to say that feminist pedagogy was democratic if by that one means that the teacher and students were on an equal footing, as if it would be possible to do away with the teacher's authority or expertise. Rather, most courses attempted to build approaches that made possible what Roberts refers to as "cognitive-affective" learning among teachers and students together. The challenge then for the feminist teacher was (and I would argue, still is) to establish her intellectual authority and at the same time to make her expertise available so that her students could make use of it to further develop their own intellectual authority. Some teachers envisioned creating a safe place for women to learn, in contrast to what was perceived to be the agonistic arena of the larger academy. Others thought that women needed to learn to disagree with one another, to stand up for what they believed. Although the "stereotypical feminist model" might lead us to expect, as bell hooks has argued, that "women best come to voice in an atmosphere of safety (one in which we are all going to be kind and nurturing)," more courses seem to have sought what hooks wants: that is, to "enable all students, not just an assertive few, to feel empowered in a rigorous, critical discussion" (1994b, 78).

As is clear in Roberts' account of her University of Wisconsin experience, no single method could do this necessary pedagogical work. As radical feminists outside the academy also found out, any method depended for success on the productive friction created through the interplay not only of the multiple knowledges of a variety of women brought to the table but the reading and writing that challenged and extended what any individual or group of women could know. For all the emphasis on process, the courses for the most part enacted an understanding that the *how* of teaching had to be in reciprocal relationship to the *what*. Students and teachers together had to be invested in recovering and discovering knowledge, and making that knowledge more fully and broadly available.

To establish a relationship of mutual, even rigorous, learning outside the academy was difficult enough. To establish such a relationship within the traditional hierarchical structure of the academy has proved more difficult. And yet, as Joseph Williamson argued, if radical academics were to change only method and content, and leave the traditional academic context intact, they would be fooling themselves if they thought they were actually achieving radical change. If women's studies programs were going to effect radical, systemic change in the academy, more would be required than innovations in method or content, as important as both have been. From the beginning, women's studies had to struggle to establish its legitimacy within the terms of the academy, even as it has challenged those terms. Early on, when students were actively demanding women's studies courses and when they were as likely to know more about women's liberation than some professors, when course materials drew on the print production of the women's university-without-walls, and when the university bureaucracy had not yet recognized women's studies as a legitimate area of study, faculty and students together were engaged in a mutual pedagogical project and could practice radical pedagogies because at least on some level they were still outside the traditional systems of legitimation. They had the freedom to innovate because on some level they were not yet touching the heart of the academic enterprise. Although the sheer fact of their presence within the university was itself a sign of institutional change, that was not going to be enough.

Initially, legitimation came as much, if not more, from outside the academy as from within. Women's studies courses were part of a larger activist network, ensuring that for a while at least the university operated as if it were permeable to the outside. Courses might include evening lectures open to the public, weekend conferences that allowed community members to participate, radio broadcasts, class projects that involved community work, community organizers who brought their expertise into the classroom, women's liberation literature that served as texts for courses, and writing produced for classes that found its way into print through the growing number of women's liberation publications. A radical feminist rhetoric that sought to break down traditional divisions between teacher and student, expert and novice, was thus not just "mere" rhetoric for early women's studies advocates but was a recognition of the real authority that students and teachers brought to the learning process from their experiences in women's liberation outside or on the edge of the academy. The rhetoric of revisionary beginning is also very much in evidence in the early women's studies courses (see, for example, Schramm 1975). But as women's studies sought to gain recognition, to establish its own legitimacy within the academy, so that it could have standing to change the university and authority to work against dominant ways of knowing, feminist academics had to rely less on the rhetoric of egalitarian authority and far more on the demonstration of authority that comes from producing institutionally recognizable and legitimate forms of knowledge. For this reason, many feminists continued to—or came to—believe that only outside the academy could they create space to allow for the necessary freedom to innovate, to create, and that would require not only breaking away from a traditionally sexist education but from the "orthodox modes of learning which have alienated so many women from conventional institutions—intellectual one-upping, ego-tripping, teacher/pupil dichotomies, smart/dumb labels," as one alternative Women's Liberation School put it (Grimstad and Rennie 1973, 123). The paradoxical challenge for those who decided to stake their claim within the university was to transform the processes of higher learning without replacing one static bureaucratic structure with another. In this sense, academic feminists did not renege on the promise of radical feminist pedagogy, but neither did they resolve the paradox at the heart of that pedagogy. Rather, in the context of institutional power relations, they attempted to appropriate—that is, borrow and transform—from the women's university-without-walls what was necessary to begin to shift the institutional center of gravity. That is a project still ongoing. What is useful to us now from this story of a beginning moment is not, as I see it, any particular pedagogical method per se but the remarkable improvisatory openness that characterized feminist pedagogy both inside and outside the university, an openness that required working with the materials and possibilities at hand to resist the congealing power of the larger bureaucratic structures and to hold open an inevitably provisional alternative space.

Notes

1. I am using pedagogy broadly, as do both Carmen Luke and Jennifer Gore in separate works: in the sense of "activity integral to all learning, all knowledge production" (Gore 1993, xii), as "endemic to all social relations...fundamental to all public/private life and all communicative exchanges, from the nursery to the playground, classroom to the courtroom" (Luke 1996, 11). In these terms, as Luke puts it, "learning and teaching . . . are the intersubjective core relations of everyday life," and they are "always gendered" (7).

2. Not only in contemporary feminist pedagogy can one find the identification of consciousness raising—either in praise or in caricature—as the Ur-feminist practice but in composition studies as well. Following Kenneth Bruffee's lead in a *College English* article from the early' 70s, Lester Faigley gives credit to women's consciousness-raising groups as one originary source for collaborative learning techniques. Bruffee observed that "on campuses everywhere, right outside the classroom door, students form their own academic clubs for collaborative study." In particular, "in the women's liberation movement...people have begun to work collaboratively in support groups—sometimes called 'rap groups' or consciousness raising groups—which subordinate figures of authority during the process of self-development" (Bruffee 1972–73, 634).

3. Although a number of early women's studies pioneers recall the importance of consciousness raising, my reading of early course materials parallels my reading of the women's university-without-walls—that is, that early courses employed a variety of methods, not all made use of consciousness raising (however defined), and when consciousness raising was part of the mix, it was often treated as an option or functioned as something akin to class recitation. I don't read this subordination of consciousness raising as a failure of nerve on the part of the faculty teaching women's studies but as both a practical matter—how to manage very large classes, in some cases—and a

pedagogical matter—how best to engage women in the intellectual work of women's studies. See, for example, Jane Roland Martin's *Coming of Age in Academe* (2000) and Marilyn Jacoby Boxer's *When Women Ask the Questions* (1998).

4. As I argue more fully in *Feminist Literacies*, the material traces of movement activism suggest that the women's university-without-walls was not a phenomenon exclusive to or created by white, middle-class, straight women alone, nor was it a phenomenon that unproblematically conjoined all women into a unified category of Woman. Indeed, the decentralized nature of the women's liberation movement, from the outset, worked with centrifugal force against an unproblematized or politically naive rhetoric of unity and commonality. Although some women argued that a separatist women's movement would require that women be "cleanly feminist," that there be a separatist women's liberation movement, most women were multiply affiliated, articulating feminism in multiple ways with other social, religious, and political commitments (Koedt qtd. in Brownmiller 2000, 33). Ironically, because criticism of women's liberation's failure to live up to its utopian aims arose simultaneously with the movement, the historian may fail to notice the multiplicity of women who were actively contributing to the midcentury reemergence of feminism. Women of color, working-class and poor women, lesbians, Chicanas, women young and old challenged from the outset what were perceived to be the oversimplifications and biases of the movement and they did so not as outsiders to but as cocreators of radical feminism. I am persuaded, however, as bell hooks has argued, that the initial moment of volatility when women sought to join in coalition across differences was not sustained (1984, 6). See also Beverly Guy-Sheftall's reflection in the *Feminist Memoir Project* (1998).

5. Getting an accurate count of often-ephemeral movement periodicals is difficult because they have not been systematically archived. Anne Mather's three-part "History of Feminist Periodicals" published between 1974 and 1975 can give a rough sense however. She determined that in the five-year period between March 1968 and August 1973 more than 560 feminist publications appeared in the United States. The majority were newsletters, but she also found sixty newspapers, nine newspaper/magazines, and seventy-two magazines and journals (Mather 1974, 82). One can also get some sense of the range of publications from such resource guides as *PM3* and *The Woman's Survival Catalog*. Many publications also provided bibliographies that listed other movement publications, suggesting not only how widely (and rapidly) "local" publications traveled but also how little competition there seemed to be among publications (Mather 1975, 23).

4

"Each One, Pull One"

Womanist Rhetoric and Black Feminist Pedagogy in the Writing Classroom

Gwendolyn D. Pough

Alice Walker: Womanist Rhetorician

"Tell the truth and shame the devil!"
— Old African American saying

This essay theorizes womanist rhetoric(s) by drawing on the creative and non-fiction work of Alice Walker—who coined the term—and black women theorists who have expanded on and developed womanist writings and thought. Although the womanist project has been taken up in a variety of areas—from fiction to theory to political activism—there has not been a detailed account of *womanist rhetoric*. Alice Walker's words, "we must say it all, and as clearly as we can," allow us to begin to theorize womanist rhetoric as a rhetoric that asks hard questions and brings out difficult issues. These words also provide the primary tenet of womanist rhetoric; it does not hold back. But what are the implications for the use of womanist rhetoric with black feminist pedagogy in the writing classroom?

When Alice Walker coined the term *womanist* in her groundbreaking collection of essays *In Search of Our Mother's Garden's: Womanist Prose*, she did so in a decidedly activist fashion. The term is at once a term of reclamation and of definition. She is reclaiming a word once used to admonish young black girls for speaking up for themselves and defining a way of being that values women of color and the unique stance they bring to feminist thought. She offers a multilayered definition, which is simultaneously complex and simple:

Womanist 1. From *womanish*. (Opp. of "girlish," i.e., frivolous, irresponsible, not serious.) A black feminist or feminist of color. From the black folk expression of mothers to female children, "You acting womanish," i.e., like a woman. Usually referring to outrageous, audacious, courageous or *willful* behavior. Wanting to know more and in greater depth than is considered good for one. Interested in grown-up doing. Acting grown-up. Being grown-up. Interchangeable with another black folk expression: "You trying to be grown." Responsible. In charge. *Serious.*

2. Also: A woman who loves other women, sexually and/or nonsexually. Appreciates and prefers women's culture, women's emotional flexibility (values tears as natural counterbalance of laughter), and women's strength. Sometimes loves individual men, sexually and/or nonsexually. Committed to survival and wholeness of entire people, male *and* female. Not a separatist, except periodically, for health. Traditionally universalist, as in: "Mama, why are we brown, pink, and yellow and our cousins are white, beige, and black?" Ans.: "well, you know the colored race is just like a flower garden, with every color flower represented." Traditionally capable, as in: "Mama, I'm walking to Canada and I'm taking you and a bunch of other slaves with me." Reply: "It wouldn't be the first time."

3. Loves music. Loves dance. Loves the moon. *Loves* the Spirit. Loves love and food and roundness. Loves struggle. *Loves* the folk. Loves herself. *Regardless.*

4. Womanist is to feminist as purple to lavender. (A. Walker 1984b, xi–xii)

I quote Walker's definition in its entirety here because I think it is necessary in order to gauge all that she is trying to accomplish. Her very rich and full definition highlights the inclusiveness for which womanist rhetoric strives. This inclusiveness is important to womanism as a rhetorical practice that does not discriminate but rather strives for wholeness in all its endeavors. The definition offers and appreciates variety and difference. Walker's definition is so complex that womanism has spawned several theoretical camps. For example, womanist theologians such as Kate Geneva Cannon, Deloris Williams, Kelly Brown Douglas, Linda E. Thomas, and Emilie Townes have drawn on the spiritual emphasis in Walker's definition and the push for wholeness, particularly the whole people that includes both men and women. Womanist theology also draws on the push toward liberation implicit in Walker's definition. Katie G. Cannon writes:

> The womanist writing consciousness does not obscure or deny the existence of tridimensional oppression but rather, through full, sharp awareness of race, sex, and class oppression we present the liberating possibilities that also exist. Our womanist work is to draw on the rugged endurance of black folks in American who outwit, out maneuver, and out scheme social systems and structures that maim and stifle mental, emotional and spiritual growth. (Cannon 1996, 135)

Womanist theology is largely about taking the skills, many of which are rhetorical in nature, that black women have used throughout time to overcome oppression and use them to conquer contemporary situations. To out wit, out maneuver, and out scheme requires a thought process that takes into consideration not only one's own feelings and knowledge but also the feelings and knowledge of others who might seek to oppress you. W. E. B. DuBois' double consciousness comes to mind as well as the image of the trickster in the black oral tradition when thinking about these "out" womanist strategies. Womanist rhetoric builds on all these legacies in the African American rhetorical and oral traditions, and womanist theologians build on those legacies as well.

Donald McCrary has written about his success using writings on womanist theology in his essay "Womanist Theology and Its Efficacy for the Writing Classroom." McCrary found that the inclusiveness of womanist theology and its push toward combining sacred and secular knowledges represented "the type of course content that could help [his] students use a greater store of their cultural and linguistic knowledge in the pursuit to become literate members of the academy" (2001, 528). The majority of his students were African American women who attended church. Using womanist theology helped him to better help them draw on their varied knowledge.

Africana womanism, coined by literary theorist Clenora Hudson-Weems, marks another theoretical offshoot of womanism. Hudson-Weems uses Africana to highlight that her brand of womanism is concerned with Continental African women and women of African descent in the Diaspora. Unlike Walker, Hudson-Weems distances Africana womanism from feminism because of the racism that surfaced in the early suffrage movement, and she cautions black women not to use feminism uncritically. She finds that "Feminism, a term conceptualized and adopted by white women, involves an agenda that was designed to meet the needs and demands of that particular group" (1993, 21). Hudson-Weems further distances her brand of womanism from Walker's by claiming that Africana womanism originates in likening black women to the continent of Africa and the legacy of Sojourner Truth and her speech "Ain't I a Woman." Hudson-Weems writes, "Neither an outgrowth nor an addendum to feminism, Africana womanism is not Black feminism, African feminism, or Walker's womanism that some Africana women have come to embrace. African womanism is an ideology created and designed for all women of African descent" (24).

Many black women find Walker's womanism to be a way to distance themselves from a feminism that rarely places black women at the center. They see womanist as an identity that is different from feminist. These women essentially ignore the last part of Walker's definition, "womanist is to feminist as purple to lavender." This is problematic for many reasons. Patricia Hill Collins offers the most compelling reason for resisting this kind of blanket rejection of feminism in her provocative essay "What's in a Name? Womanism, Black Feminism, and Beyond" (1999). She urges black women to get past the preoccupation of names and get to the work of black feminism and womanism. What it comes down to for Collins and myself is a simple matter of women being less concerned with the *what do we call ourselves* question and more concerned with the *what meaningful work can we do* question. It is a matter of putting our ideals and beliefs, be they womanist, black feminist, Africana womanist, or African feminist, into practice. Ultimately, that is what womanist rhetoric is concerned with, words put into practice, words that will mean something and provoke change.

It is useful to use Walker's own term, *womanist,* to define the rhetoric her work embodies. Womanist rhetoric is "outrageous, audacious, courageous" and "willful." It pushes past limitations, seeking knowledge beyond what is commonly accepted. It is "serious" in that it is concerned ultimately with the freedom and wholeness of entire people—male and female. A womanist rhetorician tells the truth as she sees it even if that truth is not always welcome. Alice Walker's body of work and the critical reception it has garnered highlights this push toward truth telling. From *The Color Purple* (1982) to *Possessing the Secret of Joy* (1992) and *Warrior Marks: Female Genital Mutilation and the Sexual Blinding of Women* (1993), Walker's womanist rhetoric, as the epigraph to this section notes, has sought to "tell the truth and shame the devil." She has suffered harsh criticism and rebuke, but she has been steadfast in using a variety of means to get across her message of inclusiveness and liberation. The title of her collection of essays, *Anything We Love Can Be Saved: A Writer's Activism* (1997), highlights the mission of womanist rhetoric. It is about uplift. It is about love and a push for a better world. It is about ultimately saving—whether it is saving a life, a people, or indeed the world. And it is always linked to an activist project and agenda—that is, it is about change. The titles of the essays in this volume show that Alice Walker the womanist rhetorician is not afraid to tell the truth as she sees it. The book has essays titled "How Long Shall They Torture Our Mothers?: The Trials of Winnie Mandela"; "What That Day Was Like for Me: The Million Man March"; and "Hugging Fidel." None of the essays is shy about offering a critique and positing solutions. As a rhetorician then, Walker has crossed genres and media to push her activist agenda. Like the black nineteenth-century club women about whom Jacqueline Jones Royster and Shirley Wilson Logan write, who used oratory and traversed written genres such as the essay, fiction, diaries, poetry, and drama, Walker, too, uses a variety of genres as a way to navigate audiences not always open and receptive. Using Walker as a model for defining womanist rhetoric, it becomes clear that womanist rhetoric can come in a variety of forms: a poem, an essay, a short story, a speech, a novel. For the womanist rhetorician, then, it is a decision of which genre or form will better reach her audience. Most times she will put the same message in a variety of forms to connect with and influence numerous people and push them toward change.

Writing about *The Color Purple*, Gail Upchurch states that Walker's womanist vision asserts womanism as a challenge to patriarchal dominance and rewrites "the boundaries that separate men and women" by attempting "a transcendent space where both men and women may coexist without the need for one gender to dominate over the other" (2003, 124–25). In this way womanist rhetoric is always already about pushing past boundaries and broadening awareness—the very stuff some feminist and critical educators would like to see in classrooms. Reading and studying womanist rhetorics has affected my teaching because it has made me think critically and strategically about change. Because it offers visions for a better world, womanist rhetoric ultimately makes me think about ways I can help make that vision a reality. I teach womanist rhetoric because I believe in the agenda of social justice and want to work toward a better society. When womanist rhetoric is combined with black feminist pedagogy the classroom becomes a rhetorical and political space. Issues of difference and the intersections of race, class, and gender inevitably surface, and the classroom is ultimately opened to a variety of societal issues such as racism, classism, heterosexism, homophobia, and sexism, to name only a few.

Toward Praxis: Black Feminist Pedagogy and Womanist Rhetoric

In her new book on teaching, *Teaching Community: A Pedagogy of Hope,* bell hooks writes, "Given the nature of imperialist white-supremacist capitalist patriarchy as a system shaping culture and beliefs it is simply a fact that most white folks are rarely, if ever, in situations where they must listen to black women lecture them (2003, 31). The quote from hooks raises the question, what are the liberatory possibilities of black feminist pedagogy in the writing classroom. What can we gain from black feminist teaching practices and goals? How can those gains improve our own goals for the teaching of writing and critical thinking? I maintain that the writings of black feminist educators and womanist rhetoricians can offer examples of praxis that can help us make the writing classroom a space in which critical thinking around diverse issues can ultimately lead to change. Ultimately, I hope to flesh out some of the key underlying parts of black feminist pedagogy and to begin to question the difference it can make in our writing classrooms. These kinds of inquiries inevitably lead me to questions of power and embodiment. hooks notes:

> In a class I was teaching recently, we discussed a talk I had given where many white students expressed their disdain for the ideas I expressed, and for my embodied young-looking presence, a black female with natural hair in braids. I had barely finished this comment before a liberal white male in the group attacked claiming "you are playing the race card here" (2003, 30).

Black women educators often deal with student resistance on a surface level before we even open our mouth. The resistance is intensified when we add discussion of a womanist rhetoric that "tells the truth," asks hard questions, and pushes critical thinking. Can we say it all as clearly as we can, given the racism and sexism that black women face in general, and as educators specifically, and the overwhelming resistance from students based on that racism and sexism? Is black feminist pedagogy liberatory enough? Will it be able to liberate students from their own resistance, racism, and sexism? Or, rather, will all educators need to pick up on the liberatory aspects of black feminist pedagogy and fashion a critical pedagogy that can move students forward?

Another element crucial to black feminist pedagogy is my physical presence as a black woman instructor. Because I am blessed with knowledge of Cheryl Johnson's and Shirley Wilson Logan's work on their experiences as black women teachers in predominantly white classrooms, I am able to maintain an awareness of student's reactions to the class materials and to my physical presence. Thus, I try to avoid any situation in which my presence as a black woman could stifle conversation or growth. Of course, this is not always possible.

Both Logan and Johnson write quite eloquently about what it is like for black women to teach black texts to a classroom full of white faces. Johnson's questions—"How, then, can students refigure the black woman in their consciousness? And how are they to read the African-American texts in the presence of this African-American female body?"—inform the way I teach black texts in class (1994, 412). I realize, as Logan does, that "tensions surrounding black women who teach in predominantly white institutions might be converted into catalysts for change" (1998, 46). She also notes that "difference can be a force for change. Yet it would be naïve to think that the simple presence of a Black female teacher guarantees change" (56). Both Logan and Johnson note that the space they navigate as black women in the academy is a tricky one and what they are able to accomplish with their students is contingent on their navigation of that space.

Viewing the classroom as a public space in which to grapple with, discuss, and write about wide and varied experiences and connections can open the floor for other possibilities to be explored. In combination with the public classroom, black feminist pedagogy grants students the opportunity to explore and examine subjects often missing in other classroom situations. Several of the chapters in *Talking Back: Thinking Feminist, Thinking Black* (hooks 1989) focus on teaching and learning, since the book's theme is "coming to voice" in both speaking and writing. Drawing on her own experiences as a teacher and a student in working through her ideas about pedagogy, hooks explores the ways in which marginalized voices such as her own black, female, and once working-class voice learn to talk back. hooks discusses the strong black female teachers who gave her the courage she needed to come to voice. She explores her experiences as a black woman in graduate school when she almost lost that voice owing to the racism she suffered there. More than anything else *Talking Back* is an account of hooks' personal experiences with learning as well as writing.

I find hooks' take on feminist pedagogy enlightening in *Talking Back* because she sees the need for a radical pedagogy with no holds barred. She writes, "Feminist pedagogy can only be liberatory if it is truly revolutionary because the mechanism of appropriation within white supremacist, capitalist patriarchy is able to co-opt with tremendous ease that which merely appears radical or subversive" (1989, 51). hooks realizes that radical pedagogy must be radical, that this is not something we can do half-heartedly. She also notes the need for our professional goals to be combined with our commitment to a larger feminist struggle going on outside the academy. Her forthright stance on power and authority notes that feminist teachers should not be afraid to assert their power and authority in the classroom: "we must be willing," she argues, "to restore the spirit of risk—to be fast, wild, to be able to take hold, turn around, transform" (54).

At their roots, both black feminist pedagogy and womanist rhetoric are about change—encouraging it, nurturing it, making it happen. Womanist rhetoric, with its emphasis on telling the truth, saying it loud and in as many ways possible, is an upfront and unflinching rhetorical practice. Black feminist pedagogy, with its emphasis on bringing the tougher issues of race, class, gender, and sexuality into the classroom and not shying away from the often-times volatile resistance these provoke in students, is an upfront and unflinching teaching practice. Both approaches allow educators concerned with issues of social justice to put their theories about change into praxis. This is not always an easy and simple alliance. There are tensions in the combination of womanist rhetoric and black feminist pedagogy.

For some womanist thinkers, feminism, black or otherwise, is not a place to find allies and alliances. This need to distance womanism from feminism goes against Walker's intentions, but it nevertheless exists in the ways womanism has been taken up by some writers and thinkers. This can make the alliance between womanist rhetoric and black feminist rhetoric an uneasy one at best. However, when we focus instead on the ways both practices are about doing what is needed to provoke change, we are able to navigate those tensions more smoothly. Change, however, leads to other tensions such as student resistance and the fear that facing change brings. Since both womanist rhetoric and black feminist pedagogy are about being upfront and unflinching, students may find them unsettling. The combination can lead to classroom spaces that are not always comfortable but that hold the potential for students to move past their discomfort and toward change. I move now to a classroom example intended to highlight both the tensions and the potential inherent in the combination of womanist rhetoric and black feminist pedagogy.

The First Encounter: Alice Walker Is Prejudiced Against White People

We must say it all, and as clearly as we can.

—Alice Walker, "Each One,
Pull One: Thinking of
Lorraine Hansberry" (1984a)

Several questions come to my mind as I think about teaching difference as a black woman to a classroom filled with white upper middle class students. Can I say it all clearly? Is it possible to consider issues of difference, race, class, and gender in meaningful ways? Is it within our reach? Or do we live in what James Baldwin termed an incoherent society, one where people of different backgrounds can't or rather won't talk about their differences, where difference is ignored (1985, 238). The original muse for this essay appeared when I taught two sections of first-year composition and literature at Miami University. The syllabus for both classes focused on "Love and the Black Literary Experience." Resistance was a major element in the class because the students did not want to focus an entire semester on African American literature. From day one, the course subject matter and my own presence as a young black woman instructor provided spaces for resistance among the students. For many of them it became a matter of the black girl trying to force black literature down their throats. However the resistance the students voiced in response to my syllabus request that they read Alice Walker's poem "Each One, Pull One: Thinking of Lorraine Hansberry" offered them and me an opportunity to move past their initial resistance to the course material and me and to probe more deeply their opposition to issues of oppression, race, and gender. Although I understand that my physical presence had a lot to do with my students' reactions, I have now come to understand more fully that the way I navigated my presence—bringing the womanist rhetoric of Alice Walker's poem, which was upfront and unflinching, and practicing a form of black feminist pedagogy that was radical and did not shy away from difficult topics—had a lot to do with the ways students both resisted and grappled with the issues. It was the combination of my presence, womanist rhetoric, and black feminist pedagogy that set the tone for our interchange.

If a work takes a stand against oppression, is that work antiwhite? Should white students feel threatened when asked to read something by a "minority" that critiques the power structure in the United States? Should they feel as if they are being attacked if the syllabus includes readings that don't paint a pretty portrait of white involvement in adverse historical settings of racial oppression? Should they resist a view of the world that differs greatly from their own? I asked myself those questions after my first encounter with my students' resistance to Alice Walker's poem. In one class, after a long silence when I asked what they thought about the poem, a white male student raised his hand and said, "I hated it. She [Walker] is prejudiced against white people." Others who told how offended they were by the poem followed his comment. Many of the students felt that they were being personally attacked. In both classes, I encountered verbal resistance and attempted to grab onto those feelings by asking questions such as, Why do you feel threatened? What is it that makes you think that the speaker in the poem is talking to and about you personally? Why are you offended? Why do you feel as if you're being attacked? I also offered comfort; "We will explore who the speaker in the poem is talking to and about. But first let's explore where we're coming from in relation to the poem." I had hoped to help the students begin some reflective thinking about their reactions; however, the students were not ready or, rather, they resisted the prompt. My questions were met with silence. Crickets chirped in the background. It was clear from their silence that my students somehow read me, the black woman teacher as aligned with the "we" in Walker's poem and themselves as aligned with the "them" they felt that Walker was attacking in the poem.

Because I did not want to shy away from the students' resistance and thus allow them to shy away from moving past it, I continued to find ways to make my students examine their discomfort. Seeing that my students weren't ready to make the leap, I chose another method—when in doubt move to the text. We went through the poem and selected the places that troubled them. My students agreed that the repeated phrase, "We do not worship them," was troubling. When asked why they felt troubled by those lines the class again fell into silence. I moved to some of the things Walker noted in the poem that could be referenced to the "troubling" phrase. I noted that she writes we do not worship their "power plants," "cars," "blondes," "movies," "songs," and "we do not envy their penises." I asked the class what the word *worship* meant to them and whether they felt that those things Walker wrote of should be worshiped. They offered various meanings for worship and agreed that the things Walker mentioned should not be worshiped. However, they still found Walker's poem offensive. Why?

Two other lines that the class found particularly offensive were "We do not admire their president / we know why the white house is white." The students felt that Walker was "angry," "paranoid," and "bitter." After pointing out that the speaker in the poem was not necessarily Alice Walker, I asked the students, "Why was the white house white?" Again there was silence. Because the theme of the class focused on love, they pointed out that they did not see any love in the poem. All they saw was hate for oppressors—they saw hate for white people. And the poem for them was violent. Some felt that Walker wanted to inflict on whites the same pain that had been inflicted on blacks in U.S. history. For them the poem was as simple as black and white. They refused to see anything more. And since they refused to see beyond the black/white binary, their resistance to Walker's poem became embodied in their resistance to me, their black female teacher. Because I try to encourage critical thinking in my classroom, the cut-and-dried/black-and-white response from my students disturbed me. I wanted them to read the literature and make links to their own lives as well as note differences. By the middle of that semester I had hoped that my students would be able to read Walker's womanist poem that talked about the oppression of different people, especially the oppression and rejection of people who spoke out against the systemic nature of oppression, and start to make some connections. Womanist rhetoric at its best is inclusive and takes us away from an understanding of race that is simply about black and white. The Walker poem calls up difference writ large and attacks a variety of isms, not just racism. That my students could not move past their resistance in this regard prompted me to explore other avenues.

According to Patricia Hill Collins, "Black women's struggles are part of a wider struggle for human dignity and empowerment. . . .Thus the primary guiding principle of Black feminism is a reoccurring humanist vision" (1991, 37). I wanted to promote this humanist vision. I wanted to create a classroom environment where everyone's voice was heard, respected, and appreciated. I encouraged connections, connections with each other and connections with the text. Barbara Omalade writes of a black feminist pedagogy that "offers the student, instructor, and institution a methodology for promoting equality and multiple visions and perspectives that parallel black women's attempts to become recognized as human beings and citizens rather than as objects and victims" (1987, 33). It was this promotion of equality, multiple visions, and perspectives that I wanted to guide my classroom. When reading a womanist poem that calls for an end to oppression for all people, students are faced with not only the black woman's story but multiple stories. They can choose to make meaningful connections or resist. I am interested not in "reforming" student views on difference but rather in how their views are formed and how they reach beyond their boundaries.

The Second Encounter: "Happy Darky" Versus "Angry Black Woman": Students Compare Margaret Walker's "For My People" with Alice Walker's "Each One, Pull One"

Because I was so intrigued by my students' harsh reactions to the poem, I wanted to use them as something the entire class could learn from. In her article "Toward a Pedagogy of Everywoman's Studies" Johnnella Butler writes:

> The hostility, fear and hesitancy that inevitably arise in the first few weeks of a Black Woman's Studies class can be converted to fertile ground for profound academic experiences in the humanities and social sciences. I say "profound" because the students' "familiar" is challenged, expanded or reinforced by a subject matter that vibrates with the humanness of life in its form and content. (1985, 237)

I wanted to use my students' hostility and fear as fertile ground. I hoped we could grow from it and move beyond it. I came to the next class meeting with an in-class writing assignment typed, photocopied, and ready to hand out. The students had twenty minutes to complete the assignment, which read, "Look for elements of 'Love of the People' in Margaret Walker's 'For My People' and Alice Walker's 'Each One, Pull One.'" I gave the assignment with the suggestion that they look at the different images and other strategies the two writers use to express their love of the people. In short, I informed them that they would be comparing and contrasting the two poems. The written responses I received were a variety of comments that seemed to center on how negative and angry Alice Walker's poem was and how positive and happy Margaret Walker's poem was. Excerpts from three students' responses follow:

Excerpt One

In "For My People," the poet seems to connect the people through their singing and dancing and religious celebrations. She connects them with the way they worship, plant, dig, hoe, sew and mend. In contrast, the poem "Each One, Pull One" seems to connect the love of the people to their suffering and oppression.

Excerpt Two

Margaret Walker seems happy when she talks about her people. On the other hand Alice Walker sounds angry and maybe even hostile in her poem "Each One, Pull One."

Excerpt Three

"For My People" by Margaret Walker praises the Black race for all that they do. She writes in a positive way celebrating the strength and perseverance that the Black race continued to show. She loved that they kept strong even though they were constantly reminded that they weren't up to other's standards. "Each One, Pull One" by Alice Walker on the other hand wrote in a way that seemed to denounce the actions of others rather than uplift the Blacks' actions themselves.

I found it interesting that some students honed in on the "dancing" and "singing" as well as the planting, digging, and hoeing. Their responses evoked images of the "happy darky" and the "angry black radical," one who is labeled angry simply because he or she speaks out against oppression. I tried to answer my students' comments in ways that questioned the images they cited. I also tried to get them to question why they found particular images (nonthreatening, happy-go-lucky, singing and dancing black people) more appealing than others (oppressed, vociferous, proud).

My reaction to the students in this instance was influenced greatly by their responses to other texts during the semester, readings and comments that labeled the other texts we read by black women as "whining" and "complaining." My students seemed to enjoy the readings that showed definite signs of poverty and oppression but did not make blatant complaints about society's ills against minorities. It was as if poverty, oppression, and discrimination were interesting to read about as long as the writer was not placing blame on anyone (or even implying that someone was to blame) or crying out against his/her condition. By responding to the readings in this way, my students were engaged in an open resistance to the triple threat of the black female teacher, the womanist rhetorician, and black feminist pedagogue. bell hooks writes about similar student reactions in *Teaching to Transgress*. She explores the fact that students did not want to talk about the politics of race, class, and gender: "They accept the shift in the locus of representation but resist shifting ways they think about ideas" (1994a, 144). My students, after a while, were content with the African American literature; as long as the writer was not saying it all as clearly as he/she could or making the students think or question their comfort zones, all was well. The outright, upfront, and forceful nature of a womanist rhetoric aimed at change was troubling for my students. My outright, upfront, and unflinching practice of black feminist pedagogy combined with my black female presence shook up their comfort zones.

The Third Encounter: Some Students Try to Move Past Their Initial Discomfort by Writing Longer Papers on "Each One, Pull One"

After the resistance to class discussion and the negative comments I received in the in-class writing assignments, I was surprised to see that so many students decided to write about Walker's poem. That a total of nine students decided to write longer papers impressed me. It showed me that they were making an effort to try to understand the poem instead of just writing it off as "prejudiced against white people." Each of the students worked through the poem in his or her own way. Some chose to write longer papers comparing and contrasting "For My People" and "Each One, Pull One." Some wrote explications in which they focused on the vagueness of the pronouns in the poem. They tried to figure out exactly who the "we" and "they" were in the poem.

Others tried to work through their own feelings about the poem. These are the papers I found most interesting. The students were thoughtful and self-reflective, and that allowed them the opportunity to move on to larger issues. For example, in his paper titled "What Is She Saying" one male student wrote:

> When I read this poem for the first five times, I thought it was a personal
> attack on the white race, of which I am a part of being of European decent. I

was offended, for I had never been exposed to literature that had so blatantly cut down whites.

The student moved through his initial reaction by recognizing and naming it. He wrote, "because of this I felt ashamed of my race and this frightened me. Even though I didn't commit the act written of in this poem, I felt stereotyped as if I had done them." This naming is important because it allowed the student a chance to face what was problematic for him. The student was able to identify why he felt threatened and attacked. And, in facing it, he could move beyond it. He wrote:

> "Each One, Pull One" by Alice Walker is a poem that requires deep thought and a collection of different perspectives. If it wasn't for the discussions in English class, I would have not found the true meaning of this poem. To begin understanding this poem I put myself into different economic situations. Then I understood that "we" are all victims of the power structure in the United States. However, we are also the "they" of this poem. We are constantly enforcing and contributing to the power cycle by our need for power and a feeling of self worth. We are too materialistic and not individualistic. Alice Walker is warning us not to fall in the trap of self-empowerment for we will set ourselves back.

I liked this student's concept of us all buying into the capitalist nature of society and thus contributing to oppression. The student was able to place himself in Walker's piece: "we are all victims of the power cycle." The student also thought about himself in relation to different economic situations. This is important because it helps to develop empathy. In other words, it would be hard to empathize with the "other" if one couldn't even imagine what the other's life is like. The student came to see that the poem is not just a race poem but also addresses issues of class.

Another student decided to write about the universal nature of oppression in the poem. She keyed in on the fact that the poem was larger than black and white. She wrote:

> When people read literature written by black authors, they often automatically look for symbolism of a black/white issue. Society almost expects black literature to have some political or social statement in the writing. This expectation can be blinding for the reader. Pieces that have a more universal message are restricted by readers looking for a specifically black/white statement.

The student read through what blinds most readers, addressing the larger issue. She wrote:

> "Were we black? Were we women? Were we gay?" The subject of racism against black people is addressed in the poem, but it is not the only form of prejudice in which Ms. Walker sees a need for change. Sexism and

homophobia are also forms of oppression that have been placed upon people. The inclusion of the lines concerning other forms of prejudice is what first let me know this was not only addressing black/white issues. "Were we the wrong shade of black? Were we yellow?" These two lines bring up the prejudices that exist between the races and even those that exist within a single race.

This student was able to move past the black/white issues and on to other issues in the poem that most students weren't able to see. She understood the inclusive project of womanist rhetoric and its desire to combat all forms of oppression. This knowledge is important because it opens the space of possibility not only for womanist rhetoric and the black feminist teacher but for the student as well. The spaces of possibility and the spaces in which the student can now transcend and push her own thinking are multiplied.

The Fourth and Final Encounter: Alice Walker's Poem as Read Through June Jordan's Essay "Where Is the Love?"

Even after having some students work through their feelings about the poem, I still was not satisfied or content to end the discussion there. Reading the nine longer papers and seeing that some of my students were able to comprehend the nature of multiple oppressions made me desire a similar outcome for all my students. Indeed, I was even more determined to have all my students try to combat their negative readings of the poem. I found the chance to do that in a unit of the class titled "The Politics of Love," in which students were asked to read June Jordan's essay "Where Is the Love?" I gave the students twenty-five minutes to explore the following two passages from the essay in relation to Walker's poem.

Passage One

And it seems to me that the socio-psychic strength that should follow from morally defensible Black feminism will mean that I become able and willing, without fear, to love and respect all men who are willing and able, without fear, to love and respect me. In short, if the acquirement of my self determination is part of a worldwide, an inevitable righteous movement, then I should become willing and able to embrace more and more of the whole world, without fear and without self sacrifice. (Jordan 1993, 337)

Passage Two

And it is against such sorrow, and it is against such suicide, and it is against such deliberated strangulation of the possible lives of women, of my sisters, and of powerless peoples—men and children—everywhere, that I work and live now as a feminist trusting that I will learn to love myself well enough to

love you (Whoever you are), well enough so that you will love me enough so
that we will know exactly where is the love: that it is here, between us, and
growing stronger and growing stronger. (Jordan 1993, 339)

I wanted to bring together important perspectives from the Jordan essay with
which my students were struggling: race and discussions of racism, along with
gender oppression and feminism as a political stance. I found it interesting that the
students labeled Jordan "angry" and "opinionated," the same labels they had
pinned on Walker. It was my hope that by pointing out some of the key passages
in Jordan's piece and using them as a lens, students could better see the important
aspects of Walker's poem. I wanted the students to use Jordan's words, "I should
become more willing and able to embrace more and more of the whole world,
without fear, and also without self sacrifice" to better understand what Walker
means when she says, "all of us must live or none." I wanted my students to read
Jordan's hope that "we will all know exactly where is the love: that it is here,
between us, and growing stronger and growing stronger" and understand Walker's
plea that "Each one must pull one. . .Each one, pull one back into the sun."

Some of my students were still unable to move beyond the black/white
binary that trapped them in simplistic readings of the works. One student even
labeled both works as "paranoid" and said that the writers felt "the world had
'it' in for them." However, most students were able to connect the two pieces
in meaningful ways. The following are excerpts from writing by students who
were able to move beyond simple readings of the works.

Excerpt Four

When reading "Each One, Pull One," along with the above quotes, I have
sensed that the two women are speaking of almost the same argument. This
argument is everyone in some way is discriminated against, and we need to
recognize individuality, creativity and difference.

Excerpt Five

In "Each One, Pull One," Alice Walker speaks of uniting all people and
enlightening people against prejudice and hatred. She suggests that we "pull
one back into the sun." This line suggests that we help one another to overcome our fears and prejudices and shed some light onto the closed minds of
others. We need to take the time to get to know one another and learn to love
each other. This has to be a mutual act. Jordan suggests that she will, "become
able and willing, without fear, to love and respect all men who are willing and
able, without fear, to love and respect me." This shows that every person must
be involved in the "righteous movement" for it to make a substantial change.

Although I was not explicitly teaching womanist rhetoric with this class, its concepts were present in the material, and to explore them I applied the methods of
black feminist pedagogy. This classroom encounter is an example of the ways in
which womanist rhetoric and black feminist pedagogy can interact in the

writing classroom and give students a space to think critically and move past their own resistance. The combination is not always easy and is indeed fraught with tension. But when students push past their resistance and get the concept of multiple oppressions and the need to change the systemic nature of oppression it is worth all the tension and resistance.

The poem by Alice Walker is womanist and serious, and asks hard questions. It pushes readers to want to do better, to be better people. It offers hope while making readers uneasy and forcing them to question themselves. These are the traits of womanist rhetoric. And when combined with an unrelenting black feminist pedagogy, a pedagogy that does not shy away from making students write and think about difference, even when it is uncomfortable, even when they want to resist it, womanist rhetoric can help our students move past and "transgress" their own boundaries. Ultimately, womanist rhetoric envisions hope for a better world, and black feminist pedagogy, when done properly, works toward making those visions a reality. In my "Love and the Black Literary Experience" course, students were exposed to a womanist rhetoric and black feminist pedagogy, and some of them were able to transgress their ideas about difference. Most students could look at the poem in a different light, move past their initial discomfort, and finally embrace the humanness of the poem. I charge us all to follow the title of Alice Walker's poem "Each One, Pull One" and consider seriously the pedagogical and political possibilities of womanist rhetoric and black feminist pedagogy.

Author's Note

Because I began thinking about some of the pedagogical issues addressed in this essay while I was a graduate student at Miami University, I would like to thank Susan Jarratt, Jill Swiencicki, Shannon Wilson, and Carmiele Wilkerson for reading earlier versions, offering insight, and pushing my thinking about the subject. I would also like to thank the students in my "Love and the Black Literary Experience" composition and literature classes for grappling with the complex issues that Walker's poem broached with me and for helping create a classroom experience worth continuing to think about and share with others.

5

Dissoi Logoi

Women's Rhetoric and Classroom Practice

Beth Daniell

Dissoi Logoi

The fragment *Dissoi Logoi*, by an anonymous sophist of the fourth century BCE, serves several purposes in my rhetoric classes. First, as the title implies—"contrary propositions" in English—this work shows that almost any issue has many sides: "And death is bad for those who die, but good for the undertakers and grave diggers"; "And undoubtedly it is bad for everyone else, but good for the potters if pottery gets smashed" (279). Second, the text demonstrates that universal standards for thinking and behaving do not exist: "[T]o the Spartans it is seemly that young girls should do athletics and go about with bare arms and no tunics, but to the Ionians this is disgraceful"; "The Massegetes cut up their parents and eat them, and they think that to be buried in their children is the most beautiful grave imaginable, but in Greece, if anyone did such a thing, he would be driven out of the country and would die an ignominious death for having committed such disgraceful and terrible deeds" (282).

The sophists, those earliest rhetoricians who traveled the ancient Mediterranean world teaching, well, everything, resisted the attempts of pre-Socratic thinkers to define and categorize Being, or What Really, Really Is. Instead, the sophists argued, to paraphrase Gorgias, that an essential Isness might not exist at all, but that if it did, we probably couldn't apprehend it—couldn't know it—and that even if we could grasp the ultimate What Is, we probably couldn't communicate it, words being as slippery as they are. Yet, at the same time, the sophists put much faith in the power of language: "It can stop fear and banish grief and create joy and nurture pity," this same Gorgias tells us in the *Encomium of Helen* (1990, 45).

The anonymous author of *Dissoi Logoi* not only shows that What Is is different in various parts of the world but also argues, though in a much funnier vein than most of his postmodern counterparts, that there is no actual connection between language and Being: "The true statement is the same as the false in the first place, because they are both expressed in the same words, and secondly because whenever a statement is made, if things [should] turn out to be as stated, then the statement is true, but if they should not turn out to be as stated, then the same statement is false" (287). According to the sophists, then, not only can the same thing be described as both good and bad, but the relationship between the name and the thing is tenuous at best.

Like Gorgias, our anonymous sophist plays with words—and *play* is the operative word—to trick, surprise, confuse, and amuse. On first reading the *Dissoi Logoi*, I was glad to find a fancy term for something I'd done all my life—argue the contrary propositions just for the fun of it. But over the last few years I've found this notion to be more and more significant in my classroom practice, calling into question, as it does, received opinion and challenging old assumptions. Thus I argue in this chapter that consciously and intentionally inviting diverse propositions can contribute to a feminist pedagogy that helps students write and speak and so acquire and create knowledge. I want to assert as well that a feminist spin on the *dissoi logoi* concept can help students come to voice.

Despite the devaluation of sophistic rhetoric by Plato, Aristotle, and their students, dominant versions of Western rhetoric have continued to cherish the idea of contrary propositions, but not necessarily in the same way as "the *Dissoi Logoi* guy," the name my undergraduates have given to our unknown sophist. For example, Aristotle, in explaining the usefulness of rhetoric, writes:

> Further, one should be able to argue persuasively on either side of a question . . . not that we may actually do both (for one should not persuade what is debased) but in order that it may not escape our notice what the real state of the case is and that we ourselves may be able to refute it if another person uses speech unjustly. (1991, 34)

For Aristotle and others who see rhetoric as agonistic, the *dissoi logoi* help us win by leading us to look at the opposing arguments so that we can counter them. Diverse theses help us not only find or construct the actual case but also hammer out compromise. But the sophistic notion of contrary propositions is, I have found, even more significant than that.

In the twentieth century, Kenneth Burke, for instance, argues the value of "counter-statements," those propositions that, as Tilly Warnock has explained, oppose "accepted principles of the day...[and thus] help people think critically about what they are doing with words and what words are doing to them" (1996, 90). As Warnock points out, Burke's project was peace. A man whose life was punctuated by the world wars, Burke saw war as "that most tragically ironic of all divisions," "a disease, or perversion of communion...characteristically requir[ing] a myriad of constructive acts for each destructive one" (1990, 1020). For Burke, figuring out how to do this life without killing one another in the Human Barnyard demands analysis of what is said, who says it, and what the motivation is. In order to get to this analysis, Burke believes that we need the counterstatements, that is, the *dissoi logoi*.

Similarly, Chaim Perelman, who interestingly served in the Belgian Resistance, looks to argumentation as a way to avoid violence, explaining that belief in only one right answer is the chief problem with Western epistemology. According to Perelman, "Things are very different within a tradition that follows a juridical model, rather than a mathematical model. Thus in the tradition of the Talmud, for example, it is accepted that opposed positions can be equally reasonable; one of them does not have to be right" (Perelman 1958/1990, 1085). Perelman illustrates with the story of the Talmud scholars who finally appeal to God to tell which interpretation of Scripture is the correct one. From heaven, God says, "[T]hese two theses both express...the word of the Living God" (1085). This model, a text with more than one valid interpretation, is what I try to set up in my classroom.

Feminists and the Contrary Propositions

This image of many overlapping and competing arguments existing all at the same time, this sophistic notion of *dissoi logoi*, is one I want to associate with a feminist project, as Susan Jarratt does in *Rereading the Sophists*. Like Jarratt, I do not mean to imply that that the sophists of ancient Greece were somehow feminist in their sympathies; they were not, as far as we can tell. Likewise, I do not want to imply that all women subscribe to the *dissoi logoi* concept—we all know women who rigidly hold to one unquestioned and unquestionable truth—nor that men cannot—we all know men who keep a number of diverse propositions in mind simultaneously. According to Jarratt, what women and the ancient sophists have in common is their "*other*ness," both groups existing outside the dominant tradition of language use and thereby serving as a challenge to that tradition.

Along with others who have looked seriously at issues of gender, race, and class, I assert that women and others poorly educated in the ways of Western epistemology with its pursuit of the "unicity of truth" (Perelman 1990, 1085) have learned to live with, and sometimes even value, more than one viewpoint. By virtue of the cultural and social conditions of their lives as mothers and wives, women must consider a number of competing interests. According to early research by Carol Gilligan, for example, women's moral reasoning rests on their awareness of the needs of all members of the family or the group, not on the abstract principle men supposedly use to make moral decisions (1982, 18–19). Indeed, Gilligan's work itself offers a contrary proposition: Lawrence Kohlberg's research with Harvard students posited a developmental scale to measure moral reasoning; on this scale, women almost always turned out to be less developed. Gilligan contests both the universality of Kolhberg's hierarchy and his conclusions. Gilligan's contrary proposition is that women's moral reasoning is different from, not less developed than.

Across the curriculum, women thinkers and writers have offered propositions contrary to those of the dominant group, thereby enriching the disciplines and opening new areas of research. Closer to home, Adrienne Rich has spoken for the diverse propositions, the counterstatements, that women writers present. In her essay "When We Dead Awaken: Writing as Revision," Rich valorizes the contrary perspective women bring to writing and to reading. This "other" view yields not just a different perspective but, Rich says, an often more life-affirming position to use in thinking and writing than that found in the largely male literary tradition (49). For Rich, women's writing must be *re*-vision, looking at the world a different way, presenting not the official, "masculine" facts of the case but a different, alternative set of facts. In this plea for women's writing, Rich argues for the freedom necessary for formulating the *dissoi logoi*:

> [I]f the imagination is to transcend and transform experience, it has to question, to challenge, to conceive of alternatives.... You have to be free to play around with the notion that day might be night, love might be hate; nothing can be too sacred for the imagination to turn into its opposite or call experimentally by another name. For writing is re-naming. (*On Lies* 43)

Similarly, in their article "Border Crossings: Intersections of Rhetoric and Feminism" (1995), Lisa Ede, Cheryl Glenn, and Andrea Lunsford show that women's rhetoric often begins in the *dissoi logoi*. They argue here that women's rhetoric has historically provided contrary propositions, and they offer scores of examples of women who have written or spoken against the grain—Aspasia, Margery Kempe, Mary Wollstonecraft, the Grimke sisters, Elizabeth Cady Stanton, many anthologized now in Joy Ritchie and Kate Ronald's collection *Available Means*.

In addition, "Border Crossings" provides rhetoricians with another contrary proposition: a different way of thinking about the traditional canons of rhetoric. Instead of listing the canons in the usual order—invention, arrangement, style, memory, and delivery—Ede, Glenn, and Lunsford place memory beside invention. Emphasizing that invention depends on what people remember, the authors remind us that women remember different things and remember things differently, necessarily, because their experiences are different from men's. Women's propositions, their ways of speaking and reading and writing, therefore must be different, contrary. Modeling an alternative way to use the canons, "Border Crossings" helps us envision women's writing and speaking over the centuries not as disparate anomalies but rather as a rhetoric with a history and theory different from the agonistic rhetoric of the dominant tradition.

The *Dissoi Logoi* in Women's Literacy

In addition to the work of these feminist scholars, my own research into women's literate practices underscores the value for women of contrary propositions, as I show in *A Communion of Friendship*, from which the following discussion is summarized. The women who talked with me about their literate practices are all members of one Al-Anon group in a place I call Mountain City. For readers unfamiliar with it, Al-Anon is a 12-step organization for family and friends of alcoholics. Like its exemplar, Alcoholics Anonymous, Al-Anon claims to be a spiritual, but not religious, program, and so the women who volunteered to answer my questions wrote and read as part of their program for spiritual growth.

Also like AA, Al-Anon assumes the value of literacy for self-improvement. Members write as part of the self-examination suggested by the steps. They read Al-Anon literature. Veteran members advise newcomers to read particular parts of Al-Anon publications, often offering testimonies about how such-and-such a section helped when they themselves dealt with a similar situation. At Al-Anon meetings, a written text typically supplies the topic of discussion; the talk that follows presents varying interpretations of this text. In mature groups, where disagreement is not a threat, these interpretations supply sets of *dissoi logoi*, ways of thinking and behaving contrary to usual patterns and providing an array of options for women who have known only one way. As one of my research participants said, "[Before Al-Anon] I didn't know I had a choice." From the *dissoi logoi* in Al-Anon meetings, the women who talked with me learn they have choices; from the Al-Anon spiritual message, they begin to see themselves primarily as competent human beings and spiritual seekers, propositions clearly contrary to the traditional conception of woman or wife.

The women who talked with me read not just to make their lives better but also for "distraction and play." Here they read the same genres other Americans read: science fiction, true crime, biographies, murder mysteries, and "good" novels such as *The Color Purple*, *Beloved*, and *One Hundred Years of Solitude*, to name only a few of the titles they mentioned specifically. At the center of this reading is the woman I call Lilly, who often buys the books and starts them round the circle. Lilly says: "If I have a book that somebody doesn't have, they can always borrow it. I like the discussions with the people after we've read the books. You can't have the discussion unless you're willing to share the books."

Physically sharing books is common to women's groups, according to Anne Gere's article "Common Properties of Pleasure." In the late nineteenth and early twentieth centuries, it was not an unusual practice, Gere says, for a woman's club to buy one copy of a title and either read it aloud in the group or, like the Mountain City women who talked with me, pass it around among the members (1994, 387–88). The reasons for sharing may range from poverty, to lack of control of finances, to an ingrained reluctance to buy for themselves.

Whatever the reason, such reading practices undermine the capitalistic concept of the book as commodity, Gere argues. But perhaps even more important, as Gere shows and the Mountain City Al-Anon women affirm, sharing the actual text leads to sharing interpretations of the text, a scene that calls to mind the image of the Talmud with the text in question in the middle of the page surrounded by various commentaries. Both practices—reading aloud and sharing interpretations of a text passed around the group—nurture the sense of community among the women—what Lilly calls "a communion of friendship"—that appears so important in the Mountain City women's empowerment.

The sharing, the talk, the oral conversation following a book as it is passed around the circle of Al-Anon women is arguably the most significant aspect of their reading. More than the reading itself, I submit, the talk invites the Mountain City Al-Anon women to "come to voice," to use bell hooks' phrase (1989, 6). In these conversations the women translate, clarify, and articulate their feelings on any number of issues. According to Lilly, books that "trigger feelings" become catalysts for these round-robin conversations. Lilly explains the relations among feelings, language, conversation, and understanding as she recounts her own response to *Beloved:*

> I don't think I understood it all, not intellectually. But all my feelings got it. It touched every feeling I'd ever had. Every minute little feeling, even vague ones, it touched. So when I finished reading it, I understood that book in terms of my feelings. But in terms of how it all fits together on an intellectual level, if I had to analyze it, I'd be a little lost. [But] I can talk about...how I felt about everything that happened. *It gets clearer as I talk about it* [my emphasis]. That's what books do. They touch feelings, and then I have to find words for the feelings. The only way I can find words for feelings is to talk about it with lots of people, because they often have the words that I'm looking for. The words make the feelings very clear when I can find the language for the feeling. So the words become important in terms of being able to share the feelings, and also to find some ease with the feeling in terms of understanding it. Language seems very important in terms of that.

Lilly's comment here is similar to the explanation given by psychologist James Pennebaker for the apparent healing effect of writing for people who have suffered trauma: putting inchoate feelings into words and sentences imposes an order on an experience that has been bewildering, confusing, terrifying, allowing the speaker to feel some control (1991, 166). For several of the women who talked with me, recognizing and understanding feelings, which one does through language, through talk, seems a necessary step in their recovery from their sometimes traumatic experiences with someone else's alcoholism.

In the conversations about what they read, the Mountain City women not only find the words for feelings but also practice speaking out, gaining experience in what hooks calls "talking back," which she defines as "speaking as an equal," "daring to disagree," "having an opinion" (1989, 5). Tommie calls this process "finding [one's] own language." She equates the confidence to speak one's own truth with healing, with being "restored to sanity," as the Second Step promises ("Came to believe that a Power greater than ourselves could restore us to sanity").

The conversations about the books go further than individual articulation of feelings, however. In the talk about the books, the Al-Anon women establish and reinforce relationships with one another. According to Lilly, when someone in the group reads a book that "touches feelings," that person then lends the book to someone else; when the second woman has read it, these two begin the talk about the book. Then as others read it, they join the conversation, in pairs, in threes or fours, speaking with one another with "the intimacy and intensity" of "woman speech" which hooks claims as the source of her own voice and authorship (1989, 6). Lilly explains this in her description of the talk about Ntozake Shange's *for colored girls who have considered suicide when the rainbow is enuf*:

> I saw [the play] in New York. And I literally carried it in my purse for years. It was the first thing that gave me the sense that it could get better, that something could help it get better. I started reading sections of it to people I got close to [in the Al-Anon group]. Then [later] we would take turns reading it. One time we had a gathering of about six women. What was interesting was the comments about what people liked. Some of them liked the anger. Someone liked the one about the plant—leaving it on his door—"I'm ending this affair"—and the assertiveness in terms of men—"You can water it your own damn self." What one woman loved was Sechita, who loves all the attention and knows she's manipulated men, and they go home with her, but she wants them gone in the morning because she wants her life back in order the next morning.
>
> I loved watching what people liked. And we talked a lot about it. It changed. The more conversation we added about it, the fuller everything got, because there were so many different ways to look at one poem, depending on who felt what from it.

These conversations with their multiple interpretations, their *dissoi logoi*, in turn create the "mutually empathic" relationships that Jean Baker Miller and Irene Pierce Stiver posit as necessary for both emotional and cognitive development. Feminist psychotherapists affiliated with the Wellesley Centers for Women, Miller and Stiver argue in their book *The Healing Connection* against the traditional model of separation, or individuation, as the end point of healthy psychological development. They assert instead that "connections—the experience of mutual engagement and empathy—provide the original and continuing sources of growth" (3). "Mutually growth-fostering relationships" depend on hearing and being heard, understanding and being understood,

Miller and Stiver say (19). From their clinical experience, Miller and Stiver argue that what is healing for women in therapy is the *relationship* between the client and the counselor. The attention paid to what the woman says begins the healing, for it is this attention—this human connection—that affirms the woman's self, which has hitherto been in a state of "disconnection" from others. The therapist is not required, according to Miller and Stiver, to offer "unrelenting approval" but rather to provide an audience that takes seriously the woman's concerns.

For many women who come to Al-Anon, being listened to, being taken seriously is a new experience. According to Lilly, it isn't literacy that allows people to speak, and it isn't educational level or attainment of the approved speech forms. Lilly explains, "People don't just speak. They have to be listened to first. I don't care what your language is like. If nobody's listened, you won't speak."

According to Miller and Stiver's critique, a patriarchal culture like ours mitigates against women receiving this sort of empathy and empowerment: "While many men have received a great deal of empathy that has helped them become empowered, often they have not been aware of it.... At the same time most women have not received from men the same empathic attention to their experience nor the support for their actions that would flow from mutually empathic interactions" (1997, 37). Asserting that connections with others help people become "strong, active initiators and responders" (52), Miller and Stiver seem to be describing the Al-Anon women who talked with me.

Recognizing someone else's feelings, feeling *with* the other person, paying attention to what the speaker says, empowers not only the speaker, who is taken seriously, acknowledged, and therefore affirmed, but also the hearer, who in taking seriously, acknowledging, and affirming another has an effect on the speaker. And having an effect on another human being is the most basic form of power; it is the heart of the dynamic relationship between rhetor and audience.

The *Dissoi Logoi* and Pedagogy

Reading feminist scholarship and analyzing my own research data, I have begun to understand that the *dissoi logoi*—not just an opposite proposition, but a whole array of opinions and judgments—can be something far richer than a tool in agonistic rhetoric, and I have tried to put this understanding into practice in my own classes. Perhaps it might be more accurate to say that a feminist version of *dissoi logoi* explains and enhances classroom strategies I've long practiced.

Using a strategy I borrowed from Lester Faigley, I assign response papers that students write and then share with the class. On the day students present their responses, they bring copies for everyone in the class. They read their papers aloud, with the rest of us following along. If there's time afterward, we look again at these papers to gather lists of issues for further discussion and begin to talk about those issues. Rereading these papers, I prepare remarks that respond to the student responses. As I return the papers the next day in class I talk about the important points of their readings without, I hope, seeming to lecture:

> Mary, your summary of Burke's terministic screens concept is wonderful. Your example is really clear. Guys, you might want to mark this paper "Save for final exam." It will help you study later.

> Now is probably a good time to go back and look on page 1035. I want to give you the Beth Daniell version of how to use this concept of terministic screens as you do the analysis of the text you've chosen for your project. When I was first teaching this course, I didn't make a big deal out of the *terministic* part of terministic screens, and sometimes students used it as only a synonym for worldview or ideology. But it really is more concrete than that, I think.

> Mark, I want to ask you—and the class as well—to look again at the end of *Symbolic Action*. Your negative comments about Burke's relativism are nicely phrased, and you speak to a criticism of rhetoric that goes all the way back to Plato. Clearly, you are in good company. But I think the section called "Our Attempt to Avoid Mere Relativism" specifically addresses your concern and is worth reading again. Please turn to page 1039 in Bizzell and Herzberg. I think here Burke does argue for an absolute, something that makes it not turtles all the way down. Look at what Burke says and see if you can find his bottom line.

What I am trying to do here is show the students that I am paying attention to what they say. I reward them publicly for doing good work even when they don't know they've done good work. And often when they do good work, I need to supply the academic language. In these minilectures, I rarely say that a student is wrong. Only on those rare occasions when I think a misreading will mislead the class do I intervene with an explicitly directed correction. Sometimes I supply some missing information, and sometimes I offer the contrary proposition by calling the students' attention to a particular passage, as I do in the preceding comment to Mark about Burke's relativism. Sometimes I disagree with an idea more overtly. As Miller and Stiver argue, the point isn't unconditional or unrelenting approval. The point is I listen. I take them seriously. And when I learn from them, I say so.

Once the students begin to feel safe with my comments, their readings typically become more astute. By the time we get to the feminist writers at the end of the course, students overtly disagree with one another, with, for example, some students criticizing Rich for what they see as her stridency and anger and others talking about her call for revision as crucially important for women. It is not unusual for students, not just male students, to criticize Audre Lorde for stating her reluctance to talk to white feminists. Yet, one of the most moving response papers I've ever read began, "It seems strange for me, a white heterosexual male, to identify so strongly with a black lesbian writer. But I do." After students know that difference is valued and valuable in the rhetoric class, they sometimes address directly a disagreement with another student, and even occasionally with me: "In this response paper, I want to disagree with what Josh said about the rhetoric of Christian students on this campus"; "On Thursday, Amanda criticized Bush's ethos; today I want to talk about pathos to show why people are for him"; "According to Professor Daniell, Foucault is supposed to be saying something new. But didn't Burke already say this? For example,…"

Listening to their peers' responses to the assigned readings, paying attention to how other students use the rhetorical concepts to explain the language use around them, my students see the texts that had at first seemed obscure and difficult become richer and clearer. At least this is what many of them say as they write the Introduction to the Response Folder at the end of the semester (an assignment I borrowed from Toby Fulwiler, who got it from Dixie Goswami). In this assignment, students discuss their own reading and writing over the term, as evidenced in their response papers. But I also give them the opportunity to comment on their peers' papers, if they'd like. Typically, they do. My students sound like Lilly talking about the Al-Anon women reading *for colored girls*: "It changed. The more conversation we added about it, the fuller everything got, because there were so many different ways to look at one poem, depending on who felt what from it." Sometimes they write of a classmate's consistent intelligence and insight: "I knew if I were struggling, I could always count on Annie's papers to set me straight." They talk in ways I find both moving and fascinating about how they didn't understand, say, Toulmin at all until Charlie read his response paper in class—and sometimes I just plain didn't follow Charlie's paper on Toulmin. I think to myself: "They understand some kid with a backwards baseball cap better than they understand me?" Yes, they do. And isn't that wonderful? They create meaning without the authority figure. Isn't that exactly what we mean when we talk about having students collaborate? Giving students ownership?

Being listened to by their peers and having their work taken seriously by the professor empowers students. They learn the most essential lesson of rhetoric—that your words can influence others. They learn firsthand about audience. In *Writing with Power* Peter Elbow phrases it like this:

> The wild child brought up only by animals in the woods does not speak at all. Any "back to the basics" movement in the teaching of writing needs to start by ensuring each child the most basic thing of all: a real audience for his written words—an audience that really listens and takes the interchanges seriously. (1981, 184)

They learn to "talk back," to speak out even if someone might disagree and to defend their convictions and stances. And finally, like the Al-Anon women, my students learn—or at least I hope they learn—that many interpretations, many readings, are not only possible but also desirable and that although no one right answer may exist out there waiting to be discovered, it is possible to speak or write persuasively for the interpretation that each of them deems best. I hope they learn that both rhetoric and knowledge are deeply social—a proposition still contrary to traditional classroom practice. I hope the students learn that they are smarter and more creative than they thought they were. I hope they learn that *dissoi logoi* can't exist in a world single-mindedly pursuing the unicity of truth.

A Feminist Pedagogue

But no matter what my students learn, I've learned all these lessons, and more. I've learned that the contrary propositions—or is it the students?—need freedom and trust. As the one with the immediate responsibility for ordering discourse in the classroom, I'm the only person who can set up and nurture such an atmosphere. I have learned that students learn more effectively if they can trust that I'm not playing "gotcha," ready to pounce if they make a mistake. I therefore talk a lot about how sometimes a "good" response paper helps us learn by asking questions and that we often learn more from an imperfect paper that goes out on a limb than a nice, neat one that takes no chances. I have learned that their playful responses—Richard Weaver and Audre Lorde at the local student bar, for instance—can present insightful arguments about the texts we read.

I've learned better ways of being both gentle and firm in the same note at the bottom of the page, of supporting and challenging all at the same time. I've learned to practice patience. I've learned to pay attention, especially to those women reluctant to speak and to those men too quick to claim dominion, so that I can encourage response from the former and invite a more considered rhetoric in the latter.

I've learned to listen with joy to what my students say, to revel in the *dissoi logoi* that they bring into the classroom. And I am learning on a deep level what "the *Dissoi Logoi* guy" taught thousands of years ago and what Michel Foucault describes in those last amazing paragraphs of "The Order of Discourse": that language is disconnected from the signifier, that the value of language is not necessarily in its relationship to the referent, that what my students *mean* about the texts I assign may not be nearly as important as the *event* of my students' discourse about those texts (1971/1990, 1164). It is in this event of their speaking the contrary propositions that we come into relationship, that they and I create a community that affirms and empowers.

6

Documenting Violations

Rhetorical Witnessing and the Spectacle of Distant Suffering As Pedagogy[1]

Wendy S. Hesford

Claps of thunder and dark ominous clouds trudge across the opening frames of *The Sky: A Silent Witness*, a 1995 documentary video by Midge Mackenzie, produced in association with Amnesty International. The expansive yet oppressive sky functions as a haunting reminder of human rights violations across the globe. A liturgical piano solo weaves its way down the sloping hills of Guatemala, commemorating 180 massacre victims, indigenous Quiché Indians, killed in 1982. Dozens of women and men kneel as they empty ash and bones into small coffins. Women place fresh flowers onto coarsely cut wooden boxes. Children look on with a curious sadness. A woman speaks: "My name is Juan de Paz González. I belong to the Quiché Indian tribe." González recounts how her father, a preacher, was killed by army soldiers in Guatemala, and how her family hid in ravines and mountains before coming to the city, where her husband was later kidnapped and where she was left alone with her daughter, hungry and displaced. "It was a difficult situation for me as a woman with a child," González continues. "The situation is very difficult for all one and a half million displaced here in this city, this country of Guatemala."

González's testimony, set against the backdrop of excavations, funeral rituals, and protest marches, establishes the narrative pattern followed by the other women featured in the film: name, cultural affiliation, and date of the action that led to individual and mass trauma, followed by a rhetorical gesture that highlights the importance of community and collective grieving. The film features five women of color from Bangladesh, China, Guatemala, Tibet, and the United States, and one woman from Bosnia, all of whom describe experiences of victimization and state-sanctioned violence.[2] The camera focuses on one woman at a time, with the exception of the Bosnian woman, whose face we do not see. Each face is side-lit: one half embraced by dark shadows. The slow panning between frames of the sky and the women's faces creates the illusion of a seamless visual narrative. Similarly, each woman's testimony retains the rhetorical appeal of the particular yet situates the particular within the communal—the plural—*I*. At work here, as is common to the protean genre of the *testimonio*, is a "lateral identification—through relationship, which acknowledges the possible differences among 'us' as components of the whole" (Sommer 1988, 108).

Like many human rights documentaries, *The Sky: A Silent Witness* negotiates the tensions between universality and particularity through the genre of the *testimonio*. *Testimonio* and autobiography share the "affirmation of the speaking subject," but *testimonio* destabilizes traditional conventions of autobiography through its "affirmation of the individual self in a collective mode" (Beverley 1992, 96–97).[3] Within the context of human rights documentaries, victims' testimonies bear witness to incommensurable events and also function rhetorically as empathetic markers in an effort to construct the viewer as witness. Human rights testimonies play a key role in rebuilding civil institutions, in formulating movements for reparation and restitution, and in advancing the international human rights agenda. But, we must ask, what kinds of witnesses do human rights testimonies construe? To what degree are testimonial subjects romanticized as transnational artifacts (Kaplan 1994) and/or turned into opportunistic spectacles for self-positioning or for certain political agendas?[4] If one of the prominent rhetorical features of human rights documentaries and testimonials is to create an international rhetorical space of intersubjectivity—of bearing witness—how do we account for ruptures in identification? Finally, when using human rights documentaries and testimonials in the classroom, how can we avoid romanticizing, or making a spectacle of, the "other"? That is, how can we encourage our students to be critical and rhetorical witnesses?

In this essay I demonstrate how women's testimonies about the trauma of rape warfare challenge traditional notions of identification in rhetorical theory and raise new critical questions about the ethics of representation and the pedagogical risks of testimonial travel. These testimonies and their mobilization compel us to attend much more seriously to "witnessing" as a rhetorical category and to the necessity of redefined notions of self-reflexivity and critical engagement. The call for greater self-reflexivity, however, need not lead to the creation of a spectacular, narcissistic, or melancholic rhetoric or pedagogy. Rather, as I attempt to demonstrate, this call requires attention to the limits and traces of trauma and identification, and to the *ungovernablity* of their representation. I argue that an analysis of the rhetorical dynamics of witnessing called forth by the representation of human rights violations (namely, women's testimonies about rape as a military tactic) will enable us to create productive critical and pedagogical encounters. We need to be able to account for cultural differences, to examine the politics of the production, circulation, and consumption of texts across national boundaries, and to foreground the methodological and pedagogical crises posed by representations of individual trauma and mass atrocity. I argue that attention to the methodological and ethical challenges posed by testimonials' use of witnessing as a rhetorical strategy enable us to productively examine what I call the *crisis of reference* and the *crisis of witnessing*.

I use the term *crisis of reference* to describe how trauma and violence often throw truth-telling genres into crisis (Egan), a process that Rothberg refers to as "traumatic realism."[5] The concept of the *crisis of reference* highlights the inability of representations to capture, as in fix or make static, the truth, and more particularly, it refers to the paradox of representing trauma. I use the term *crisis of witnessing* to refer to the risks of representing trauma and violence, of ruptures in identification, and the impossibility of empathetic merging between witness and testifier, listener and speaker. Human rights testimonials as documentary forms of evidence might be said to conjoin legal and dramatic forms of persuasion, a conjoining captured by the phrase *crisis of witnessing*. A critical approach to the *crisis of witnessing* as it pertains to the representation of human rights violations prompts us to question the presuppositions of both legal and dramatic realism that urge rhetors (advocates) to *stand in for* the "other," on the grounds that such identifications risk incorporation of the other within the self. Little critical work exists on the pedagogical reception of human rights testimonies in the classroom; this neglect, in part, stems from assumptions about the authenticity of firsthand accounts and the referential nature of testimony as legal evidence (Kennedy 2004, 49). In developing an analysis of the functions of human rights testimonies and the multiple and often conflicting identifications they (dis)enable, we move closer to articulating a rhetorical pedagogy of witnessing that attends to the issues raised so forcefully by *The Sky*.

Ungovernable Locations: The Crisis of Witnessing

In *Testimony*, Shoshana Felman and Dori Laub observe that the twentieth century has been marked by events that produced a "crisis within history which precisely cannot be articulated, witnessed in the given categories of history itself" (1992, xviii). Felman and Laub allude to the limitations of disciplinary conventions and categories in understanding atrocity and point to how trauma may throw into crisis existing paradigms and patterns of communication. In terms of the reception of representations of mass trauma and torture, scholars in memory and trauma studies have called for a critical stance of bearing witness, wherein the witness (listener or viewer) "does not take the place of the other" (Chun 2002, 158). For instance, Dominick LaCapra characterizes the desired response of the "secondary witness" as "empathetic unsettlement." The "secondary witness," as LaCapra puts it, "should reactivate and transmit not trauma but an unsettlement . . . that manifests empathy (but not full identification) with the victim" (1999, 722). Similarly, Ulrich Baer argues that "empathic identification can easily lead us to miss the inscription of trauma because the original subjects themselves did not register the experience in the fullness of its meaning" (2002, 13).

In *Spectral Evidence*, Baer uses *ungovernability* to describe the "break-down of context that, in a structured analogy to trauma, is staged by every photograph" (2002, 11) and by the "structuring *absence* [that] defines . . . [traumatic] experiences" (12). His position contrasts with modernist photog-raphy criticism, which he argues is characterized by a melancholic strain caught in a rhetoric of doom, a stance that laments the loss of the referent and the "real." Baer argues that the "real" cannot be limited to the notion of pho-tography as impending loss; rather, there is a trace of the *ungovernable* in every photograph. Aware that viewers project narratives onto photographs, and that images elicit narrative impulses, Baer is less interested in the connotative dimensions than in how "photographs can capture the shrapnel of traumatic time" (7). Rather than pointing to a loss, Baer argues, "every photograph is radically exposed to a future unknown to its subjects" (7). Thus trauma signi-fies the *ungovernable*, which, like the past, is an unstable referent (107).

Critical works in life writing studies—a broader category under which the testimonial genre is often located—and feminist ethnography have engaged these *ungovernable crises of reference and witnessing* primarily in terms of the mediated nature of the testimonial genre—the editorial processes of col-laboration and mediation, for example, and the circulation of testimonials.[6] Critics have pointed to the problem that the privileged speak *for* rather than *with* the oppressed, thereby situating themselves as an authenticating pres-ence, and the equally problematic assumption that the subject can speak *only* for herself, a stance that ignores how rhetorical conventions and discursive systems shape the construction of subjectivity and agency. Feminist critics in particular have questioned such conceptions and propose that we consider not only the social location of the speaker or writer but also the material-rhetorical context into which the utterance or text is projected.[7] The emergent focus within life writing studies and feminist rhetorical studies toward "how one gets heard" is essentially a turn to the rhetorical analysis of listening. For example, Krista Ratcliffe advocates a rhetorical listening that "locate[s] iden-tification in discursive spaces of both commonalties and differences" (1999, 204) and "turns hearing (a reception process) into invention (a production process), thus complicating the reception/production opposition" (220). This negotiation speaks to the rhetorical dynamics of witnessing and the intersub-jectivity of testimonial acts.

Rhetorical listening as theorized by Ratcliffe significantly "abandon[s] a fixed (ad)vantage for a mobile . . . politics of listening" and thereby recog-nizes multiple positionalities (1999, 51). But how are we to understand this mobility? And for whom are these movements forced, coerced, elected? To what extent do representations of human rights violations position viewers rhetorically as "voyeurs of the suffering of others" (Ignatieff 1997, 10)? To what extent does a mobile rhetoric of listening reflect a generalizing of otherness, which depends, in Edward Said's words, on a "flexible positional superiority" (qtd. in Shome 1999, 594)? To look at human rights documentaries and testimonials through the lenses of feminist rhetorical criticism and rhetorical pedagogy suggests a need for a reorientation in these fields to the geopolitical. More specifically, it calls for a pedagogical recognition of the possibilities, limits, and risks of identification.

Absent Presence and the Risks of Identification

Midway through *The Sky*, an unnamed woman speaks explicitly, though briefly, about the trauma of rape warfare. We hear her voice but do not see her face. She speaks through a screen of dark thunderous clouds:

> In Bosnia on September 3, 1992, the soldiers came to take the young women. They said they would beat us and rape us and kill us. I was raped by two of them. They brought more soldiers to rape me. I cried and screamed. I wanted to kill myself. They said it was war. There is no law and order. In my dreams, it's happening to me again. I have these bad dreams all the time.

This woman recounts the horror, haunting memories, and lingering trauma of rape warfare, dreams that expose the wounds and that function as evidence—archives of memory that establish her authority and ethos. The visual absence of her body reminds viewers of the vulnerability of victims in speaking out, even as her testimony *stands alongside* the thousands of women who could not speak out: those who were killed or who kept silent out of fear for their lives and for the social stigma that a rape victim carries in patriarchal cultures. Absence and presence are configured not only in terms of the belatedness of trauma but also in terms of the witness, whose rhetorical function is to give trauma a presence.

But this scene from *The Sky* also unsettles the relationship between viewer and speaker and functions in ways that parallel formulations of *empathetic unsettlement* (LaCapra) in trauma and memory studies. This scene marks a point of tension in testimonials, which, as Gilmore notes in another context, often "invite and rebuff identification" (1994, 23).[8] Thus we might ask: Does the visual absence of the rape victim in *The Sky* provide an opportunity for our rhetorical presence? As the unidentified woman speaks, the film captures a reflection of the sky on the surface of water. This reflection reverses, distorts, and contains the sky; it establishes boundaries where there are none and therefore draws attention to both the *crisis of reference* and the *crisis of witnessing*. The sky functions as an image-metaphor for trauma's unattainability; trauma is often conceptualized as always out of reach, unknowable, shifting, yet always present. The primary motive for the testifier's anonymity may have been protection, but her refusal to become a visual text also places the viewer in a curious rhetorical relation to this refusal. The film does not permit view-ers to appropriate trauma or the suffering of others through the spectacle of visual identification; however, the speaker's verbal testimony bears the cultural stigma of identification as a rape victim. The visual absence yet auditory pres-ence of the material body also figures the psychological dislocation associated with traumatic experiences—the experience of "going elsewhere"—and a dis-location of another sort, namely, the historic absence of rape as a human rights violation within international law. It was not until 1996, after intense lobbying by human rights and feminist activists, that The Hague International Criminal Tribunal for the Former Yugoslavia recognized rape as a war crime (Freeman 1999).[9] International recognition and coverage of rape warfare in Bosnia, however, stands in marked contrast to the relative invisibility of wartime rape in other contexts, such as Latin America, where it was a common practice throughout the 1980s.[10] Thus, this scene not only attests to the risks of testify-ing but also serves as a reminder of how voices speak through or are silenced by the image (Shohat and Stam 1994, 214).[11]

Significantly, in *The Sky* the woman who testifies to being raped by sol-diers in Bosnia does not identify the perpetrators or her own ethnic and/or reli-gious affiliation(s). This lack of identification requires viewers to contextual-ize this absence within the complex identity politics, cultural mythology, and history of the region.[12] As Lynda E. Boose notes, "In the Balkans—and espe-cially Serbia—a type of racial ethnicity is largely assumed to be synonymous with religious difference, and ethnic identity synonymous with national boundaries" (2002, 75). In other words, the absence of identification generates its own question. How are viewers to understand the range of possible identi-fications and differences? Bosnians. Croats. Serbs. Muslims. Bosnian Serbs. Bosnian Croats. Bosnian Muslims. Croatian Serbs. Croatian Muslims. Serbian Croats. Serbian Muslims. The absence of identification might be said to fore-ground the tragic irony of the Balkans, in which, as Boose puts it, "all three of these peoples actually belong to the same racial and linguistic group, Southern Slavs"—a connection that Serbian epic culture denies in its struggle to retain heroic uniqueness constructed around fantasies of racial purity and denial of interethnic marriages and cultural hybridity (76).[13]

In this scene from *The Sky*, then, absence creates the consubstantial space for rhetorical witnessing. Significantly, however, this space is not predicated on the identification of victimization alone but on the *crises of reference and witnessing*. This scene therefore raises complex questions about the dynamics of rhetorical identification in human rights discourse and about what it means to witness the suffering of others in increasingly transnational and transcultural contexts. The rhetorical art of witnessing opens up a much needed critical space in both feminist rhetorical studies and life writing stud-ies to examine the methodological and pedagogical strategies employed in making visible and audible the traumatized experiences of "foreign" women. What is the role of the silenced, violated, and "foreign" female body in North

American feminist rhetorical scholarship and pedagogy? How might our understanding of audience need to be reconfigured to account for the spectacle of distant suffering? What happens when traditional understandings of rhetorical identification and presence reach their limit? I take up these questions in the next section through an analysis of a rhetorical stance that exemplifies identification through incorporation and projection—an instantiation of rhetorical witnessing that belies empathy as an ethical and critical practice. It is precisely such spaces that teachers risk creating when we introduce human rights testimonies into the classroom, especially if issues of representation and reception remain elusive.

Spectacular Cultures: Epistemological Violence and Consumption

Catherine MacKinnon's 1993 article "Turning Rape into Pornography: Postmodern Genocide" exemplifies the critical risks in representing trauma, the pedagogical problem of contextualization, and the spectacle of violence in North American coverage of rape warfare in the Balkans in the early 1990s.[14] MacKinnon argues that Serbian soldiers in a Serbian-run concentration camp for Muslims and Croatians in Bosnia-Herzegovina turned rapes into pornography as tools of genocide. The article includes the testimonies of Croatian and Muslim women survivors, who attest to the horrendous conditions in the camps, the presence of pornographic materials, and torture and rape. The testimonials depict in vivid detail practices of torture and traumatized bodies; the spectacular nature of the stories in particular raises questions about the role of trauma narratives and, more broadly, testimonials in feminist criticism. In contrast to *The Sky,* MacKinnon produces a *crisis of witnessing,* but never engages it as such. For instance, MacKinnon constructs a fairly simplistic cause-and-effect relationship between the consumption of pornography and the sexualization of torture. A "pornography saturated Yugoslavia," she argues, fueled the sexual atrocities in this genocide. Pornography was a "motivator and instruction manual" (1993, 28). She describes the Serbian-run detention centers for Muslims and Croatians in Bosnia as "rape theatres," where rape and torture were staged for private viewing (29). As she puts it in another context, rape in Bosnia is "rape to be seen and heard and watched and told to others: rape as spectacle . . . rape as genocide" (1998, 49–50).

The only photographic image in the article is that of a soldier holding an assault weapon aimed out a window. On the wall next to the window is what looks to be a page from a pornographic magazine of a topless woman in a provocative pose. The caption reads: "Serbian soldier practicing his aim." One might argue that the visual absence of victims combats the victimization of women (and the article is explicit in pointing out that survivors are not named for their protection) but also that the pornographic image reproduces and thereby privileges the perpetrator's gaze. The women's testimonials become carriers of multiple exploitations; they become rhetorical proofs, points of authenticity, and documentary evidence in service of MacKinnon's antipornography argument. The inclusion of the pornographic image as a backdrop to the soldier's cocked firearm codes looking as an act of violence. Similarly, survivors' testimonies, which might be read (heard) as sites of possible change and agency, become pedagogical spectacles within the rhetorical context of the essay. One testimonial from the essay, for instance, describes a woman having to "remain kneeling" as she is raped and beaten. There is no sense of the woman as anything but an individual "kneeling." Rhetorically, MacKinnon positions herself as if branded by the violence in ways that resonate with the classical art of forensic rhetoric, in which advocates (lawyers) would attempt to approximate the position of victims to persuade audiences to action. She expresses "shock, a clarifying jolt" (1993, 25) at descriptions of rape in Bosnia. "Turning Rape into Pornography" likewise projects onto its readers the position of victim in this rape theater.

By failing to position the women's testimonies in a communal or activist context, MacKinnon reproduces a model of spectacular uniqueness and individuality. She employs the particularities of rape warfare in Bosnia, as conveyed through the anonymous women's testimonies, to support a "universal" claim about pornography. Using rape victims' testimonies to privilege the rhetorical gaze of North American feminism as somehow beyond nation or nationalism, MacKinnon's essay reveals nationalism as a kind of spectacular narcissism. As the photograph of the soldier's cocked gun alongside the pornographic pinup makes clear, MacKinnon is more interested in linking human rights violations (in this case, rape warfare) to her antipornography stance than in exploring these women's testimonials for what they say about the complexities of women's victimization and agency and the politics of nationalism and transnational feminism. For example, MacKinnon's conflation of rape, pornography, and prostitution across cultural and national locations (for instance, comparing rape warfare in Bosnia-Herzegovina with Linda Lovelace's coerced role in *Deep Throat* (1993, 25); comparing "ethnic rape" with brothels all over the world (26); comparing snuff films with filmed torture scenes in Bosnia; and comparing Bosnia with the Holocaust, and both with pornography and violence against women) ignores the complexities of cultural location and agency and creates a universalized misogyny (as pornography) at work worldwide.

It is not only the reproduction of the rape scene as pornography that erases women's agency but also the lack of control over how their testimonies will be reproduced in criticism. As North American feminists engage representations of human rights violations against women across the globe, many based on third-hand accounts,[15] we need to be mindful of how rhetorical acts of witnessing may function as new forms of international tourism and pedagogical appropriation (Lugones 1990). We need to be mindful of the rhetorical and pedagogical dynamics of circulation and the incorporative power of reception.

Likewise, as teachers, we risk constructing our students as voyeurs, or as one with the "other," if we do not attend to the rhetorical and cultural contexts from which testimonies emerge and how our own locations and agendas shape their current reception. For example, for an upper-level undergraduate course in rhetorical criticism and the analysis of social movements, I designed a course called "Human Rights, Visual Rhetoric, and the Trauma of Representation," which focused on contemporary literature, public policy, and documentary films about human rights violations and activism. The course was organized in terms of four case studies, one of which focused on fictional and documentary representations of the trauma of rape warfare in the Balkan conflicts of the early 1990s. Women's testimonials about the trauma of rape warfare, as depicted in the videos *The Sky: A Silent Witness* (1995); *Calling the Ghosts: A Story about Rape, War, and Women* (1996); and Slavenka Drakulic's fictional work *S: A Novel About the Balkans* (2001b) highlighted for me the pedagogical struggles that we face in becoming critical witnesses rather than merely consumers of others' suffering.

For instance, students had a particularly difficult time reading *S: A Novel About the Balkans*, in which Drakulic, a native of Croatia, recreates rape scenes in ways that made many students uncomfortable. S, the protagonist of the novel, is a twenty-nine-year-old Muslim, the daughter of a Muslim father and Serbian mother. We first meet her in a Stockholm hospital in 1993, where she gives birth to a son conceived during her rape by Serbian soldiers in Bosnia. As part of their group project, a number of students in my course worked through their discomfort by analyzing the network of looking relations in the novel. Students applied the filmic concept of the gaze, a concept I had introduced earlier in the quarter, to analyze how the novel positions men with the power of looking and how it treats the role of the male gaze in acts of sexual violence in the detention camp. The group concluded that "The women of *S: A Novel About the Balkans* are presented as objects rather than as subjects of action." Students expanded their claim by turning to the controversy surrounding Drakulic's literary and journalistic representations of rape warfare. A number of Bosnian and Croatian women's and feminist groups who had been working with victims of genocidal rape, for example, noted Drakulic's early silence on the issue, her claim made to *Ms.* magazine in October 1992 that the rapes were isolated incidents, and her alleged manipulation of testimony in an op-ed piece for the *New York Times* (Drakulic 2001a). Students compared the range of responses, including positive U.S. reviews, and used these comparisons to highlight the politics of representation and the role of cultural and national contexts in shaping reception. Additionally, one student whose family immigrated from Serbia found the portrayal of victims and perpetrators of rape warfare as portrayed by *Calling the Ghosts* biased, in that the video did not explicitly address the Serbian women who were rape victims. There are numerous ways to trouble essentialist identifications; one of the ways I addressed this student's concern was to diversify the positions represented by including responses from and background on antiwar Serbian feminists and activists.[16]

The Trauma of Identity: Wounded Attachments[17]

Unlike MacKinnon's essay, the 1996 award-winning documentary *Calling The Ghosts: A Story about Rape, War, and Women,* directed by Mandy Jacobson and Karmen Jelincic, directly engages the problem of representing trauma, and the critical, pedagogical, and political limits, possibilities, and consequences of identification.[18] The film employs the testimonies of Croatian and Muslim women interned at the Serbian concentration camp of Omarska to explore the trauma of rape warfare in Bosnia-Herzegovina.[19] The filmmakers did not turn their cameras on for seven months but instead focused their energy on building trust with the women they met. Jacobsen and Jelincic state that they were interested not in *what* happened to the women, but in *how* they were making sense of their experiences and channeling their pain into issues of justice. As filmmakers they sought to counter dominant representations of war that focus solely on its ethnic dimensions. Their intention was to use media to influence public policy and to do so in a way that did not recreate a victim narrative but that depicted how the women responded to victimization (Jacobson 2003, 5).

Calling the Ghosts focuses on two middle-class women; an attorney, Jadranka Cigelj; and a civil judge, Nusreta Sivac, childhood friends who were captured, tormented, and tortured by former neighbors and who, as Jacobson puts it, "defy all those stereotypes about peasants and mad savages" (2003, 4). By focusing on the experiences of middle-class legal professionals, the film works against Western expectations about what a sexually abused Muslim woman might look like. In the first scene, Cigelj washes her face before swimming in the ocean. Water, as a sign of purification, functions ironically against the horrific story of "ethnic cleansing" that follows.[20] As Cigelj speaks, it is clear that washing cannot wipe away the memories: "There was a period of self-questioning before me. To stay silent or to speak . . . If I stay silent, how moral would that be? When I remember the night when I was taken out my own broken bones start to hurt. If I speak how good is that for me? I would actually have to expose myself." This statement articulates the intersection between embodied memory and speech acts: the individual's trauma is implicated in the social, regardless of whether she "chooses" to speak. Yet, as Cigelj notes, "Without the live witness, one can only speculate about the crime. The crime has not been filmed with a camera. It is only recorded in the memory of the witness." And yet, Cigelj and the filmmakers know all too well what price survivors pay for their testimonies. As the film slowly pans in on the face of an old woman in a headscarf, visualizing how violations and abuses cross generation lines, Cigelj states, "In order to expose the crime, you violate the witness. You don't force her, of course—you beg her to speak. But you do make her live through it again." In reliving the trauma, in the name of giving evidence, the witness and the viewer, perhaps unavoidably, are implicated in recreating the spectacle of trauma.

Recognizing the problem of voyeurism embedded in many representations of rape warfare, *Calling the Ghosts* addresses the question of spectacle and foregrounds the *crisis of witnessing* in its highly ambivalent critique of the media. The film provided the pedagogical occasion for my class to consider their own subject-positions as viewers and the shaping of the U.S. response to the situation in the Balkans by certain cultural and national scripts.[21] On the one hand, the film condemns the news media's insatiable voyeurism. A long, slow shot pans a still photograph of a group of women of different ages as Cigelj speaks: "Journalists and TV crews would come, always with the same question: 'Are there any women here who were raped?' I mean, as if one could possibly divide women between those who were raped and those who weren't. As if they were in some sort of display." This critique of voyeurism intersects with the camera's pan across the picture, implicating the viewer in the desire to know if these unidentified women were raped. At the same time, the film credits news reporters for bringing to international attention ethnic genocide in Bosnia and, indeed, for saving the lives of many women at Omarska. A scene in a refugee camp explicitly confronts the ethical choices of filmmakers and reporters. A group of women and children crowd around the camera as a woman yells, "I am telling you: If you are going to help, then shoot! If not—then don't film us." As the film cuts to a train pulling away from a station, the viewer is left with only the ambivalent and unresolved issues surrounding the need to publicize this violence, and the costs of such publicity. For instance, there is a powerful scene in which Nusreta Sivac directly challenges cultural fantasies and the voyeuristic gaze that links violence to the "other": "It bothers me when someone says raped women . . . . Abused women, women victims of war, find some other appropriate term. But raped women—that hurts a person, to be marked as a raped woman, as if you had no other characteristic, as if that were your sole identity." Here Sivac not only alludes to the reductive label that casts women who have been raped as spectacles but also points to the use of the category raped women as a form of social stigma, itself attached to that spectacularization. This scene thus shows how rape scripts the perception of women and how its representation further traumatizes women.[22]

Despite an explicit critique of voyeurism, however, the film clearly recognizes the crucial role that news reporters played in saving the lives of women in Omarska and, more broadly, in bringing this violence to international attention. As a result of the publicity surrounding a visit by a group of reporters to the camp, the majority of women still held there, including Jadranka and Nusreta, were released. The film also shows Jadranka working with the reporter Roy Gutman, who first publicized the death camps and later the rape and torture of women. But in another scene, Jadranka watches a television news report that features both her testimony and a refutation by the commander of Omarska, Zeljko Mejakic, who tortured her. The irony is chilling, for on television, they appear similarly calm and authoritative, Mejakic as credible as Jadranka. It is only within the wider context of the film that his credibility—his delivery—is undermined. But *Calling the Ghosts* does more than position these women as victims or injured subjects; it also grapples with the notion of testifying as a collective act. Against a visual backdrop of their home city of Prijedor and the Omarska camp, Cigelj and her friend Sivac identify their torturers by name and provide specific details about their incarceration, release from Omarska, and subsequent resettlement in Zagreb, Croatia. There, they join with other women to create support communities for providing legal aid and the gathering of testimonials of others. Turning from victims to activists, the women dramatize the "epistemological travel" in testimonial work, a mobility signaled initially by Cigelj's dilemma, "To stay silent or to speak?" Through these images, testimonials reconfigure the atomistic self as a plural *I* (where the *I* becomes exchangeable with the *we*) and construe a "collective 'I' witness" (Sánchez-Casal 2001, 87). In this sense, one might argue that the testimonials in *Calling the Ghosts* contest the formulation of the sovereign subject of liberalism and its established universalism through the articulation of collective experiences. As Patricia Zimmermann notes, *Calling the Ghosts* "rejects victimization, isolation, individualism, and silence. . . . [The film] refuses to only speak its pain" (2000, 73). These women's collective material-rhetorical acts of reclaiming their lives through testimony and witnessing are indeed political acts of empowerment.

Calling the Ghosts focuses on women's agency, activism, and healing in a communal context. This depiction contrasts with MacKinnon's statement that constructs rape victims as injured individuals, radically alone (1993, 30). Although the film shows us victimized bodies, we also see bodies surviving the wounds. For example, *Calling the Ghosts* features individual and group interviews, montages of many women's faces, and close-ups of stacks of 3×5 photographs of tortured body parts. Cigelj's dilemma, whether to speak or stay silent, articulates the relationship between the spectacle of trauma and oral testimonials as both empowering *and* voyeuristic, collective *and* individual. The material presence of women's bodies and their excruciating experiences of torture produce important tensions between witnessing and spectacle. To find testimonial narratives and images of suffering simultaneously empowering *and* voyeuristic is not to remain undecided about their role but rather to recognize their complex rhetorical and pedagogical dynamics. To explore these tensions pedagogically enables us to consider both the potential and the limits of empathetic identification. In my teaching, I am careful to distinguish between what Meg Boler refers to as "passive empathy" and testimonial reading practices. Boler uses the term *passive empathy* to refer to those instances in which concerns are directed to a fairly distant other, whom, presumably, we cannot directly help. The limitations of passive empathy are that it may re-create a consumption-based model of identification, hinder recognition of one's own implication in social forces that the other confronts, and fall short of providing any basis for social change. In contrast, testimonial reading practices emphasize the social hierarchies that define reader/writer and listener/speaker relationships and inspire an empathetic response that motivates action and a commitment to rethink one's assumptions and world views (Boler 1997, 261).

The social functions of memories of collective trauma are complex and must not be seen in isolation from the economic conditions and the internationalization of identity politics that figure prominently in the conflicts.[23] For instance, the ultranationalist Slobodan Milosevic went to great lengths to polarize people by manipulating the economy. Hence, when considering the mobilization of identity categories, we need to take into account the economic motivations of the leaders of regions involved in the conflicts. Moreover, as Susan Woodward notes, nationalist politics emerged in areas more integrated with Western markets and was pushed by politicians who had support from Western sources for their reforms. This Western drive overflowed into areas that were less able to cope with liberalization strategies, and thus adverse political and economic consequences emerged (Woodward 2000, 24). In short, the Balkan Wars challenge us to recognize how injury claims and identifications based on historical processes of domination are mobilized as structural elements of national policy, and as tools of war as well as tools of peace. When teaching this material, I introduce layers of discursive frames, including an overview of the economic and geographic history of the region. The case study approach enables interdisciplinary inquiry into economic, political, legal, cultural, and literary practices. Rhetorical analysis of these various discourses and forms of representation unites the case studies at the methodological as well as thematic level.

Rhetorical Pedagogy: Transnational Acts of Witnessing

One of the final scenes of *Calling the Ghosts* features Cigelj and Sivac's trip to The Hague for the opening of the UN International Criminal Tribunal's prosecution of crimes of ethnic violence.[24] The convening of the Tribunal features Judge Elizabeth Odio Bento addressing the panel of jurists. She states that this is the first time in human rights law that rape has been listed as a human rights violation. Bento emphatically states that "There can be no justice if there is no justice for women." At this moment, as rape becomes recognized as a human rights violation, women become distinct subjects of international human rights law. They become postnational citizen-subjects in the sense that their identities are not defined exclusively by the nation-state. Their citizenship and identities, however, are not defined solely in terms of suffering and injury either. In fact, *Calling the Ghosts* works against a dichotomous conception of women's agency between those who act and those who are acted on. The film exemplifies how women's agency, as Inderpal Grewal puts it in another context, is "differentially constructed within formations that come not only from state and nation, but also from geopolitics, economics, religion, sexuality," and so on (1998, 516). Testimonials certainly can, and often do, serve to claim a legal identity, especially when the context for the testimony is juridical. But testimonials also function in extrajuridical ways and contexts, as acts of memorialization and as sites of healing and cultural resistance. If one of the rhetorical appeals of a documentary like *Calling the Ghosts* is the hope of social justice and the promise of human rights, the film also foregrounds how the juridical does not relieve the wounds of atrocity or attachments to identity, and in so doing highlights the *ungovernability* of trauma. *Calling the Ghosts* reveals how social desires for retributive justice are dependent on configurations of identity as "wounded attachments," even as the documentary seeks to counter that dependency.

Walking through an amusement park in The Hague, Cigelj and Sivac select a postcard from several large racks. They send the postcard to former friends of Sivac with whom she had worked at the court, with a message that reads "we hope that you will join us shortly in this lovely city." Cigelj and Sivac use The Hague as a symbol of human rights to remind the postcard recipients, and the viewer, of the (promised) ability of international law to hold accountable those responsible for ethnic genocide. This message thus both re-marks and re-claims identity categories between Cigelj and Sivac and their "former" friends, the Bosnian Serbs. The postcard signifies women victimized by rape warfare as juridical subjects, a rhetorical move that reclaims a collective identity in opposition to the degrading and dehumanizing denial of subjectivity produced by acts of violence and torture (see Scarry 1987). This collective identity is asserted, in part, through the articulation of injury and justice within the literal and figurative space of international law. Interestingly, the articulation of the juridical subject here is packaged within the rhetoric of tourist and consumer culture. The postcard as an image metaphor signifies a chosen, rather than coerced, mobility—yet in this scene, it also signifies experiences of displacement and enforced movements.[25] The postcard reveals tensions between a return home and continued displacement. The postcard is sent from a place other than one's home, indicating movement away from the domestic sphere, a self-consciously ironic move for refugees forced to flee their homes. In this way, the postcard signifies both movement and the preservation of borders. The deprivation of writing space yet mobility of the post resonates with the imposition of geopolitical borders as well as their transgression.

The postcard scene in *Calling the Ghosts* also reproduces the process of making the private text public. The postcard is a rhetorical situation—an open letter—that has a destiny, an addressee, and an audience. But the rhetorical situation is *ungovernable*; the postcard can be intercepted, interrupted, read by unintended audiences. For Derrida, the "tragedy" is that "everything becomes a postcard" that never reaches its destination (1987, 23), which speaks to the inadequacy of representation, the limits of narratability, and the risks of speaking out. The public reproduction and exposure of the private represented by the postcard points to yet another pedagogical risk of testimonial travel: the anxiety and material consequences that surround its interception/ reception. Will the postcard reach its destination? Who might intercept the postcard and its message along the way? Hence, we need to consider, in both the literal and theoretical sense, the "irreducible twists in any sending system" (Bass qtd. in Derrida 1987, xii). What role do we play as interceptors of the postcard, as international witnesses of the testimonial narratives of victims of rape warfare?

The postcard scene prompts us to think about our own complicity as a nation, how the global economy and international politics, including the interests of the United States, have intervened in supposedly local conflicts, and how such conflicts are configured rhetorically. The scene also urges us to consider what it means for human rights and humanitarian practices that genocide has taken place under the watchful eye of humanitarians (Ranck qtd. in Simon, Rosenberg, and Eppert 2000, 188). The complex politics of humanitarianism necessitates a rethinking of not only international political and economic relations but also disciplinary borders, methodologies, and pedagogies that are out of sync with the geopolitics of globalization. For instance, the postcard scene might be used as a critical occasion to formulate a pedagogical approach to cross-cultural and transnational reading practices that does not simply intercept or colonize the "other" but that considers how, as Paul Jay puts it, "cultures are exchanged along with commodities" (2001, 34). Human rights testimonies risk voyeurism and commodification, and I do not want to minimize these risks, but the "you" to whom the testimonies are addressed opens up the possibility for alternative forms of listening, witnessing, and "unforeseen memory" (Simon, Rosenberg, and Eppert 2000, 19). Testimonials ask us to consider, as Roger Simon puts it in another context, "How and why it would matter if accounts of systematic violence and its legacies were part of [our] memorial landscapes?" (17). Therefore, one of my pedagogical goals is to enable students to develop a critical stance of rhetorical witnessing that inspires a commitment to rethink one's own assumptions and world views, that fosters distinctions between one's own losses and those of others, and that accepts ethical obligations without having to stand in the shoes of those to whom one is obliged, an obligation, that is, not rooted in guilt or pity or facile empathy but rather in ethical responsibility. If we take our cue from scholars who address the methodological and ethical challenges posed by testimonials, we might begin to fashion a transnational rhetorical pedagogy by witnessing the national, cultural, and discursive frameworks and limitations of our disciplinary orientations, methodologies, and pedagogies. For example, Renata Jambresic Kirin, a Croatian scholar, frames her study of the testimonies of displaced persons of Croatian and Serbian nationality not as a search for something "'sensationally tragic,' silenced and kept hidden from the public eye, and finally scholarly revealed" (1996, 67). Instead, Kirin suggests that our goal should be not "just to turn silence into speech that compels listeners, but to change the nature and direction of exile discourse . . . to turn the 'passive' voice . . . into an active powerful one, which can, with force of argument, participate in political discourses from the local to the parliamentary level" (1996, 67–68).

Transnational readership markets and pedagogical spaces enact identifications and disidentifications characterized by *crises of reference* and *crises of witnessing*. If we look at rhetorical (dis)identification as a fundamentally social process that presumes both discontinuity and continuity with the past, we come to realize the need for a rhetorical methodology and pedagogy that encourages a relationality based on the recognition of the partial and mediated nature of remembrance (Simon, Rosenberg, and Eppert 2000, 19). *Calling the Ghosts* suggests that the international community had better negotiate the enormous risks of identification and consumption of the spectacle of violence. Our role as scholars and teachers is not simply to turn passive or silent voices into compelling speech but to reconfigure witnessing in rhetorical and ethical terms. This entails recognition of the ongoing need for the call to action—a continual *empathetic unsettlement* predicated on the incompleteness of the present and the *ungovernability* of the past. Finally, transnational rhetorical acts of witnessing have the potential to open new critical and pedagogical spaces to offset indifference, national denial, and the averted gaze of peoples, governments, and countries in the face of violent conflicts and war.

Author's Note

I wish to thank Kay Halasek, Leigh Gilmore, Theresa Kulbaga, Joy Ritchie, Kate Ronald, and anonymous readers for comments on an earlier draft; Amy Shuman for conversations about the limits of history; and Wendy Kozol for numerous readings, conversations, and collaborations that greatly informed this work.

Notes

1. My title evokes Boltanski's *Distant Suffering: Morality, Media, and Politics* (1999).

2. Taslima Nasrin from Bangladesh describes being beaten and tortured by fundamentalists with whom, she argues, the government was complicit. She was targeted for speaking out against violence against women; death treats forced her to flee her country. The other three women of color are Judy Richardson, an African American civil rights worker who was jailed in the 1960s for her participation in marches against racism; Tsultrim Dolma, a Tibetan Buddhist nun who was beaten by the Chinese government for her work on behalf of human rights and the fight for Tibetan independence; and Lu Jing Hua from Beijing, who was arrested, taken to a detention center, and tortured by the Chinese government for her participation in demonstrations at Tiananmen Square.

3. I use the term *testimonials* to refer to narratives told in the first person by a narrator who recounts the trauma of human rights violations. In particular instances, I pre-

fer the term *testimony* to indicate the oral presentation and legal prominence of testimonial narratives within the international human rights movement. As Beverley notes, "The word *testimonio* translates literally as 'testimony,' as in the act of testifying or bearing witness in a legal or religious sense" (1992, 94). In "The Margin at the Center," Beverley uses the term *testimonio* to refer to a "novel or novella-length narrative in book or pamphlet (that is, printed as opposed to acoustic) form, told in the first person by a narrator who is also the real protagonist or witness of the events he or she recounts, and whose unit of narration is usually a 'life' or a significant life experience" (92–93). Like Beverley, I am not particularly interested in formulating a rigid generic definition of *testimonio*; but like Beverley, I recognize important distinctions among the textual categories that the genre *testimonio* may include: autobiography, autobiographical novel, oral history, memoir, confession, eyewitness report, nonfiction novel, life history.

4. I use the term *transnational* to highlight the material-rhetorical relationship between local and global spheres and listeners and speakers in diverse parts of the world. See Inderpal Grewal and Caren Kaplan's "Global Identities: Theorizing Transnational Studies of Sexuality"(2001) for an important cautionary discussion of the ways in which the term *transnational* is used in the academy.

5. "Traumatic realism," Rothberg explains, "is marked by the survival of extremity into the everyday world and is dedicated to mapping the complex temporal and spatial patterns by which the absence of the real, a real absence, makes itself felt in the familiar plenitude of reality. In the wake of modern and postmodern skepticism, traumatic realism revives the project of realism—but only because it knows it cannot revive the dead" (2000, 140). Rothberg is likewise interested in the perplexities of representing mass violence and trauma, and the demands of such representation, which include "a demand for documentation, a demand for reflection of the formal limits of representation, and a demand for the risky public circulation of discourses on the events" (7).

6. See, for example, critical works by Behar, Beverley, Carr, Kaplan (1994), Sánchez-Casal, Sommer, and Yudice, among others.

7. See, for example, Bose and Varghese, Bow, Carr, Chow, Fernandes, Grewal and Kaplan (2001), Hesford and Kozol, Jarratt (2000), Kaplan (1997), Roof and Wiegman, and Spivak, among others.

8. Susan Jarratt argues that the rhetorical moves of diasporic postcolonial intellectuals create a sense of disidentification with the audience. This de-identificatory rhetoric tends to disperse subjectivity and representativeness, thereby challenging assumptions of social similarity and presumed identification—the coming together of rhetor and audience—of traditional rhetorical theory.

9. A UN Commission of Experts appointed in October 1992 by Secretary General Boutros Boutros-Ghali to examine the violations of international humanitarian law in the former Yugoslavia published a report that described ethnic cleansing carried out by Serbian military forces. The report also highlighted the systematic nature of rape and sexual assaults committed by Serbs against mostly Muslim women. The report noted that "It is clear that some level of organization and group activity was required to carry out many of the alleged rapes" (qtd. in B. Allen 1996, 47). On June 27, 1996, based on the historical evidence and eyewitness accounts that Jadranka Cigelj and

others had gathered, as represented in the film *Calling the Ghosts*, the Tribunal indicted eight male Bosnian Serbs for the rapes of Bosnian Muslim women (Enloe 2000, 135). Efforts to indict and prosecute war crimes suspects have remained limited, primarily because of the difficulty of taking suspects into custody. The Tribunal cannot compel suspects to appear but instead can only hope for arrests if they leave the protection of officials in their country (Copelon 1988, 72).

According to Amnesty International's 2003 annual report covering events between January and December 2002, ten trials were conducted before the tribunal, involving a total of thirteen accused under international prosecutions for war crimes (Amnesty International, 2003a). Twenty-four publicly indicted suspects remain at large; most reportedly are in the Federal Republic of Yugloslavia (RS). Some 10,000 potential suspects were listed in local investigation files of domestic prosecutions for war crimes, of whom 2,500 had been reviewed by the Tribunal Prosecutor. Thousands of cases of disappearances remain unresolved. (See Amnesty International, "Key Figures of ICTY Cases" (n.d.), for an overview of those indicted since the inception of the International Criminal Tribunal for the Former Yugoslavia.) In a November 12, 2003, news release, Amnesty International expressed serious concern over the closing down of the Tribunal and over the planned War Crimes Chamber at the newly established State Court (Amnesty International, 2003b). The concern is that the War Crimes Chamber "will address only a handful of the thousands of crimes under international law committed in the past decade . . . . Amnesty International opposes the closing down of the Tribunal until effective alternatives are established by the international community to bring all those responsible for crimes under international law to justice in fair and effective proceedings."

10. See Enloe (2000, 108–52) for a discussion of other contexts in which government officials have used rape and the threat of rape to terrorize domestic populations. Copelon argues that the visibility of rape in Bosnia is a result of its association with "ethnic cleansing" and genocide (1988, 64). She is critical, however, of the emphasis on genocidal rape as unparalleled and of the "notion that genocidal rape is uniquely a weapon of war." She argues that to "exaggerate the distinctiveness of genocidal rape obscures the atrocity of common rape" (69).

11. Notably, it is the bodies of only women of color that are visualized in *The Sky*. At the level of individual motive, invisibility may be read as a protective visual rhetoric; however, at the larger cultural level, absence might be read as a "power-concealing rhetoric" (Middleton qtd. in Glenn 2002, 285). In other words, the visualization of bodies of women of color plays into the politics of racial representation that renders whiteness invisible and situates the "First World" as the rescuer of the "Third World" subject, including "Third World Subjects" within the United States (Grewal 1998, 502). One might also argue that the United States is imaged in *The Sky* as the "normative interlocutor" (Shohat 1998) through the figure of Eleanor Roosevelt, who as the delegate from the United States and chair of the UN commission, helped write the 1948 Declaration of Human Rights.

12. Aida Hozic observes the power of mass-mediated imagery of "distant violence" in the production of global crises. Hozic argues that the "attention and media space given to war-torn areas is proportional to the propensity of the international community to intervene in their troubles" (2000, 229)—hence the international focus

on ethnic violence in Sarajevo over other regions in Bosnia, or Somalia, Rwanda, or Chechnya. Initially, victims of persecution by Serbian nationalists welcomed media attention, expecting publicity to persuade the international community to intervene. Soon, however, many began to realize that the voyeuristic nature of news media exposed Bosnians to "an unwanted parody of genuine witnessing" (Weine 1999, 183) without adequate responses from international agencies and governments.

13. Some of the strongest support for survivors has come from antiwar feminists. Feminists have been divided, however, over the objectives of their nation-states. Although I do not have space in this essay to detail how nationalism has divided feminists in the region, is it important to note that there are opposing views among feminists in the successor states about who was doing the raping and why. See Benderly (1997) for a detailed discussion of this issue.

14. It is important to note the common assumption among North Americans that the "former Yugoslavia" is an Eastern bloc country, which contrasts with the perception of Yugoslavia as Western by the Eastern bloc. Since Yugoslavia severed its ties with the Soviet Union in 1948, in the words of Vida Penezic, it has been "precariously balanced between the blocs and a founding member of the nonaligned movement" (1995, 59). Penezic further notes that these perceptions reflect and emerge from a dominant American Cold War paradigm, which configured the Western bloc as a "free world," progressive and enlightened, and the Eastern bloc as communist and bad. Cold War discourse has therefore helped secure perceptions of Yugoslavia as an Eastern bloc country.

15. The accounts in "Turning Rape into Pornography," for instance, are based on original research conducted and translated by Natalie Nenadic and Asia Armanda.

16. As mentioned earlier, the war heightened conflicts among Zagreb feminist groups. Four women's groups retained MacKinnon as their attorney. These groups were Kareta (a radical feminist group), Bedem Ljubavi (Wall of Love, a Croatian women's group), Zene BiH (a Bosnian refugee women's group), and Biser (International Initiative of Women of Bosnia-Herzegovina). Their stand, as Benderly characterizes it, "is that rape is a distinctly Serbian weapon for which all Serbians—even feminists who oppose the war—are culpable" (1997, 66–67).

17. The phrase *wounded attachments* is taken from Wendy Brown's *States of Injury*, in which she critiques the limitations of identity politics and argues that identity has become overly attached to woundedness. In my book-in-progress *Spectacular Rhetorics*, I address Brown's argument in more detail. For my purposes here, I would simply point out that Brown's critique does not address the internationalization of identity politics: how trauma marks and reshapes identity in ways that affect communities, and how the reclamation or reconfiguration of identity may foster social change, justice, and healing. In other words, injury and identity may not be as productively separated as Brown seems to suggest. I share Brown's skepticism about the potential of identity and rights claims to address historical inequities at the structural level. However, what Brown doesn't account for, which is crucial to my argument, is how rights claims and identities are combined in new ways in the context of new nationalisms.

18. *Calling the Ghosts* was Mandy Jacobson's debut documentary. A South African–born New York filmmaker, Jacobson hooked up with Macedonian director

Milcho Manshevski, whose feature film *Before the Rain* (1994) won numerous awards. Apparently, Manshevski put Jacobson in touch with Karmen Jelinicic from Croatia, with whom she collaborated on the film. Jacobson notes in an interview that the film's title refers to an interview she and Jelinicic had with four women who had been in Omarska with Jadranka Cigelj, and who told a story about "calling the ghosts." As one woman noted, "Dika and I were sitting around and we were calling the ghosts. We only wanted to cheer ourselves up a little but it wasn't working. So we were calling the ghosts to come. All was silent. And the next thing, a Chetnik soldier came in. And I quickly gathered all the candles and pieces of paper and hid them in my skirt. The Chetnik said 'Are you calling the ghosts?' To which we said, 'No, sir, we do nothing of the sort.' Then he said 'What's burning?' And the only skirt I had was in flames."

19. Although the numbers are still in dispute because of the difficulty of gathering evidence, there is little question about the magnitude of these crimes. Enloe writes, "the European Union's investigators calculated that in 1992 alone, 20,000 Muslim Bosnian women and girls had been raped by Bosnian Serb combatants. By the time of the cease-fire in 1995, the number of women from all communities who endured wartime rape was estimated to be between 30,000–50,000. The numerical uncertainty reflected the ongoing gendered politics of silence and denial" (2000, 140). For further discussion in English of rape and the Bosnian war, see B. Allen, Bernard, Drakulic, Ramet, Rejali, Stiglmayer, and Vranic. See also Nikolic-Ristanovic and Samantha Power.

20. I use the term *ethnic cleansing* in this sentence to highlight the metaphor of purification; however, throughout the essay I have chosen to use the term *ethnic genocide* over the term *ethnic cleansing*. Controversy lingers over the use of the term *genocide* to describe atrocities of the wars in the Balkans. The conclusion that Bosnia has suffered genocide has been reached by many nongovernmental organizations such as Amnesty International, Helsinki Watch, and UN commissions. These agencies and commissions concluded that 90 percent of the ethnic cleansing has been committed by "Serbs," and they have provided concrete evidence of a systematic Serbian policy to get rid of Muslims. But as Power notes in her discussion of the controversy surrounding the term, the Bush administration avoided the word because a "genocide finding would create a moral imperative" (2002, 288). Power continues, "The day after the ITN footage of Keraterm [concentration camp] aired, Bush told a news conference: 'We know there is horror in these detention camps. But in all honesty, I can't confirm to you some of the claims that there is indeed a genocidal process going on there.' Policymakers preferred the phrase 'ethnic cleansing.'" (Power 2002, 288).

21. See Steven Weine's, *When History Is a Nightmare* (1999) for a useful analysis of official U.S. rhetoric and response to the conflicts in Bosnia-Herzegovina. See also David Campbell (1998) for additional coverage of national scripts that shaped the U.S. response to the Balkans conflicts.

22. Marsha Freeman (1999) discusses the dilemma of double victimization, that is, legal efforts to prosecute war criminals confront the difficulties of finding victims willing to testify while needing to protect those witnesses from the possibilities of community retaliation. Critics of the Tribunal charge that not enough attention has been paid to the physical and emotional needs of witnesses, making it difficult and often dangerous for women to testify. For instance, the statute creating the Tribunal does not provide for either compensation or rehabilitation for survivors. For more on

this point, see Copelon (1988, 72). For further analysis of the politics of representing rape, see Hesford (2001).

23. For further exploration of the economic conditions that facilitated the conflicts in the former Yugoslavia see M. Brown, Chomsky, N. Davidson, Haynes, Magas, and Power, among others.

24. The official title of this judicial body, established in 1991, is the International Tribunal for the Prosecution of Persons Responsible for Serious Violations of International Humanitarian Law Committed in the Territory of the Former Yugoslavia.

25. According to Amnesty International's 1999 annual report, efforts to facilitate the return of Balkan refugees who had fled the armed conflicts of 1992–1995 were expedited by intergovernmental organizations in 1998. This effort, however, met with limited success because of persistent human rights abuses and bureaucratic opposition by local and national administrators. At the same time, pressure from host countries has forced approximately 88,000 to return despite being unable to go back to their homes. Even with these policies, as of 1999, approximately 1.2 million people were still either refugees in other countries or remained displaced within their country of origin.

7

Objects, Memory, and Narrative

New Notes Toward Materialist Rhetoric

Marguerite Helmers

We have only to speak of an object to think that we are being objective. But, because we chose it in the first place, the object reveals more about us than we do about it.

—Gaston Bachelard,
The Psychoanalysis of Fire

In "Empty Shoes," Ellen Carol Jones writes about the poignant significance of the mounds of empty shoes of all sizes left to bear witness after the Holocaust. Each shoe signifies the life history of the owner. Each shoe tells the spectator that a living human once pressed a foot into the leather and walked to school or to temple, a life peremptorily shortened by violence and hatred. Citing Sidra DeKoven Ezrahi, Jones notes that in museums such as the United States Holocaust Memorial Museum, relics such as the shoes become "both metonymies and the authenticating evidence of our foothold in buried worlds" (Ezrahi qtd. in Jones 2001, 216). She goes on to question whether the shoes, called "object survivors" by the museum, allow access to a painful past or preclude any real knowledge of events because of their very tangibility. Ultimately, the shoes attest to the trauma brought on by memory, by the "resurfacing of the events" under the museum's direction (Liss 1998, 71). The museum creates a display area for the shoes. The shoes are removed from everyday use into a new context; they are three times removed, from the owner, to the camps, to the museum. In her work on the Holocaust memory, Andrea Liss comments that re-presentation of objects within a public exhibition re-creates the object's meaning because that object is deployed within a new discourse, that of aesthetics:

> The aestheticizing activities of the museum must create bridges for guarded, imaginative projections and (im)possible witnessing. . . . The metonymy is eerie, deadening; the theatrical effect materializes the real into its evocation. (1998, 78)

Shoes also signify at the Vietnam Veteran's Memorial in Washington DC. Of the many objects left at the wall—photos, letters, stuffed animals—broken army boots sometimes rest against the names carved into the smooth black wall, the life that once occupied them physically absent from space and time, yet present in the space-time of memory. People leave things at the wall to articulate the meaning of a particular life and death, writes Kristin Ann Hass (1998, 2). The wall becomes a personal shrine in a public space, enacting the tension at the root of all wars: that between official culture and private lives. Memorials can never "represent all of the conflicting impulses—sorrow, sacrifice, shame, pain, pride, suffering, victory, loss" (40). Thus, individuals must narrate and present their own pain and memory.

One day, in an assignment that asked students to find their own special object and to share it with the class, a student brought in his running shoes. It was the second semester of his first year of college. He wore the shoes in high school on the cross-country team. They were stained and the laces frayed. He no longer wore them, but he kept the shoes all the same, for they represented his lived experience—and one might also say his performed role—as a runner. Running represented solitude and freedom, his ability to push his body to its limits. I was stifled: my initial temptation to read the shoes as a clichéd symbol of achievement in athletics was silenced when I considered that, of all the things in this young man's room that he might have selected, he chose the most bulky and difficult to carry to the classroom with the books in his backpack. He selected an object that represented his ability to fly the confines of the four walls and my official assignment.

"There is no shorthand for reading the meanings of everyday objects used to make memory," writes Hass about the shoes and beer cans and bears left as testimony in public places (1998, 90). "There is no shorthand because there is no history of speaking with things" (90). Hass is right: things do speak. Material objects tell stories, hint at lives, remember events, weave into memory. "Leaving something at the Wall is a communicative act, a complicated kind of speech," Hass asserts (30). The speech act is authored by the possessor of the object and by the selection of position, location, and time. The speech act is received by the (absent) loved one and by ambient, unintended (but surely not unanticipated) witnesses. These witnesses incorporate the object into their own narrative space, evaluating its significance, remembering, and telling.

As materialist feminist rhetoricians would argue, written expression and oral speech acts are material, deriving from human activity and lived experience. Therefore rhetoric is material; each speaker (or creator) and each respondent (or audience member) is contextualized by discourses, which are construed as

Michel Foucault posits, as ways of speaking about particular subjects at particular times. To this emphasis on language I believe we can add "ways of imaging" particular subjects at particular times so that we capture the image (photographic, painted, or molded into a three-dimensional object) as an aspect of discourse. All discourses are derived from ideology, the structures of belief and value that adhere to various societal groups in various epochs, and thus objects and linguistic artifacts express ideas about lived experience and the ideology of cultures.

It is also helpful to keep in mind that the object is not the only physical presence in the rhetorical situation of a rhetoric of objects. The speaker, author, or creator is a material being—a *body*—as is the respondent. The respondent draws on her or his personal history and lived experience to create meaning. This potential for differing discourses meeting at the site of the object allows for diachronic readings of the object as text, yielding new meanings.

In this essay, I consider the fertile ground of an object-based rhetoric and the insights I have gleaned from working with material things in my classrooms. Although Richard Enos proposes that rhetoricians include "sources that are not only visible but tangible" in his argument for an "Archaeology of Women in Rhetoric" (2002), he eventually recategorizes the tangibility of rhetoric as a way of speaking about the evidence of the past that supports a reading of rhetorical texts. Fieldwork that uses inscriptions on pedestals and vases as indications of women's roles as rhetors is one way to manage evidence, but it does little to explain how those objects themselves were created, distributed, used, and understood in everyday practice or the experiences and lived contexts of those who created the objects. To this end, the collection of essays in *Rhetorical Bodies* explores further the implication of tangibility in *"material rhetoric."* It is evident, though, that the contributors to this collection variously define the term *material rhetoric,* with definitions engaging the rhetoric of the body to considerations of embodied rhetoric. Celeste Condit notes that, among the definitions, Michael McGee has urged rhetoricians to "think of rhetoric as an object" (1999, 326), whereas Susan Wells defines the rhetoricians' project as providing an embodiment for forgotten discourses—or "reanimation" of "persuasive practices" (1999, 71). From this group of essays, Barbara Dickson's decision to interpret rhetoric's materiality as a way of reading, "a mode of interpretation that takes as its object of study the significations of material things and corporal entities—objects that signify not through language but through their spatial organization, mobility, mass, utility, orality, and tactility" (1999, 297), bears the most on my project: to differentiate a rhetoric of things from semiotics and associate it as a means of feminist material rhetoric. Cultural studies would read the object's process of production, dissemination, and reception, its histories of distribution throughout the material worlds of consumerism and function. Semiotics would study the structural form of the object together with its various associations or significations.

I am curious about how objects participate in human interactions that involve language, image, emotion, and gesture. Each of these rhetorical practices is embedded in historical processes. Certain discourses are available to speakers at particular points in history; these discourses are embodied in networks of power that authorize certain speakers to have voice and disenfranchise others. Similarly, what can be examined or studied at any particular point in history is also the result of a discourse of power. In rhetoric, the object and the body is only recently being considered as a site of discourse. This work is connected to work in cultural studies, anthropology, and religious studies through those who study history, memory, public culture, narrative, and visual culture, and thus it is, given the space available to me in this text, incomplete. Nonetheless, it is a necessary beginning, for rhetoricians study words and signs but do not often concern themselves with the physical vehicles that carry the words and are signs in themselves. The problem with studying objects, writes Roland Barthes, is that the objects are themselves so ordinary that they must be defamiliarized. He refers to this as "the obstacle of the obvious" (1988, 184). A redeployment of the object into new contexts—for example, the gallery, the classroom, or within a new cultural framework of understanding—allows readers to describe the object's significance.

Consider that the words of Aristotle are carried for us in a text that has been translated and edited and footnoted, displaying layers of human intervention and thought. It has been printed in a union print shop and bound to a size that might fit in the palm of our hand or the side pocket of our suitcase. We do not need to travel to the great libraries at Alexandria or Oxford. We can read Aristotle's *Rhetoric* on the bus, at the airport, or in bed. The book symbolizes our mobility and the economies of advanced capitalism. It also represents the shift in literate practices away from the privilege of the few to the right of the many.

Alberto Manguel emphasizes that the book may be studied as an artifact without emphasizing its content. Among other ways, books "declare themselves" by their size, he writes. "From the very beginning, readers demanded books in formats adapted to their intended use" (1997, 125):

> Of all the shapes that books have acquired through the ages, the most popular have been those that allowed the book to be held comfortably in the reader's hand (128). . . . My hands, choosing a book to take to bed or to the reading-desk, for the train or for a gift, consider the form as much as the content. Depending on the occasion, depending on the place where I've chosen to read, I prefer something small and cozy or ample and substantial. (125)

Thinking about "the form as much as the content," we can also consider the many uses to which books are put that have very little to do with reading. During the hot summer when I was studying for my comprehensive examination in graduate school, some of the hundreds of books in my small apartment propped open the door to allow a breezeway. At other times, lacking a proper writing desk, the largest of the tomes became a hard surface on which to edit.

I found out at a young age that the book provided an excellent defense against intrusive riders on the bus. I've often given books to people as gifts, and, at times, I buy a book simply because it has a nice design. Even in nineteenth-century America, as Ronald Zboray and Mary Saracino Zboray point out, "published texts themselves often mattered less . . . than the meanings they ascribed to the printed goods they used" (1996, 588–9). Books were valued as objects that participated in social relations: "books could be textually inert, but socially rich in their uses as people recruited them for household purposes other than reading" (603). For example:

> Books preserved flowers and leaves—and the memories of loved ones and shared experiences they often represented—pressed between pages. Books could also become an accessory in games attending courtship rituals, as Calista Billings noted in 1849: 'we played *Bumblebee* or place a book on anyones hands & try to take it off & hit their hands before they can get them away or a forfeit, for forfeits write the character of some one in the room.' (603)

The rhetoric of the object differs from the project of cultural studies in that it considers objects at the nexus of social relations and communicative processes. Cultural studies views objects within "an historically transmitted pattern of meanings embodied in symbols, a system of inherited conceptions expressed in symbolic forms by means of which men communicate, perpetuate, and develop their knowledge about and attitudes toward life" (Geertz 2000, 89). As Bill Brown describes in his essay "The Secret Life of Things" (a precursor to his book *The Meaning of Things*), "[p]eople shape, code, and recode the material object world . . . they make things meaningful and valuable" (1999, 2). People do this through, for one, processes of selection. (Brown focuses on Virginia Woolf's 1920 short story "Solid Objects," in which the protagonist gradually devolves from a successful public life to seek objects cast off in corners and curbs, pieces of glass, ceramics, detritus of modern existence.) Luc Sante's unusual book *Evidence* opens with a comment on the role of just such detritus in contemporary life:

> Time in its passing casts off particles of itself in the form of images, documents, relics, junk. Nobody can seize time once it is gone, so we must make do with such husks, the ones that have not yet succeeded in disintegrating. These forms repose in cardboard boxes and closets, in old houses and attics, in filing cabinets and mini-storage warehouses, in museums and libraries, in archives. In a great city such as New York there are collections of artifacts and boneyards of information everywhere. (1992, ix)

Sante's book of historic New York police department photographs was prompted by the questions that the photographs asked him: "Why had they been taken? Who took them? What sort of truth were they supposed to represent?" (xi). These are historical questions about the past, about the way that we look at images from the past.

The work of materialist feminist art historian Jennifer Gonzales reminds readers that any meaningful study of the object recognizes that it is implicated in a visual rhetoric. Objects are seen and held. They are placed by actors and agents in positions that testify to a publicly articulated significance, a timeline, and a narrative:

> A rhetoric of objects can thus be defined as the use of material culture within a context of presentation or display (such as commercial market, museum, private collection, or art installation) for the sake of producing a visual and material argument at a particular historical moment and within a legible semantic "code." (1999, 186)

The object takes on a value as a fetish, representing the lost owner. It may be accorded a value that greatly outweighs its monetary exchange value, it is domesticated, and it participates in a process of bricolage in which it combines and recombines with other objects to represent human emotion. Citing Walter Benjamin, Brown points out that, "[a]ny newly purchased object . . . can be declared by the manufacturer to be *collectible*," thereby "obliterating the commodity-like characters of things" (Brown 1999, 11). Most important for my argument here is that objects have traces of the narratives of their collection, the story that marks them as significant. Thus, Sante's collection of photographs becomes meaningful to the rhetorician based on the story of his collection of the images.

Rhetoric in Private and Public Spheres

As Andrea Lunsford points out in *Reclaiming Rhetorica*, the rhetorical tradition "has never recognized the forms, strategies, and goals" that are outside of the mainstream logical discursive tradition (1995, 6). Many alternative forms have been used by women and writers of color. For example, the rhetorical language of quilts and their role in directing slaves to points of safety along the underground railroad has been studied by Jacqueline Tobin and her colleagues. African American historian and singer Bernice Regan Johnson has similarly explored the role that spirituals played in the quest for freedom. June Hadden Hobbs explores hymnody as a rhetorical practice in *"I Sing for I Cannot Be Silent"* (1997). Further recent work by feminist historians has examined the Bayeux Tapestry (Suzanne Lewis), needlepoint (Maureen Daly Goggin), clothing styles (Carol Mattingly), and the *Godey's Ladies Book* (Nicole Tonkovich). Although different in method and rhetorical purpose, each of these works nonetheless shares an important emphasis on the dialectical nature of rhetorical work. Rhetorical practices, whether through needle, note, or language, allow "intersections . . . among private, social, and public domains" (Royster 2000, 234–35).

There is a double problematic in working with objects, especially with everyday objects not part of the artistic or rhetorical tradition. Certain objects, not only those that are strictly decorative, suffer from a negative characterization as domestic, trivial, fashionable, bourgeois, vernacular, and fetishistic (Cullens 1999, 206; 213). As Christopher Reed notes, that which is domestic is "perpetually invoked in order to be denied" (1996, 16). Indeed, as Daniel Miller observes, "The deeply integrated place of the artefact in constituting culture and human relations has made discussion of it one of the most difficult of all areas to include in abstract academic discourse. The mundane artefact is not merely problematic but inevitably embarrassing as the focused topic of analysis, a practice which always appears fetishistic" (1987, 130). Miller's invocation of the fetish implies that the artifact cannot be dissociated from emotion or personal use, a traditional fear of rational scholarship. The object is negatively categorized as something that cannot be evaluated without self-interest, and thus it must be presented apologetically.

Similarly, traditional rhetorical theory is not a theory of the vernacular, for it tends to rely on manifest, public speech, that of political figures, published writers, or corporate advertising in popular venues. Among resistant discourses of race, class, and gender, contemporary feminist discourse offers rhetoricians the opportunity to focus on opposition, disruption, and particularity; the feminist refusal to be essentialized or universalized allows the vernacular to be written and spoken. In the object studies of aesthetics and art history, the privileged objects are the sculptures, paintings of the Masters. The ordinary or everyday—especially the mass-produced—is eschewed as banal and kitsch, a symbol of the alienation and reification of the possessor (alienation because he or she did not craft it; reification because the owner is similarly objectified as working the mass-production machine). Contemporary feminist artists such as Judy Chicago, Faith Ringgold, and Alma Lopez use alternative forms to inscribe persuasive messages. Chicago's work, such as the famous painting *The Dinner Party*, argues for the inclusion of women at the forefront of power. Ringgold's quilts piece together images from African American history, blending the domestic form of the quilt with the public forum of arguments over inclusion and contribution. In a controversial work that angered the Catholic Church, Lopez's photo-collage *Our Lady* reinscribed the passive Virgin de Guadalupe with the consequences of her passivity, demonstrating that the daughters of Eve were destined for objectification through an emphasis on the body. Lopez's work digitally blended the image of a real woman in a floral bikini with the traditional blue cloak and halo of the Virgin de Guadalupe, found in Mexican folk art and religious iconography. Each of these artists uses material forms—paint, canvas, fabric, thread, digital photographic collage—to write with and against the grain. Their art allows them access to a public sphere of display, criticism, and news coverage. Their works are all intentional creations of persuasive material. Art work, as well as the grander displays of public memorials, are embodied rhetorics, in other words, rhetorical messages that take a physical form (Blair 1999).

Nan Johnson's *Gender and Rhetorical Space in American Life, 1866–1910* provides a crucial intermediary step to my own exploration here. In this work, Johnson defines rhetorical "space" contextually, as the opportunity for a rhetorical act to have power within or beyond the private sphere (2002, 175 n1). Less interested in the physical locations in which demonstrations of oratorical or written ability are visible, Johnson instead explores the ideological conditions under which identity is constructed and performed. The relationship between "gender identities and rhetorical behavior" is linked to cultural attitudes about what women are expected to achieve in a historical epoch (2). American women in the nineteenth century were constrained by expectations that their sphere was the domestic, yet this did not prevent many women from taking on strong roles in political debates. If women exercised rhetorical ability through letters, reading aloud, or conversation, then how did these forms provide a means to power (4)?

I extend the exploration of alternative forms of communication and spheres of rhetorical influence to what is perhaps a more ethnographic focus on the actions of rhetorical agency in every day life. To list just a few examples, in cemeteries, roadside memorials, private altars, and the tokens that deck the office cubicle, the American public invests public space and objects with narrative meaning to redefine the public and private spheres. The materials create a liminal space between official culture, arguably barren and monoglossic, as Mikhail Bakhtin argues, and the riot of emotional associations present in personal lives, diffuse and heteroglossic. As I explored in my work with virtual memorials devoted to the memory of Princess Diana, the writers were anxious to inscribe a personal space in a public narrative. The flowers, candles, stuffed bears, and notes left at various Diana sites across Britain and America attested to the power of an object-based communicative act. The explanations of the ritual presentation of tokens at sites of commemoration were explained in the official press as acts of mass hysteria, dismissed as demonstrations of a particularly feminine excess and irrationality (the *lack* of good judgment). Yet, Diana's death was certainly not the only instance of devotional communicative processes in cultural life. As I noted earlier the Vietnam Veteran's Memorial has become a locus of devotional activity. Private objects are regularly brought into the public sphere to attest to the life of the departed and the living. These ordinary objects—dog tags, six-packs, baby shoes, and Christmas-tree ornaments—are invested with extraordinary associations that infuse the banality of daily life and consumer products with spiritual meaning. As Marita Sturken points out in her work on cultural memory, "the artifacts left at the memorial are talismans of redemption, guilt, loss, and anger" (1997, 78). When they began to appear, the Park Service classified the objects as "lost and found," Sturken writes. "Later, Park Service officials realized the artifacts had been left intentionally and began to save them.[1] The objects thus moved from the cultural status of being 'lost' (without category) to being historical artifacts" (79). She cites the comments of the manager of the NPS archive:

These are no longer objects at the Wall, they are communications, icons possessing a substructure of underpinning emotion. They are the products of culture, in all its complexities. They are the products of individual selection. With each object we are in the presence of a work of art of individual contemplation. (79)

As the archivist notes, the ordinary objects inscribe the trace of the self that was present at the moment of devotion. He uses rhetorical terms to describe their presence: the objects communicate and indicate an element of rhetorical agency because they have been selected for presentation at the Wall. They embody an ethos, the rhetorical presence of the giver. They are invested with pathos, an emotional appeal from the giver to the dead, and from the object to the witness. Thus, the Vietnam Veteran's Memorial is both a physical space and a rhetorical space in the sense that Johnson defines it. It provides the opportunity for a rhetorical act—the presentation of a token—to have power beyond the private sphere. The objects represent the lived experience of the person who leaves the token at the Wall, of the wartime experience of the veteran whose name is inscribed on the Wall, and of the audience who visits the Wall and perceives the talismanic token in that place at that time.

I am not asserting that the study of these object talismans is strictly feminist. The work of material feminists, however, contributes to an understanding of the ways that discourse is implicated in relations of power and derives from the multifarious experiences of speakers. Objects derive from and form social groupings; bringing them into the space of the classroom enriches the potential to create the classroom as a social space. People gather around objects to converse, share viewpoints, and, at times, initiate collective action.

Reflections on Objects and Power

In anthropology and in religious studies, a number of scholars have directed attention to the ways that ordinary people commemorate private, national, and global events ranging from births or deaths to wars. Among them are several women who have studied the creation of home shrines and altars. Although I will not stress that shrines are an effective pedagogical practice for deploying feminist rhetoric in the classroom, I do believe that they occupy a liminal space between domestic, personal spheres and public culture that is essential to demonstrate. In contrast to stumbling on Enos' "terra cotta ladies" reading scrolls in perpetuity on a vase in the British Museum, these personal object assemblages are found at home rather than in the museum—a significant removal from officially sanctioned objects arranged in official space.

Shrines are found almost anywhere in the house or yard. Domestic altars may be simple or elaborate, explains Teresa Palomo Acosta, "with each one conveying the experience of its maker":

They generally consist of a major image—usually a special rendition of the Blessed Virgin Mary or a favorite saint—set in the center. Votive candles, which convey a sense of the sacred, may remain continuously lit. Images of other saints or martyrs, family photographs, artificial flowers, ex-votos, and such personal items as stuffed animals or knickknacks, gifts to the altar maker from family members or friends, are arranged in various positions around the central image. (n.d.)

The creators of the home altars select the objects to include and rearrange the distribution of images to accord with their emotions or with significant events in their family lives, "reflecting daily events, catastrophes, losses, romantic complications, illnesses, births, deaths, and relatively minor disturbances and celebrations" (Cash 1998, 66). Once selected and arranged, the creator uses the altar to communicate to the Virgin or to the saints. Often, as folklorist Kay Turner points out, the devotions are written (1999, 133). "The *altarista* . . . transforms the saints arrayed on the altar into confidants and maintains an aura of intimacy by disregarding the formal language of church ritual and addressing saints in the vernacular, changing their names, for instance, from San Antonio to "Tonito" and referring to the altar as her "altarcito" (Acosta n.d.).

Writing about altars in New Mexican Catholic Hispanic homes, the *santera* Marie Romero Cash points out that the "makers and keepers of these shrines are almost always women, perhaps because the home is still the traditional female stronghold and the saints offer company during the day (or a life) when husband and children are absent" (1998, 46–47). Furthermore, Kay Turner has noted that "home altars represent flexibility in contrast to the church's institutional rigidity" and are therefore a "women's tradition in a male-dominated Church" (1999, 46). Cash, in turn, echoes Turner when she writes, "Institutional religion and home religion (*religion casera),* personal and communal life, coexist in the *altarcitos de casa* . . . an altar is embraced by and intertwined with family life (1998, 57).

Shrines can work visually like a family tree, Cash notes (1998, 66). In addition to placing the images of family members next to the images of saints, the saints in turn become like family members to whom the penitent communicates. Providing the physical manifestation of the spirit, the shrine allows unmediated communication, contact outside the official authority and structure of the Catholic Church. Shrines "are talked to, dressed up, punished, and rewarded," comments Cash (67). Turner explains that the altar provides the space for a "relationship with divine allies" (1999, 30). The *altaristas* position themselves so that they "belong" in the space that they occupy. As Philip Sheldrake describes, "'[b]elonging' involves both our connection to specific places and also our existence within networks of stable relationships" (2001, 49). The irony of the *altaristas'* position, however, is that the hegemonic, patriarchal discourse of the Catholic Church disenfranchises women's voices. Thus, the voice of the *altarista*, expressed through the creation of the shrine, is resistant to that power. However, the voice is not subversive because it continues to maintain a relationship to the discourse of the wider community, which includes the Catholic Church, ancestors, current extended family, and friends. The *altarista*'s "agency, the ability to make choices and act in situations, is located in others" (Fleckenstein 1998, 112).

Until recent decades, the parish was the organizing space for many individuals. "People belonged to it from birth to death and beyond—their ancestors were already in the churchyard and they would doubtless be buried there in turn" (Sheldrake 2001, 49). This strong sense of connection to place was doubled by the connection to spirit through the objects of home. It is a "commitment to human contexts and being accepted within them" (50), writes Sheldrake. A sense of place involves a sense of belonging to an integrated environment, which Marilyn Cooper referred to in composition theory as an "ecology."[2] Looking to rhetorical history, Susan Jarratt finds that Quintillian considered the sense of place in rhetorical practice:

> Space, he reflects, is not only a container for things but a place wherein people meet, relate, feel each other's presence: "For when we return to a place after considerable absence, we not merely recognize the place itself, but remember things that we did there, and recall the persons whom we met and even the unuttered thoughts which passed through our minds when we were there before." (2002, 35)

Using Quintillian's conception of space as an example of a mode of thinking about physicality and memory in rhetorical discourse, Jarratt extends his configuration to questions of feminism. Feminist historians must be wary of uncritically assigning feminine values to traditional sites of women's experience. She writes:

> We must look closely at specific features of place and gender, and seek to uncover the ideologies determining their meanings. Where we find familiar elements—separate or intimate spaces, cultivation of the person, emotional intensity, interest in natural beauty—we should ask a number of questions: are they exclusive to a feminine world in a particular time and place [?] . . . what material conditions support them? what social and political functions do they perform? (2002, 15).

As Acosta notes, predominantly female scholars have directed attention to "the significance of Mexican American women's home altars in terms of both ethnic heritage and women's culture." Thus, the altars are, to use Jarratt's words, indicative "of a feminine world in a particular time and place." The altar-making tradition is linked to folk arts, "such as corridos, communal jokes, and foods made of "bits and pieces" (Acosta n.d.):

> According to this view, altaristas have employed a conscious strategy to fashion an art of survival and beauty for a people whose culture continues to struggle against domination or appropriation. (Acosta n.d.)

Amalia Mesa-Bains argues that the shrine "springs from the experience of the émigré, the curandero and the lost devotional. In the experience of separation and expatriation lingers the sense of loss" (qtd. in Cash 1998, 67). "Altar makers have established a creative and spiritual 'space apart,' which is a means for women to meet their artistic and religious needs and challenge the 'powerlessness' to which male-dominated cultural institutions have consigned them." Often, the altar materials are passed from mother to daughter, a gesture that attests to the power of life history in family. This interaction between female family members is a key feature of personal altars. Kay Turner includes in her book *Beautiful Necessity* an altar titled "Woman Rising" (1974) by Mary Beth Edelson that featured "story-telling" boxes. The drawers held testimonies from many women, messages to be held tangibly and read. Women were invited to write their own stories and leave them with the installation. The effect was interactive and discursive and it also served to slow time because the piece demanded interaction and contemplation. "You couldn't just zip through and see the work," said the artist (qtd. in Turner 1999, 136). Altars are also forms of communication. Like prayers, Cash writes, altars "are mediators, collaborative forms crafted to reach across the abyss between known and unknown." (1998, 56):

> Fragmentation and accumulation, layers and repetition, are the underlying collage esthetics of the shrines, as they are of women's work, women's lives, and (more self-consciously) feminist art in the 1970s. They are classic examples of collage, bricolage, or liturgical patchwork, random clusters with an organic logic testifying to the power of repetition and imitation . . . [Fragmentation] is used to reveal and heal dissonance between past and present, between expectations and reality. Eclectic accretions of recontextualized *recuerdos* are placed in what might be called "bilingual" (double-tongued) or "polyvocal" (many-voiced) arrangements. Because placement is the tool with which new wholes are created from fragments, the specific juxtaposition and superposition of images and objects are particularly fascinating. (73)

Turner's work includes altars that are acts of patchwork, that transform the ordinary into the sacred: a rattle (1999, 132), feathers (125), stones (132), a shell (88), playing cards (86), photos of a friend waxed and formed as candles (133), a statue of Wonder Woman (107), an image of Barbara Streisand (124). The woman who created the Streisand altar saw the image as a reminder of her quest for self-identity, Turner writes. Without irony, using the image of another became a reminder that identity can be transformed from within and not imposed from without:

> In creating altars to popular figures—Madonna, Frida Kahlo, Princess Diana—women sacralize the secular for their own purposes of self-knowledge and self-understanding. Meanings are subjective, invented, imagined—not imposed. (123)

Viewers often recognize objects that assume a different meaning within the sacred space of the altar, but rather than impose the traditional meaning on the objects, they are encouraged to seek the meaning of the objects within the articulated system of the piece. For example, in the image of Marlene Terwilliger's altar *We Share the Moon* (1991; in Turner 1999), I discover pieces of a deck of Alice in Wonderland playing cards that I purchased from the Levinger catalogue in 1995 or 1996 and with which I have never played. Mine sit in a box somewhere, yet I recognize them in the photo of this display as "my cards." Terwilliger and I share an identity as consumers within a capitalist culture; she has used her cards partially in the way that they were marketed—to build a house of cards—but she has displaced them in a shrine to her deceased sister in which they are no longer "my cards, too," but a house that has fallen from absence and loss.

Certainly, in this century, which opened with war and terrorism, the American flag is another such symbol that unites and divides. It is a form of expression deployed to illustrate personal conviction and participation in a national discourse. The flag is a national symbol that works across public and private spheres and distinctions of gender, race, and class; yet it is for many a perpetual symbol of American cultural, economic, and ideological domination of other countries. Similarly, the yellow ribbon on my neighbor's tree attests to the son or daughter, husband or wife who has been sent overseas to fight in Operation Iraqi Freedom. Although the yellow ribbons are recognizable cultural symbols for military personnel deployed in combat, they are also the personal evocation of a life lived locally, intimately, within the space of home and family.[3]

Pedagogy, Objects, and Power

The study of liminal/public and private spaces is effective as a pedagogical technique, as is the introduction of material creation in the classroom. As a pedagogical strategy for deploying a feminist rhetoric, creating "sacred spaces" for languages and images can potentially draw students into new understandings of the relationship of objects to personal and public histories—without returning to the philosophies of expressivist pedagogy that decontextualizes and depoliticizes the writer. There are implications in the study of talismanic objects and the rich meanings of public and private spaces for rhetorical pedagogy, and I offer some here.

First, materialist feminist rhetoricians are enjoined without apology to consider the study of the everyday in classrooms. This does not mean an exclusive authorization of the domestic as woman's space, for, as we have been cautioned by Susan Jarratt and others, the domestic is a constructed sphere that has been identified with restrictive roles for women. Rather, focusing on the objects of the everyday presents the rhetorician with an opportunity to exercise a certain kind of mindfulness in which things are brought out of habitual use to explain their role in daily ritual and identity formation. Such modes of collaborative inquiry are similar to the ideas of reflexive practice that Donna

Qualley sets forth in *Turns of Thought*. It implies a way of looking, seeing, thinking, and turning back on the self. Qualley refers to reflective practice as "recursive and hermeneutical" because the teacher repeatedly returns to the classroom to interpret the moment:

> reflexivity is a response triggered by a dialectical engagement with the other—an other idea, theory, person, culture, text . . . . In the process of trying to understand an other, our own beliefs and assumptions are disclosed, and these assumptions themselves can become objects of examination and critique. (1997, 11)

Second, feminist rhetoricians should explore opportunities to absorb everyday language and images into creative pedagogical practices. One of my colleagues, a poet inspired by the Southwestern *altaristas*, involves her students in creating artistic collages combining word and image, artifacts that could be called *word shrines*. The object is a common heuristic for poets and teachers of poetry, who often use objects as vehicles for teaching description and for eliciting memories. The poet Susan Goldsmith Wooldridge offers yet another consideration for the creative process, to think of words themselves as objects, thereby erasing the metaphysical distinction between three-dimensional piece and the presence of the word. As she writes in *Poemcrazy*, "The word *poem* comes from the Greek *poein*, to make. In a collage, as in many poems, you reassemble fragments of found or collected images to make a new image of your own" (Wooldridge 1996, 139). Citing the collage boxes of artist Joseph Cornell (1903–72) as her muse, she asserts that "you don't make art, you *find* it, accepting everything around you as your material" (139).[4] The everyday, the discarded, the well-worn, the used, even the precious become transmuted into a communicative act. As an exemplification of the rhetorical principle of *kairos*, the found object represents an opportunity that presents itself to the creative person. At the point of apprehension, the object qualitatively changes the life of the bearer, positing a future that contains the object in a new way with new understandings. As John Smith notes in "Time and Qualitative Time," *kairos* involves the recognition of the rhetor that there is an appropriate time to speak, "which means knowing *when* to speak, *when* to be silent and *when* to use the specific devices of discourse contained in the science of rhetoric" (1986, 12).

In addition, because the objects invoke histories that are public and personal, the object may be used as a way to explore differing concepts of historical representation. Objects embody the history of their manufacture (a word broadly employed here to mean both machine-made and personally crafted modes of creation), the history of their use, and the history of personal associations and emotions given to it. The personal "history," as the quotation from Gaston Bachelard that heads this chapter suggests, is less a story about the object than about the holder and beholder. Some of these histories are articulated as narrative, others are exploratory, and still others are factual. Histories invite the writer to consider origins, audience, purposes, and designs and to resituate the article of inquiry in new contexts, amidst new audiences. In rhetorical pedagogy, then, creating the collage of words, things, or words and things, brings to bear the powerful forces of history and memory.

As a third option for pedagogical exploration of a rhetoric of objects, feminist rhetoricians may initiate inquiry into the relationships between the ubiquitously published images of celebrity icons (here constituting "the every-day") and what we might construe as the mysticism surrounding the ancient orthodox icons of religious tradition. In earlier work, I examined the ways that worship of celebrity icons can be traced to reverence for traditional icons of the Orthodox Church (Helmers 2002). *Icon* derives from the Greek *eikon*, "to resemble." In Orthodox tradition, the icon is invested with spirit. The viewer extends the gaze *through* the image to an inner, inscrutable *ousia* (essence). In Orthodox tradition, therefore, reverence for the image of Christ is ontologically the same as reverence for the embodied Jesus. In contrast, Western modes of viewing separate self from that which is viewed—object—in order to take in elements of form, design, texture, and color. The response is aesthetic. When an image of a movie star or athletic superstar is proffered as an extension of self, we tend to degrade it as kitsch or inauthentic. Yet, to follow Turner's example, the image of Streisand within the space of the altar is no longer an outward representation of the star but a reconstructed image of the self of the *altarista*. Such a redefinition of the object into new contexts that are fused with personal narrative and histories is rhetorical.

In her work on creating a spiritual classroom, Kristie Fleckenstein describes the ways that a teacher can enable the discovery of a "spiritual center" in pedagogy. The spiritual center is the "individual's ordering principle" without which the individual is alienated from self and others, "resulting in an erosion of a meaningful existence" (1997, 26). Contrary to the modernist vision of the object engendering alienation, Fleckenstein's work suggests that the object, meaningfully chosen and appreciated, may enter into a spiritual connection between self and other. Fleckenstein argues that exploratory peda-gogy is essential to developing a spiritual center. She lists "intuition, imagery, and somatic learning" among its techniques and links its aims to liberatory pedagogy (27). At the heart of successful pedagogy is affect, "emotions, feel-ings, moods, beliefs, personality traits" (27):

> In a writing classroom that incorporates affect, topics such as a writer's self-image, a student's personal history with writing (including childhood and family experiences), and the writer's personal as well as rhetorical goals obtain legitimacy. (27)

A fourth mode of rhetorical inquiry that can integrate the material object with feminist goals is the study of physical space. As I argued earlier, altars are intelligible because they occupy a space apart that is at the same time part of a dominant discourse and a discourse resistant to hegemony. Although the objects within them may be everyday objects, they take on new meaning when they are redeployed in a new network of meanings and associations. The object can give rise to a chain of individuated ideas, images, emotions, and associations without the need for proof or ordering according to a prefashioned sequence or hierarchy. Thus the object participates in this process of centeredness by privileging metaphor and allusion. In *The Body in Pain* (1987), Elaine Scarry considers how creative actions, such as telling stories or creating objects, construct the conscious world of humans. Manufactured objects are "extensions of the body into the world" and become "ways of knowing it" (Solnit 2001, 29). Whereas Marshall McLuhan saw the object as the sign of the inevitable alienation of the human self from the body, Scarry's work suggests a way to reconnect the body with the spaces and objects around it.

The consequence of this pedagogy is a sense of self that orders and constructs reality but that, in turn, presents students with the opportunity to explore the connections between personal and collective memory. Citing the remark "Sensitivity to life is the highest product of education" from the 1915 philosophical exploration *The Holy Earth* by Liberty Hyde Bailey, first dean of agriculture at Cornell University, Ruth Wilson comments that "teaching at its best is a quest for touching and enflaming the spark of enthusiasm for life" (n.d.). Wilson draws our attention to the *ousia*—the soul—of the teaching process, just as Fleckenstein asks us to consider the *ousia* of material reality by asking in what way does "personal reality become a shared reality that, in turn, becomes a personal reality" (1997, 30)? Intentionally invested things like the shoes of the Holocaust, the boots of the Vietnam Veteran's Wall, and the track shoes from the student's backpack tell us something of their lives and histories. As talismans of loss or anger, joy or guilt, they speak across time and culture. Rhetoric should allow us a means to read their significance.

Notes

1. The officials overseeing the development of a memorial after the Oklahoma City bombing on April 19, 1995, recognized quickly the significance of testimonials and objects left by mourners. On the question of preserving the chain-link fence that surrounded the wreckage of the Alfred P. Murrah Federal Building in Oklahoma City and the objects of devotion that were placed in it and near it, see Edward Linenthal, *The Unfinished Bombing*.

2. Objects achieve a power by participating in economic and social exchanges and by occupying significant space. In this latter sense, space is construed as physical and psychical space, that which has been appointed as having meaning by individuals or groups. Gaston Bachelard's impressionistic study *The Poetics of Space* is based on phenomenological philosophy, which he uses to explore the constructive role of the imagination in creating the world. In Bachelard's conception, images are not objects but are *lived*, connected in space and perception to the observer. A second, related writer who illuminates the relationship between human and object is Marcel Mauss, whose *The Gift: The Form and Reason for Exchange in Archaic Societies* has been influential in describing exchange values of ordinary things.

3. In *Culture in the Marketplace: Gender, Art, and Value and the American South-west*, Molly Mullin points out that the American flag was forbidden as a symbol in Native American art, not by the artists themselves, but by the art dealers from the eastern United States. The flag was not considered "authentic" by the modernist transplants to the Southwest who interacted with the natives (86, 93–4, 116–18).

4. German artist Kurt Schwitters (1887–1948) also used found objects to create collages. Recently, Davy Rothbart created the magazine *Found* devoted to collecting bits and pieces of forgotten and abandonded life, such as Polaroid photographs, tickets, and love letters. Offered with only minimal commentary in the pages of the magazine, the newly recontextualized items become poetry and art, sometimes funny and often incredibly sad. Examples from the magazine can be viewed at *www.foundmagazine.com*.

8

Making Room for New Subjects

Feminist Interruptions of Critical Pedagogy Rhetorics

Shari Stenberg

During the last two decades, rhetoric and composition has appropriated radical pedagogy rhetorics to help the field recast itself from a domestic service provider for the university to a public agent of student empowerment and civic-minded cultural participation. Although rhetoric and composition scholars trace the intersection of literacy, democratic participation, and critical consciousness as far back as the sophists (Jarratt 1991b), it is the theoretical credibility delivered by the Frankfurt school critical theory, Gramsci's concept of the organic intellectual and counterhegemonic practice, and Freire's notion of conscientization that have helped composition and its teachers achieve a sense of disciplinary insiderness and status we could not garner on our own (Worsham 1998).

The writing teacher has traditionally occupied the feminized role of either the (current-traditional) disciplinarian/grammarian or (expressivist) nurturer/midwife. Susan Miller's metaphor of the bourgeois mother/maid aptly depicts the writing teacher's work in the private sphere to prepare students for "real" academic work in the public world; she at once embodies comfort and power, nurturance and discipline, but her work is always limited by the domestic sphere in which it takes place. To achieve greater disciplinary credibility, compositionists have thus sought out a more "crisply masculine" (S. Miller 1991) identity, designed to promote us from the home (or classroom) to the public sphere (or discipline).

Critical pedagogy rhetorics lend the writing teacher new status as the "transformative intellectual," who is conceived as a public figure located in a classroom that is a democratic public sphere, a site in which students are prepared to become active, critical citizens (Aronowitz and Giroux 1991). In this way, then, the teacher as critical pedagogue is lifted out of the devalued private sphere; the sad woman in the basement who cleans and disciplines student language (S. Miller 1991) becomes the transformative intellectual who provides students a language of critique and fosters in them a sense of critical agency (see McLaren; Giroux; Aronowitz).

In some ways, this project and role may seem ideal for feminist teachers; critical pedagogy rhetorics privilege the pragmatics of experience and voice and are predicated on an ethic of care, solidarity, and liberation (Giroux 1983). At the same time, they do not limit women, as do some versions of feminist pedagogy, to the role of maternal nurturer. Ideally, critical pedagogy helps students "make the turn from the personal back out to the public" (Jarratt 1991b), in part by insisting that the teacher is a public, intellectual figure.

But something, as feminist rhetors in education and composition point out, has been overlooked. The fact that the key terms of radical pedagogy—democracy, the public sphere, citizenship, voice—are regarded as inherently "good" in American culture has prevented critical pedagogy rhetorics from examining the ways that this vision has historically excluded female subjects. As Carmen Luke argues, the rhetorics of critical pedagogy have been articulated in epistemic relation to liberal conceptions of equality and participatory democracy, which are "located squarely in (male) individualism constitutive of the public sphere" (1992, 29). While male–authored critical pedagogy rhetorics grant lip service to gender and subjectivity, little attention has been granted to the masculinist ideology that shapes the standpoint from which radical pedagogy scholarship is written or to the gender privilege to which public speech and writing have historically been tied (Luke 1992).

Feminist rhetors argue that we cannot move (female) teachers out of the "basement" without altering the structure that has for so long feminized the teaching of writing in the first place. It is not enough to be given opportunity to speak and to participate in the public sphere when the discourses and networks of gender and power relations that infiltrate that classroom (liberatory or not) remain unchanged. To make room for female subjects in the project of radical pedagogy, feminist rhetors have relied on the tactic of "feminist interruption," to render visible the ways that critical pedagogy discourse excludes the subjects it seeks to empower.

Nedra Reynolds defines feminist interruption as a means of asserting agency used to draw attention to women's identities as marginalized speakers and writers and to illuminate the ideological workings of discursive exclusion (1998, 60). Rather than a rude or dismissive behavior, Michelle Ballif, Diane Davis, and Roxanne Mountford promote interruption as a positive intervention, a *critical affirmation* allowing us a richer means of "attending to [the] conversation" (2000, 931). Carmen Luke and Jennifer Gore, for instance, argue that their collection *Feminisms and Critical Pedagogy* is designed as a "*productive* and *enabling* intervention towards a re-visioning of pedagogical relations" (1992, 2, my emphasis).

Although Reynolds contends that verbal interruption is often most effective, since physical presence heightens the impact, she argues that feminists in composition studies need also to investigate the kinds of interruption possible in written texts (1998, 71). I will answer her call in this article, examining the ways feminist rhetors including Gore, Luke, Ellsworth, and Payne have interrupted the three central metaphors for the "critical" teacher: public intellectual; emancipatory authority; and bearer of critical knowledge. I extend this work through interruptive narratives that depict the tensions I have experienced in seeking to "try on" and "make fit" the ideal subject of critical pedagogy, a subject that does not, I contend, leave adequate room for (embodied) feminist teachers. Ultimately, I hope to show how these interruptions stretch, alter, and reconstruct the subject position of critical teacher and, in this way, make room for female subjects.

The Teacher as Public/Transformative Intellectual

As Jennifer Gore argues, little direct attention is granted in critical pedagogy discourse to the ways a teacher must alter herself and her practices to assume the role of critical pedagogue. Instead, emphasis is placed on mastery of the social vision espoused by critical pedagogy theorists; in these visions, however, we find implications for the behavior and subjectivity of the ideal teacher.

Giroux describes critical pedagogy as "designed to educate the citizen for intelligent and active participation in the civic community" and contends that these ideals have not "found their way, in general, into the day-to-day practices of schools, either historically or in more recent times" (1983, 168). He calls, then, for teachers to enact a pedagogy based on the principles of (public) critique and action and grants them the status of "transformative intellectuals" to do so. According to Giroux and McLaren, the transformative intellectual is:

> one who exercises forms of intellectual and pedagogical practice which attempt to insert teaching and learning directly into the public sphere by arguing that schooling represents both a struggle for meaning and a struggle over power relations . . . . [T]ransformative intellectuals treat students as critical agents, question how knowledge is produced and distributed, utilize dialogue, and make knowledge meaningful, critical, and ultimately emancipatory. (1986, 215)

Whereas Giroux and McLaren argue that this construction "dignifies" teacher work, feminist rhetors have intervened to ask whose work is really dignified by the label transformative intellectual and to examine the roots of classic Greek education from a feminist standpoint. In doing so, feminist rhetors evoke "dangerous memory"—a practice promoted within critical pedagogy discourse—as a tactic to turn the project back on itself. According to Giroux and McLaren, acting as "bearers of dangerous memory" requires teachers to link "knowledge to power by bringing to light and teaching the subjugated histories, experiences, stories, and accounts of those who suffer and struggle within conditions

that are rarely made public or analyzed through the official discourses of public schooling" (1986, 227). Although rarely enacted within critical pedagogy
rhetoric, feminist rhetoricians have put this vision powerfully into practice.

For instance, in "Feminist Politics in Radical Pedagogy," Luke relies on
dangerous memory to illuminate the subjugated history of women in classic
Greek education, a tradition that not only excluded, but militated against,
women's civic participation. In the liberal democratic state, to publicly critique
and act, to speak and be heard, were privileges of men, not women. And even
today, when critique and action are waged by women, it is largely "organized
and articulated in discourses and texts defined and regulated by men" (Luke
1992, 30).

An October 2003 *New Yorker* profile entitled "The Student"—who happened to be Senator Hillary Rodham Clinton—provides an apt example of this.
As Elizabeth Kolbert demonstrates, the Senate abides by deeply entrenched
laws and by traditions, which are governed by senior men. One such tradition
requires a "freshman visit" to fifty-year Senator Robert Byrd, who in 1993 as
chair of the Senate Appropriations Committee refused to sign off on Rodham
Clinton's bold health-care reform legislation. Byrd saw her then, as he puts it,
"through a glass darkly, as the Scripture says" (Kolbert 2003, 67).

The profile, however, marks his changed opinion of Clinton from those
days. He praises her "hard work and deference," both of which he advised her
on during her freshman visit. For following the already-established rules and
traditions, and not making the mistake again of seemingly "overstepping" her
position, Byrd names her "the perfect student" (Kolbert 2003, 67). Her ability
to critique and act in this forum are dependent on her ability to play by rules
regulated by men.

Academic women can likely identify with a similar requirement to play by
already-established rules and to, as Jennifer Gore and Carmen Luke put it, "identify their feminist position with a paternal signifier" (1992, 4). Perhaps Cixous
states it best: "the moment women open their mouths . . . they are immediately
asked . . . who is their master and where they are coming from: they have, in
short, to salute . . . and to show their identity papers" (1981, 51). This is true,
as well, for those women seeking to enact or contribute to critical pedagogy.

Although critical pedagogy discourse may claim to "give voice"—or, as
some have described it, to donate space—to female teachers and students, it
does so without rearticulating the masculine public subject or challenging the
subordination of the private in relation to the public/political. As Sue Jackson
interjects, "Why does Henry Giroux place an emphasis on 'public life'? What
does this mean? Does [critical] pedagogy give consideration to private lives, in
particular the private lives of women?" (1997, 460).

As much as critical pedagogues may call for the illumination of subjugated experiences and stories, the scholarship does not tend to make room for
the stories of the (largely female) teachers who seek to enact its visions. Dominant educational discourse continues to make women's lives and experiences

invisible and unwelcome. As Luke and Gore argue, despite the fact that teaching has historically been "women's work," it remains in the "theoretical and administrative custody of men" (1992, 2).

The invitation of women into the public sphere, as feminists have long argued, does not mean they are excused from the "caretaking" positions of the private; they are simply required to fulfill both roles. Moreover, making space for women in the public sphere—or arguing that teachers are public intellectuals in public spaces—does not adequately challenge the division that has kept them outside in the first place. Consequently, as Luke argues, "women end up doubly inscribed in marginal public positions and in 'natural' caretaking positions in the private" while the "public man" is liberated from domestic work and is thus "free to defend public, universally human interests as a full time (pre)occupation" (1992, 32).

In fact, Jennifer Gore goes so far as to pose the following problem to critical pedagogy discourse: "'Whose interests are served by dignifying teachers' work?' 'Dignifying' in whose eyes?" (1993, 101). She asks, in fact, whether the construction of teacher as intellectual functions in the interest of students, teachers, democracy, or male theorists (101). Not only does critical pedagogy risk privileging male theorists at the expense of female teachers—who are left with the burden of unpacking and enacting these largely abstract social visions (see Gore; Lee; Gallagher)—but it also risks reifying the dynamic whereby women are limited to public roles that are mere extensions of their traditional private duties: nurturer, caretaker, servant.

As Jackson contends, although humanizing education promoted by Freire is designed to teach women and men to take into consideration their own needs and the needs of others, Freire does not give consideration to the ways women have traditionally prioritized the needs of others over their own. "Women have long been tied to a caring and nurturing role," she writes, "where we are expected, and have learned to expect of ourselves, that we will always put others first. The journey along the path of liberation for men has often been at the expense of women"(Jackson 1997, 464–65).

At the same time (female) teachers are expected to serve and meet the needs of (male) critical pedagogy theorists, they are also expected to assimilate to the construction of the male, public intellectual—a move that often requires the teacher to deny those aspects of herself deemed "female." As Susan Bordo contends, "any celebration of 'female' ways of knowing or thinking may be felt by some to be dangerous professionally and perhaps a personal regression as well. For, within the masculinist institutions we have entered, relational, holistic, and nurturant attitudes continue to be marked as flabby, feminine, and soft" (1993, 233).

Further, even a female teacher who seeks to model herself as a "public intellectual" cannot control how she is read—based on her specific, embodied location—by her students, colleagues, and superiors. Although critical pedagogy may make mention of the issue of gender, it does not, as Luke contends, address "the politics of gender the structure, the possibilities (of critique) for women teachers and female students" (1992, 39). Consequently, feminist rhetors have intervened to call attention to the entrenched and naturalized construction of the critical pedagogue and to "bring to light" their own subjugated histories, experiences, and stories as they struggle to step into this subject position (Giroux and McLaren 1986). In doing so, they challenge the private/public dichotomy that exists not only in our culture and institutions but also in critical pedagogy discourse.

I dreaded the arrival of the fall semester. I was eight months pregnant, a condition that left me constantly mindful of the way my "private" self was read as separate from, and alien to, the public world of intellectualism, of the academy. I walked into the classroom wearing a carefully chosen dress I hoped would mark me as professional, even as my belly marked me as mother. I left the section in the syllabus titled "other business" for last; under those bolded words, I explained how I would handle my six-week "family" leave. The rhetoric was deliberate: I would treat my leave as part of the business of the course—not part of my private life colliding with my public life; I would describe it as a family, not maternity, leave—hoping to evoke Bill Clinton's work on the Family Leave Act, to highlight my (public) rights to a private life. A life I felt guilty about making visible, about wanting. Maternal, maternity seemed dirty words in this context; as much as I already loved this being in my womb, I wanted to sever my body, and its connotation of motherhood, from the classroom.

Certainly I "knew" better, that I was abiding by problematic (and archaic) assumptions about the body, and yet, I also was not naive to my surroundings—an institution, however committed to issues of "diversity," which is still dominated by Western, masculinist norms of intellectualism and professionalism. An institution in which the agency of female subjects depends on the degree to which we are able to cloak, or overcome, bodies marked by difference—bodies that insist on being visible.

I chose a seat behind the table, slouching to hide my belly. When a student commented on my size, comparing me to her sister-in-law, I quickly deflected the remark. When another student asked why I didn't take the elevator—I was out of breath after climbing three flights of stairs—I choked out an uncomfortable laugh and changed the subject. I wanted my body—and any other reminders of me as a member of the "private," caretaking, sphere—left out of the classroom.

The (Disembodied) Bearer of Critical Knowledge

Above all, the critical teacher is one who "excavate(s) the 'subjugated knowledges'" of her students (McLaren 1989, 241), "employ(s) critical analysis and utopian thinking" (238), introduces students to "a language of empowerment and radical ethics that permits them to think about how community life should be constructed around a project of possibility" (Giroux 1988, 166). This means that the teacher not only must understand oppression better than her students but also must spark in them a commitment to changing societal structures and promote processes for doing so.

Although critical pedagogues are not positioned as experts in the traditional sense—indeed, they are to learn from their students and begin with student knowledge (see Shor; Freire)—they are, according to Giroux, "bearers of critical knowledge, rules, and values through which they consciously articulate and problematize their relationship to each other, to students, to subject matter, and to the wider community" (1988, 90). In this way, a critical teacher is thought to have knowledge about culture that his or her students do not. As Shor writes, "the dialogical teacher is more intellectually developed, more practiced in critical scrutiny, and more committed to a political dream of social change, than are the students" (1980, 95).

Of course, the notion that the critical pedagogue can occupy a position from which he can see better than his students and lead them to rationality and reason stems from the myth that a universal and central social location is available to him. As feminist rhetors have argued, the critical pedagogue is constructed as an androgynous, colorless, disembodied, heroic teacher, who is beyond the sexism, classism, and racism he critiques. And, as feminist Jane Durie suggests, this "essential body of humanness" really refers to a "white, male, heterosexual, able bodied, middle class [subject]—from which all 'others' are given meaning" (1996, 140).

Through tactical interruptions, feminist rhetors not only have called attention to the exclusionary tendencies of this idealized subject and vision but also have illuminated the contradictory effects of such objectives. Perhaps the most notable example of feminist interruption is Elizabeth Ellsworth's oft-cited article "Why Doesn't This Feel Empowering? Working Through the Repressive Myths of Critical Pedagogy." While much has been written about this piece, its interruptive tactics are worth examining here both because of the openings the article created for other feminist voices and because of the fraught response it evoked from male critical pedagogy theorists. Indeed, as Erica McWilliam points out, Ellsworth's piece "marked a reconfiguration of critical pedagogy as a form of rhetoric," carved an opening for many (often marginalized) voices to discuss dissonance between pedagogical aims and outcomes, and challenged the often "self-congratulatory and somewhat evangelical tone" that characterized the rhetoric of critical pedagogy (1997, 221).

In order to disrupt the "generic" critical teacher, who can somehow exist above oppressive social formations, Ellsworth highlights the complexities involved in assuming this subject position as she experiences them from her social location as a white, middle-class, able-bodied, thin woman. Consequently, she contends, she can "never know" about the experiences, oppressions and understandings of her students better than they can (1992, 101). Instead, she argues:

> it made more sense to see my task as one of redefining "critical pedagogy" so that it did not need utopian moments of "democracy," "equality," "justice," or "emancipated" teachers—moments that are unattainable (and ultimately undesirable, because they are always predicated on the interests of those who are in the position to define utopian projects). (100)

The preferable goal, she contends, is to "become capable of a sustained encounter with currently oppressive formations and power relations that refuse to be theorized away or fully transcended in a utopian resolution—and to enter into the encounter in a way that both acknowledged my own implications in those formations and was capable of changing my own relation to and investments in those formations" (Ellsworth 1992, 100). In other words, Ellsworth rewrites the critical teacher as one who is necessarily implicated in the social formations she hopes to alter, whose knowledge is always partial, and, consequently, whose "self" and whose pedagogical aims require ongoing self-reflexivity and revision.

The male theorists she interrupted, however, didn't see it quite this way. They accused her of "misreading the tradition" and being unable to "move beyond self-doubt" (McLaren 1988, 72). McLaren goes so far as to contend that Ellsworth used critical pedagogy theory "as a scapegoat for failed practice" (72).

But others saw the interruption differently—not as a threat to the project, but as a "'postcritical' turn that enabled a new generation of feminist analyses" (McWilliam 1997, 221). McWilliam defines postcritical work as that which "refuses the final vocabulary of ideological critique while insisting on the importance of the struggle against real material conditions of oppression and marginalization" (221). It is a position working both within and against, which also requires writers to "perform" their critiques in such a way that points to their own "lack of innocence" (221).

As a result of these efforts, we have a growing body of scholarship that looks different from more mainstream critical pedagogy scholarship; not only is it more locally grounded, but it is often built on moments of struggle, indecision, even failure. In this scholarship, the teacher is not the hero, but rather she is a learner along with her students, a work in progress. Although some might read this work as lacking certainty or clarity, that is exactly the point. As Gore and Luke argue, the indeterminacy that stems from the poststructuralist feminism that informs these efforts is not the same postmodern deferment. "Rather," they write, 'it is an indeterminacy that lies in its rejection of certainty promised by modernist discourses, a rejection of a self-certain and singular subject, and a rejection of knowledges that promise answers which lead to closure" (1992, 7).

I am committed, as a writing teacher, to highlighting the ways that culture "writes" us as embodied subjects. I hope to foster in my students an awareness of discourse as always socially constructed, always working on and through us, in a way that serves some and disempowers others. I long to spark a commitment in students to reflect on, even change, societal structures. And yet, I have learned that in the private, Midwestern institution in which I teach, discussions of race, class, and gender usually evoke defensive reactions on the parts of white students in my class and risk positioning the one or two students of color in the class as token representatives of their groups.

I am stuck. I want to call attention to these issues, and yet I want to do so in a way that best facilitates collaborative inquiry, that doesn't result in debilitating anger.

Critical pedagogy discourse does not address the visceral responses I feel on mornings when race will be the topic of discussion in my classroom. It tells me that students may resist my "morally responsible" choice, but it doesn't address the complexities of negotiating a pedagogical moment when a student asks her classmates, "How many of you considered not coming today when you saw the word race on the syllabus?" and the majority of students raise their hands.

I have thought about giving up, and giving them not what they (presumably) need, but what I believe they want: topics that make them comfortable, topics that allow us to forego discomfort in the classroom. But I am not quite there yet. And so this semester, I try a different approach. I include a unit entitled "Figuring the Body," which includes discussions and depictions of the "ideal" body. We can't, I figure, discuss these issues without discussing intersections of race, class, and gender. The unit comes last in the sequence, after we've approached "safer" topics. Still, the night before we begin the unit, I worry about who will be made uncomfortable, about who will feel her body is overly visible as we discuss—abstractly, of course—issues of the body, plastic surgery, piercing, tattoos.

We look at two images in class: one of two thin, laughing, white females. They are obviously models, dressed alike, and their black, low-cut dresses contrast with the white backdrop. On the opposite page are two Latino men, large, shirtless, laughing. They are clearly enjoying each other, taking pleasure in a shared joke. I am the (disembodied) "problem poser." I ask them questions: "Which photo do you like better? Why?" Some like the photo of the men. They seem real, they say. They seem human. A few men joke and whisper; they prefer the image of the women. "What is the effect of juxtaposing these images?" I ask. We tease out the distinction between these two "human" seeming men, and the two "objectified" women. We talk about the way runway models often seem more like clothes hangers than people. We talk about the way women learn themselves as objects. "You don't know how hard it is for us!" one woman tells the men in our class. She says it as a joke, but she is serious.

*I push onward: "How would the meaning of the photos change if the gen-
ders were reversed?" I immediately regret the question.*

*"It would be gross!" one man retorts. His remark hits the issue squarely
on the head: fat women are not human, either. They are regarded with disgust
in our culture; they are bodies out of control.*

*Though I lead us through an "intellectual" discussion of how fatness is
read in our culture, I am aware of Mary's silence. She is usually involved,
engaged. Today, she does not contribute at all.*

*Darlene approaches me after class, "It's such a sensitive issue; I'm wor-
ried about how Mary might feel. She sure was quiet today." I tell her that we
need to make these issues public, to challenge our assumptions; it's the only
way change will occur. And yet, I am worried about Mary, too.*

*I share the worry with two colleagues after class. Both have wise offer-
ings: "Discomfort is okay," Greg advises, "as long as it's not shaming."*

*"In African American communities, a larger body is accepted, even pre-
ferred," Nainsi reminds me. "Don't assume she was offended."*

But I can't put Mary out of my head.

*The right choices, critical rhetorics tell us, will be clear. But I am filled
with uncertainty. Does this mean I have failed the critical project? Or that I
have discovered a need for revision, a possibility?*

The Emancipatory Authority

Proposing an alternative pedagogy means negotiating the traditional dynamic
in the classroom where the teacher has authority over her students. Whereas
feminist pedagogies have tended to reject teacher authority as inherently negative, favoring a nonhierarchical arrangement whereby the teacher "shares"
her power, critical pedagogues contend that the teacher can never escape his
position of authority (Gore 1993, 97). The teacher can, however, use her
authority to lead her students toward critical consciousness by acting as an
"emancipatory authority" who strategically uses her agency in the name of
social change and student empowerment.

Although critical pedagogy discourse poses a crucial difference between
the "directive liberating educator on the one hand, and the directive domesticating educator on the other" (Shor and Freire 1987), there is little discussion
of how the teacher should enact liberatory authority. McLaren and Giroux
contend that it is (simply) a matter of setting one's mind to it; that is, the realization of critical pedagogy's goals depends on teachers' making the "moral
choice" put before us to employ teacher authority in a manner that promotes
individual agency and social transformation. As Gore contends, the discourse
"functions through a general assumption that the right choices will be clear"
(1993, 116).

Thus, the responsibility for advancing emancipatory authority rests squarely on the teacher's shoulders, and as the exchange among Ellsworth, Giroux, and McLaren above suggests, the teacher who is unable to assume the role of critical teacher is positioned as somehow having failed—or misunderstood—the tradition. Consequently, feminist rhetors have stepped in to interrupt this notion of authority by making visible the contexts in which critical pedagogy is enacted, narrating the complicated ways in which pedagogical relations are necessarily structured by institutional discourse and embodied subjects—not by sheer (individual) will or knowledge—and calling attention to what (and who) gets lost in this articulation of authority.

Feminist rhetors have relied on what Chris Gallagher calls "institutional literacy" to interrupt the calls for emancipatory authority. As Gallagher argues, "institutional literacy" means that we are able to "read institutional discourses (and their resultant arrangements and structures) so as to speak and to write back to them, thereby participating in their revision" (2002, 79). It requires that we ask, What is at stake and for whom? Who is served by these calls and who is not? Feminist rhetors use their (alternative) institutional literacy to point out that whereas critical pedagogy demands that teachers not assume domesticating authority, the institution has long domesticated and disciplined female subjects. In fact, this pedagogy of domestication often commences in the "domestic" sphere.

Michelle Payne offers a brave—particularly in a system that devalues any writing that could be deemed "confessional"—account of her personal history in which she learned to doubt her own authority: "Very early in life I was convinced that I was as gullible, naïve, irrational and emotional as my father and younger brother said. Whenever I had an opinion about something, they would argue with me, sometimes through intimidation, always to the point of me getting 'emotional'" (1994, 104). As Payne contends, it is often difficult for a female teacher to understand herself as an authority, in the first place, let alone transform herself into the kind of authority required by critical discourses.

Of course, as Linda Brodkey and Michelle Fine point out, we are most "attracted to discourses that promise to represent us to ourselves and others as empowered" (1996, 118). In the discourse of a Penn Harassment Survey they studied, they found that women tended to deny their experiences, typically offering narrative accounts attempted to "rise above" the scene of the harassment— and to rise above their embodied selves. Brodkey and Fine conclude that the new generation of women "is equipped with a striking sense of entitlement and yet beset by fears that their female bodies are liabilities [and] their minds are male" (128). So long as their bodies, and their experiences as embodied subjects, are cast aside or hidden, they will be granted authority.

Acting as a liberatory authority often involves a knowledge of when to "fade" from the foreground to the background, when to, as Ira Shor names it, "wither away." But female subjects have already learned to render themselves invisible; how does one give up authority she has never felt in the first place? As Lil Brannon argues, the male critical teacher maintains his privilege through a "double-move": he resists the image of the all-knowing, distant, authoritative figure but paradoxically gains power by becoming the "star"— the heroic, emancipatory teacher (1993, 460). Even when he "withers away," his authority is taken for granted. Female teachers, in contrast are often read first and foremost as caretakers, nurturers—not intellectuals or authorities. "Withering away" may be read as a "natural" behavior; the female teacher is not "able" to take center stage. Moreover, occupying a more assertive stance of imparting critical knowledge might easily be read as outlaw behavior. Payne reminds us that "a female teacher's authority . . . is tenuous no matter which pedagogy she embraces" (1994, 109).

Espousing "critical" knowledge is risky not just inside the classroom but outside as well. Despite the lip service granted in many contemporary universities to multiculturalism and diversity, the daily practices of most institutions are far behind the ideals espoused, and feminist and critical knowledge—especially spoken too loudly or in the wrong places—is still regarded as dangerous. As Luke writes:

> the very gendered divisions of power and authority that enable and deny
> female academic mobility still tend to render a feminist language of critique
> politically counterproductive for women, who still continue overwhelmingly
> to depend upon men for sanctioning of research topics, allocation of research
> funds, decreeing what knowledge counts as relevant and citeable, for thesis
> examination, degree granting, promotion, and tenure. (1992, 38)

Critical pedagogy scholarship does not tell the stories, or address the complexities, of women who put themselves at professional risk by seeking the role of "emancipatory" authority. Indeed, although critical pedagogy may (claim to) offer female teachers an alternative to a subject position defined by service, teachers who seek to enact critical pedagogy often find themselves in the precarious position of serving the vision of the (male) critical pedagogy theorist on the one hand and the (male) institution in which they work on the other. In either case, the female teacher is required to serve a vision that at best excludes and at worst works against her.

In addition to highlighting the institutional contexts of their work, feminist rhetors also question what and who is excluded in the name of emancipatory authority. Because the emancipatory authority is one who has mastered the "right" knowledge and makes the correct moral decisions, this category severs from it knowledge and subjects who experience uncertainty, who are in progress, indeed, who are embodied. To be sure, critical pedagogy scholars do call for recognition of embodied subjectivities, of what McLaren calls "refleshment": critical pedagogy needs to "counter the tendency of some critics of modernity to dissolve agency, claiming that we are always already produced and finalized as subjects within discourse" (1988, 66). This means recognizing modes of resistant subjectivity, so that as we "reveal" to students how they are inscribed by conflicting social relations, we do not reduce individuals to the "static outcomes of social determinations" (66).

Forgoing attention to what it means to enact "refleshment" in local sites, McLaren goes on to articulate what this pedagogy of refleshment must *not* be. It must not, he argues, enact a "flabby pluralism," which "constitutes a simple acceptance of the existence of a variety of perspectives and paradigms; a pluralism which regards different perspectives as virtually incommensurable; and the 'decentered anarchistic pluralism' which celebrates uncertainty or lapses into a brooding and nihilistic retreat from life" (1988, 71). I am struck here by his use of the signifier "flabby," which he links to uncertainty, brooding, lack of authority. Even in this article striving to legitimate embodied knowledge—flesh (or flab—excess flesh) has been linked to devalued ways of knowing, feminine ways of knowing. We want, according to McLaren, to eliminate that which is soft, excessive, feminine from our pedagogies, since it leads only to paralysis.

Feminist rhetors challenge this notion, embracing bodies, knowledges, and moments that have been deemed "excess" in our classrooms. One particularly effective interruption is found in Mimi Orner, Janet Miller, and Elizabeth Ellsworth's "Excessive Moments and Educational Discourses that Try to Contain Them" (1995), in which they examine the "excess"—moments or knowledges typically repressed in classrooms and scholarship—to discover how attention to the repressed might inform and transform their work.

In and beyond Orner, Miller, and Ellsworth's piece, feminist rhetors have invited excess into their scholarship, insisting that, as McWilliam writes, "identity formation is the social production of a desiring body that matters, not a troublesome excess baggage in pedagogical work" (1997, 224). That is to say, feminist rhetors challenge the rational, logical, masculinist norms of critical pedagogy by reappropriating those characteristics typically associated with the "feminine"—bodies, emotion, desire—as legitimate aspects of pedagogical work (see Orner; Worsham (1998); McWilliam). As I argue elsewhere, this requires that we embrace and listen to "messiness"; the clashing of our multiple social locations; the sting of our complicity in the oppressions we teach against; the frustration and relief of accepting that the results of our teaching may not be immediate or clear. Embracing excess means acknowledging that our pedagogies will be interrupted by the tension we feel in our stomachs or the tightness that rises in our throats, by the weight of student silence, by the undoing of what we thought we knew. As Joy Ritchie writes of her feminist rhetoric class, "we need to have freedom to speculate, to be tentative, to be inarticulate. But we also need to be conscious of our rhetoric—how we speak, how much we speak, who has not spoken, and who is silenced" (Ritchie and Ronald 1998, 235). It is this combination of "messiness" and of self-reflexivity that can lead us to a new conception of feminist authority, that can open space for new pedagogical possibilities.

The grotesque body is open, protruding, irregular, secreting, multiple, and changing; it is identified with non-official "low culture" or the carnivalesque, and with social transformation. (Russo 1997)

I questioned my choice to make bodies visible, public in our classroom. But bodies are a public issue, I reminded myself. They're everywhere; Botox ads are now a part of mainstream advertising; Victoria's Secret models sell lingerie and the ideal body during prime-time TV; Britney Spears and Christina Aguilara bare their flesh to prove their legitimacy as adult singers. And yet, the body remains deeply private, deeply privatized, in our educational institutions. As much as I wanted to support McLaren's idea of "refleshment," I could not conceive of a way to do so without making those whose bodies are already marked as visible, as devalued, as different, even more visible.

I thought about my own protruding, irregular, pregnant body in my classroom the year before, how I wanted to separate myself from it, to shed it. Now, a white woman, no longer pregnant, smaller, more invisible, I could once again position myself as the disembodied facilitator. We could discuss these issues without evoking my own discomfort, without my own body's coming (so much) into view.

Mary kept her head down in class the next day. When it came time to workshop, she turned her piece over to me and asked that it not be made public. She wrote it as a diary entry and shared that class on Tuesday had made her feel awful. She wasn't sure why; she had heard these comments countless times before. It made her wonder if she had "anything to contribute"—she who shared earlier that her goal was to write a book someday. She blamed herself for not speaking back to those views she disagreed with, for not representing the experience of a "fat person."

As the other students workshopped their papers, she retreated to the private sphere of the bathroom. I followed her. We stayed there, talking, for fifteen minutes. I shared how angry it makes me that so many women—of all shapes and sizes—are hurt by these ideals. This is why I want to make those ideals visible, expose them for their falseness, for their dangerous ways. I told her how valuable her insights are to our class; I apologized for the topic, since it seemed to have silenced her. No, she said, she was excited about discussing these issues, but when discussion began, she couldn't open her mouth.

"Maybe it's time for me to do something," she said.

"What do you mean?" I hoped her answer would not be culture's answer: make yourself smaller; deny your body food, deny your flesh.

"Maybe I need to speak back," she said.

I told her that she could use any of her future assignments to do that work. And I offered to throw out the rest of the "Figuring the Body" readings. My loyalty was to her, not to a critical agenda.

And anyway, more "critical" work happened in the bathroom that day than happened all semester. Critical, at least, to Mary and me.

Toward an Interruptive Subjectivity

> . . . it is the gaps and ruptures in practice—the breaks, confusions and con-
> tradictions that are always a part of the interplay in teaching—that offer the
> greatest insight and possibilities for change. (Orner 1992)

The feminist interruption is not a mere disruption, an opposition, or challenge;
it is rather an opening that allows for reflection on critical pedagogy's ideal
subject(s) as well as room for new subjects to enter the dialogue. Critical pedagogy rhetorics insist that teachers become public intellectuals, bearers of
critical knowledge, and emancipatory authorities; they don't, however, attend
to the social, institutional, and affective barriers that particular teachers
encounter as they seek to assume these "critical" identities. Rather than reject-
ing entirely these social locations—which certainly offer a positive shift away
from the nurse/maid subjectivity—feminist rhetors rewrite them as always in
process, always requiring negotiation, always informed by the complex social
contexts. In so doing, they make visible the masculinist assumptions and values implicit within these critical ideals.

By promoting the public intellectual without accounting for or challenging the ways women have historically been excluded from public roles, critical rhetorics only perpetuate this exclusion. Showing the ways women struggle to serve as public figures, even as they are often read as representatives of
the "private" helps make visible the work that remains if we hope to alter not
only our conception of the teacher as service figure but the public sphere in
which she works. As I demonstrate in my narrative, the moment where my
desire to act as a public intellectual and my pregnant body collided illuminated the revision still required if female teachers are to assume the role of
public intellectuals. It was not a moment of "failure" but a moment when subjugated histories and experiences needed examination.

Similarly, whereas critical pedagogy rhetorics express a certainty that
acquisition of "critical knowledge" means teachers will engage in the right
practices that will best serve their students, feminist rhetors interrupt to show
how our critical agendas can actually work against our critical projects and
our students. When Mary seemed silenced by our discussion of bodies, I could
not simply believe that I was doing the right thing—that disseminating my
critical knowledge was more important than her experience of my pedagogy.
Her interruptive silence, and my uncertainty that accompanied it, did not lead
to apathy or deferment of the project; rather, it reminded me that critical pedagogy must be worked out in the local space of our classroom, with—not
apart from—my students and their needs.

And finally, although critical pedagogy rhetorics require us to position ourselves as emancipatory authorities, feminist interruptions remind us that our
abilities both to emancipate and to act as authorities need to be reconsidered,
always in the institutional contexts in which we work. In the end, I couldn't

give Mary critical knowledge or empowerment. I could work out of my partial knowledge only to help her reflect on how culture has shaped her, and how she could use her words to write back. And at the same time, Mary could help me think about how to use my pedagogy to write back (to dominant ideologies and to critical pedagogy rhetorics), to create a classroom that better enables students like her.

Ultimately, feminist rhetors remind us that moments of "excess"—uncertainty, anger, frustration—will necessarily seep into our pedagogical work. But rather than dissecting or ignoring these moments—or worse, assuming that they render us unable to participate in critical projects—feminist rhetors remind us that we can and should embrace them as possibilities to bring in alternative knowledge, to revise our own classrooms and the project of critical pedagogy, and to make the role of critical teacher more hospitable to new subjects.

9

Taking Sides

Nancy Welch

Philosophers have only interpreted the world in various ways.
The point, however, is to change it.

—Marx 1845/1941

Christ is dead, Marx is dead, and myself, I don't feel so good.

—Graffiti on a wall, Paris,
May 1968

We are afraid to appear ridiculous, and this may kill us.

—Slogan from the
French Women's Movement

Going to Activism School

At a recent meeting of the Feminist Research Network, just before the start of
the Conference on College Composition and Communication, Susan Miller
remarked that lately she'd been thinking she shouldn't send her students to
graduate school; she should send them to activism school instead. I don't
know what prompted her remark. At that moment—late in the day as the room
grew warm and the lively discussion about feminist rhetoric had lulled—I was
in a kind of haze. Was Miller arguing for a new breed of rhetorician—rhetor-
anarchist-activists whose voices are trained for the next Seattle? Was she echoing Marx's famous assertion that we must do more than fight phrases with
phrases? Or was this less a call to the streets and more an expression of late-
day, late-capitalist, preconference weariness? I can't say; I wasn't following
the discussion closely enough. What I can say, though, is that her words
startled me into attention, stayed with me through that conference, and through

the whole of the year that followed—a year I think of as having been spent in activism school.

Some necessary background: It's only recently that I've defined myself as a rhetorician at all. Though I was mentored by remarkable women (two of whom are editing this collection) who view rhetoric as central to our enterprise, my studies immersed me in writing as a practice of inquiry, a practice I associated much more with (feminized) composition than with (masculinist) rhetoric. The humble appellation of compositionist seemed better matched to my proletarian credentials—vocational high school, secretarial school; later, a degree from an urban, open-admissions university, a doctorate from a large Midwestern land-grant institution. Since my first try at college was a nighttime basic writing class, I've pointed to composition as the link between who I was and who I have become. Yet, paradoxically, it's likely that I've preferred composition over rhetoric not for its attachment to workaday scenes and on-the-ground struggles but instead (in classrooms that promote inquiry and downplay argument) for its distance. A one-step distance from daily arguments and daily demands is what that first college class—Monday and Wednesday nights at Boston's YMCA on Huntington Avenue—offered me. There, after a day of typing other people's words, I found space and encouragement for my own.

Elsewhere I've described such writing classrooms as "critical exile" and "potential spaces" where students can "sideshadow" the dominant narratives that compose their lives (see Welch 1997; 1998; 1999). At the same time, I've been careful to note my critical distance from the assumptions of the solitary artist's garret. Here, though, I'll admit that there has been something of the garret in my thinking and in my teaching—understandably, I think, since if you've never had a garret and have been told that you are not cut out for one, it can seem like a very precious thing. The university seemed to me to be one big, beautiful garret. It was a place where I did not have to wear pantyhose and no one would ever say to me, "Nancy, get your [steno] book. Nancy, take a letter." It was (when I shut my eyes to who emptied my wastebasket each night and who taught composition side by side with me) a realm removed from the major sources of antagonism in my life: bosses, bills, layoffs. I can remember explaining to my father, pink-slipped by a company he'd been with for more than twenty years, the concept of tenure:

"You mean they can't fire you?" he asked.
"Well, there're some technicalities, but no, they can't fire me."

At that he nodded and said nothing. A job for life—how could you argue with that?

It's difficult to unpack all the reasons why I've started to ponder what my relationship to argument might necessarily be.[1] Such a summary would have to include events in my workplace (health-care benefit cuts, a faculty downsizing program) and events countrywide (the repeal of welfare, a hijacked election).

Such a summary would need to include the problems I faced when I sought forums for action (an anarchist network whose insistence on consensus resulted in a group both homogenous and small) and scattered, surprising victories (collective bargaining rights for the University of Vermont faculty). Such a summary should also include my husband (with whom I learned the rhetorical pitfalls of arguing with managed-care bureaucrats) and my students (those in my literacy politics course who asked that future classes focus more on public intervention; my advanced nonfiction writing students who say they're afraid of sounding "pushy" and "like a know-it-all" yet love Jamaica Kincaid and June Jordan for the forthrightness and bite of their words). Such a summary would need to acknowledge all the ways in which I do not have, and no longer desire, the luxury of distance from the world.

In an essay that aims to mediate between the crudely constructed poles of rhetoric as inquiry, a Platonic search in common for truth, and rhetoric as confrontation, the clash of competing perspectives, Dennis Lynch, Diana George, and Marilyn Cooper trace through the twentieth century a "general effort to expand rhetoric's horizons" (1997, 62). Over the past year, that's what I've sought to do—expand my understanding and practice of rhetoric. Through antiwar organizing in diverse coalitions of union rank-and-filers and university students, religious pacifists and lifestyle anarchists, revolutionary socialists (my own orientation), and wary ex-Marxist-Leninists, I've learned something of what it means to link arms with others in a common fight while arguing out the differences among us. I've learned to run the risk of raising a slogan—something I've particularly shied away from since 1991 when, at the start of the first Gulf War, I marched under the deadly slogan "Sanctions, Not Bombs." I've thought a lot about the means of persuasion within fledgling coalitions, and I've come to believe there is something at stake in winning particular arguments, such as the argument that our local antiwar coalition not insist on pacifism (and hence opposition to the Palestinian intifada) as a point of unity to which all must adhere. Whereas the dominant trend in twentieth-century rhetorical studies, as described by Lynch, George, and Cooper and as experienced in my own late-twentieth-century education, tended away from confrontation and toward the ideal of mediation, my recent efforts to expand my studies have been in an opposite direction. Schooled in that rhetoric of inquiry, I'm now trying to learn more, much more, about taking a side.

Yet I'm doing so, I also realize, at a moment when it's considered regressive for a feminist and an academic leftist to profess a desire to argue at all. Notwithstanding individual voices in the field[2] who argue for a return to what Andrea Greenbaum calls the "muscularity of argumentative discourse" (2001, 154), agonistic rhetoric, so stubbornly gendered as muscular and male, is routinely dismissed both in the specialized field of rhetoric and in the mainstream discourse of liberals, progressives, and (chastened) radicals. Such rhetoric is doubly disdained as antithetical to a properly feminist stance and as an encumbrance to an appropriately postmodern position that, as Diane Davis puts it, shares with Tomas in *The Unbearable Lightness of Being* the belief that "missions are stupid" (Kundera 1984, 313; qtd. in Davis 2000, 164). How did we reach this place where to argue a position, and particularly a position explicitly linked to current events and material consequences, is to be charged with a lack of sophistication and appropriate politics? How did we come to a place where Miller's counsel that students consider "activism school" is heard as reactionary, not vanguard, advice?

I have to say that much of my own teaching, particularly through revision exercises with names like "Unending the Ending," is likewise about opening up sealed-tight conclusions and unpacking assertions. With Arundhati Roy, whose essays from the global economic justice movement have served as my guide, "I'm all for . . . tentativeness, subtlety, ambiguity, complexity. I love the unanswered question, the unresolved story . . . the tender shard of an incomplete dream. *Most of the time*" (2001, 11; my emphasis). Most of the time I relish messy, contradictory ethnographic detail that has the power to unseat this or that general principle. So do my students who are particularly drawn to the open-ended and receptive form of the collage. But I've also observed that my students are reluctant to come to conclusions, and that when they do, they are quick—sometimes too quick—to concede that an opposite conclusion might also be true. They appear to be in agreement with Gary Olson's (oddly assertive) argument that we repudiate "thesis-flexing rhetoric" and pursue instead a "more dialogic, dynamic, open-ended, receptive, non-assertive stance" (1999, 14). But at what cost?

To get at these questions, I'll examine two strands in feminist rhetoric that have shaped the ambivalence about argument I've encountered in the classroom and in activist organizations. Though these two strands—the maternalist, which associates women biologically or socially with peacemaking, and the postmodern or "third sophistic," which eschews any solid ground on which to stake a claim—appear worlds apart, they share a deep distrust of fixed positions and first principles that is born from the problems of participating in social movements. Before I examine the shared tenets and history of these rhetorics, I want to sketch the context in which I'm ultimately taking issue with both. It's a context that has changed and charged my teaching, bringing me to the urgent belief that we musn't repudiate assertion, musn't relinquish our willingness to take a stand.

Cool Colonialism and the Diffident Left

On my desk is a CD featuring a new game for Macintosh users called "Tropico." In "Tropico," the CD's jacket explains, "you take a trip to a third world island AND RULE!" Promising "pure, dictatorial fun," the jacket depicts a verdant island, its beach densely dotted with church and houses in sumptuous colonial style. A jet hovers overhead while cruising out of the lagoon is a large yacht, or battleship, it's hard to tell. When my husband first dropped this CD in my lap, I was watching TV. In one part of the world, U.S. war planes shelled a country already decimated by two decades of war; in another, teams of fit, athletic Americans competed to cross deserts, climb mountains, and claim a million-dollar prize. Though it is unfashionable among academics to speak of imperialism except with a wry tone and arched brow—"We have to stop it with all this knee-jerk talk of imperialism," one cultural studies scholar told me, "or else no one will take us seriously"—I can't think of any other word that fits.

Apparently, neither can the *Wall Street Journal* and the *New York Times,* which have been running features and columns trumpeting the virtue of U.S. rule over unruly nations that also happen to be resource rich. Just to provide a small sampling:

- In "The Answer to Terrorism? Colonialism," the *Wall Street Journal*'s Paul Johnson argues for a return to the "'respectable' form of colonialism" that once held Iraq, Syria, Sudan, Iran, and Libya under "special regimes" (2001).

- In "How to Keep Afghanistan from Falling Apart: The Case for a Committed American Imperialism," featured in the *New York Times Magazine,* Michael Ignatieff calls the war on terrorism "an exercise in imperialism" (2002, 28). He then chastises the administration of George W. Bush for not pouring *enough* money into the imperialist project: "[E]mpires don't come lite. They come heavy, or they do not last" (26).

- In an issue of Harvard's alumni magazine, Stephen Peter Rosen details with breathtaking frankness how contemporary "imperial wars" must be waged through the use of "unconventional weapons" and a "maximum amount of force . . . for psychological impact to demonstrate the empire cannot be challenged with impunity" (2002, 31).

Here and elsewhere, if there is mention of Vietnam, it's as a "syndrome" from which the United States has, thankfully, recovered.

While imperialism is enjoying such a renaissance some of the Left's most influential voices dismiss the word as the shabby remnant of a bygone era. "Imperialism is over," argue Michael Hardt and Antonio Negri in *Empire* (2000, ix), which, ignoring the concentration of wealth and might that has been the hallmark of the "New World Order," celebrates the (largely mythic) potential for global capitalism to erase borders, hybridize identities, and diminish state power. As the United States wrapped up its bombing of Afghanistan and turned toward "regime change" in Iraq, psychoanalytic theorist Slavoj Žižek told students on my campus to forget the slogan of the May 1968 general strikes in France: "Be realistic! Demand the impossible!" The efficacy of oppositional politics, he argued, crumbled with the Berlin Wall. He did not consider that most of the audience had not heard the news of the student–worker. alliance that virtually shut down France nor of the student–worker campaign that twenty years later helped bring down South African apartheid.

Several prominent academic and activist feminists have likewise joined in disdaining "recycled" '60s radicalism, advocating a politics of opportunity rather than opposition. ATTAC's Susan George wrote of the post–September 11, 2001, climate as one that's brought a restored belief in government, creating the chance for a "new, updated global Keynesian strategy" (2001b, 2), while Ellen Willis approved of the use of U.S. troops to "defeat patriarchal culture" in Central Asia (2001). The anarchist activist and poet Starhawk called on George W. Bush to employ "the carrot as well as a stick" (2001, 7), never mind that forms of the carrot, such as IMF policies aimed at privatizing public services and resources while lining the pockets of a few, are what she, Susan George, and others had dedicated themselves to protesting. Thus the vacuum that's created when phrases like *imperialist war* and *oil pipeline* are evacuated is refilled with—what else can we call the notion that the antichoice, anti–affirmative action, antiwelfare Bush can be the liberator of women?—confusion.

Confusion is what I too felt, deeply, when a student recounted trying to speak up in a class against the U.S. bombing of Afghanistan. When the professor challenged her to say why, she fell mute while a classmate hissed, "Fucking stupid peacenik." This is a student who, in two writing classes plus an independent study with me, had reveled in inquiry, using her writing to pry open ruling arguments and probe the corners of experience. But when called on to defend a tentatively held belief in a hostile setting, she could not; her rhetorical education had not prepared her even to imagine arguing in the face of such express opposition.

I don't want to paint too grim a picture, since I have, in this same period, encountered voices of passionate opposition and incisive critique: Colleen Kelly of September 11 Families for Peaceful Tomorrows, who speaks against the use of her brother's death in the World Trade Center as a pretext for more killing; the University of North Carolina Chapel Hill's Progressive Faculty network, whose forum on Christian and Zionist, as well as Islamic, fundamentalisms challenge the ability of a Bush and an Ashcroft to defend women anywhere; Arundhati Roy and Barbara Kingsolver, whose email-circulated essays lay out in clear, accessible terms the corporate oil interests driving U.S. policy and also insist on globalizing expressions of grief and fear; the nearly 100,000 people—many of them Arab and Muslim—who, despite real threats of detainment and deportation under the U.S.A. Patriot Act, turned out in April 2002 for the largest Palestinian rights rally held in the United States. These examples of arguments advanced in the most difficult, painful of circumstances are ones I've urged my students to seek out.

Yet—as North Carolina's Progressive Faculty network found when their antiwar teach-ins were denounced by right-wing pundits Rush Limbaugh and David Horowitz and as members of Berkeley's Students for Justice in Palestine also discovered when they were met with academic sanctions and criminal charges for a nonviolent protest in the birthplace of the campus free speech movement—those who have engaged in protest have faced reprisals while receiving equivocal support from the traditional defenders of academic freedom. The American Association of University Professors recently sent out a flyer that sits now on my desk next to my copy of "Tropico." "It's unfortunate," the flyer warns, "but highly respected professors and researchers, who have a right to academic freedom, face legal action each time they stand before a class, present research or publish work." The flyer continues not with a call to collective action or even to a conference; instead, it offers academics a chance to purchase professional liability insurance.

It's in the hope of finding an alternative to such embarrassed diffidence, mistaken opportunism, and embattled silence that I've turned to feminist rhetorical theory. What I've found, however, is much of the same wariness of positions and principles that marked Žižek's antiactivism speech on my campus, much of the same fear of appearing ridiculous that prompted the cultural studies scholar to warn, "No one will take us seriously." I've also found something else—let's call it a shared problem with history—that has helped me to see how we can claim what's been invaluable in feminist rhetorical practices *plus* intervene in this pervasive reluctance to have anything to do with (knee-jerk, unsophisticated, sloganeering) rhetoric at all.

Contemporary Feminist Rhetorics: Between the Failed Revolution and the Shabby Deal

At a Washington, DC, rally for Palestinian rights, held in late April 2002 just days after the Israeli Defense Forces had bulldozed Jenin and other West Bank refugee camps, a woman with a long commitment to joining peace activism with feminism said to me, "Why do all the signs have to be so negative?"

The signs she pointed to were carried overwhelmingly by Arab women and men, many accompanied by young children and pushing strollers. "End the Occupation," "Stop the Genocide," the signs said. I tried to explain why I saw these signs as positive. Just imagine the worldwide sigh of relief if the United States would just let up. Or imagine how different a place northern Vermont would be for many women if people publicly proclaimed "Don't" and "Stop"—emphatic, resolute—to rape, domestic abuse, and the punishing dictates of welfare reform. The woman shook her head: "There's too much arguing here," she replied.

For many of the women I work with, political activism is defined by both pacifism and a strand of feminism associated with maternalism—the equation of women with mothering and what's understood as the related task of peacemaking. Sabina Lovibond, in a critical assessment, cites the work of developmental psychologist Carol Gilligan as a foundational figure in a politics rooted in maternalism. Intervening in the models of cognitive and moral development put forth by Jean Piaget, Lawrence Kohlberg, and William G. Perry, Gilligan urged a *"sensitivity to morally significant detail"* (a sensitivity defined as feminine) to counter "a legalistic reliance on abstract principle" (a reliance considered distinctly masculine) (Lovibond 1994, 780; Lovibond's emphasis). Working from this opening is Sara Ruddick who argues in *Maternal Thinking* against allowing "rule-dominated 'fairness'" to "override care and sympathy" (1989, 96) and who highlights "maternal practice" as a "'natural resource' for peace politics" (154), since caretaking trains one to value above all the preservation of human life.

Of course, the equation of women with peacemaking predates Ruddick and Gilligan. Participants in the Women's Strike for Peace in the United States in the early 1960s highlighted their identities as mothers and defenders of the family in arguing against nuclear proliferation (Tickner 2001, 58). Local activists I've spoken with point to the Women's Peace Camp at England's Greenham Common in the early 1980s and similar peace camps that popped up amid antinuclear campaigns in Vermont as exemplary of political action nurtured by women's capacity to create life. It was also at this time, according to local activist lore, that consensus-based affinity groups became the prime means for organizing. Abhorring argument as both masculinist and militaristic, individuals were to assemble according to affinity for one another. Predisposed to agree, affinity group members would have no need for argument.

Yet, such an idealization of community and consensus can have, as numerous compositionists have explored (see, for starters, Trimbur; Leverenz; Harris; Wells (1996)), the profoundly conservative effects of deflecting debate and ultimately dividing people according to strict identity markers. In addition, political conservatives such as Francis Fukuyama, champion of neoliberal globalization, have readily latched onto the equation of women with peace, asserting that in an aggressive and dangerous world, women must be barred—protected from—the political arena (Tickner 2001, 60). In rhetorical studies, too, the advancement of a tie between men and aggression and women and receptivity—elaborated in the last decade by Elizabeth Flynn, Catherine Lamb, Olivia Frye, and Jane Tompkins—has had the unintended effect of making women scholars vulnerable to a conservative backlash. For example, Robert Connors, in response to Gesa Kirsch's excruciatingly controlled critique of his "Teaching and Learning as a Man," sets up Kirsch as a "discipline and punish" dominatrix (1996a, 971). Similarly, G. Douglas Atkins dismisses Cynthia Selfe's sharp (and smart) response to his "On Writing Well" as nothing more than "personal anger" arising from "envy" for her lack of "a good pen" with which a "Freudian might have a field day" (2000a, 418, 421–22). It's not only Fukuyama who uses the equation of women with the soft strokes of nurture to ban them from public voice and participation.

There's one further difficulty I've encountered with maternalist rhetoric, and especially its founding disavowal of abstract principles and conceptual unities, that I can get at best through an anecdote. Recently, participants at a gathering of women union activists swapped stories of their families' experiences with labor struggles. Looking around the table, dropping her voice, one woman said, "Well, maybe I can tell this story in this group, though I don't think I could tell it anywhere else in this state." She then launched into a tale that involved a grandmother, a shotgun, and a (soon-to-be-dead) scab. In this tale, with all its (to recall Gilligan) significant detail, was a direct challenge to the myths that women are predisposed to peace and that peacemaking is always preferable to confrontation. The catch is that adherents to maternalist feminism would have difficulty hearing this challenge, at odds as it is not only with the foundational belief about women's peacefulness but also with the foundational belief that they do not operate from any foundation, any abstract principles, at all. The other women around the table gasped, cheered, and launched into their own family stories of women's fightback—careful, however, to preface each tale with "I wouldn't tell this story anywhere else."

In contrast to such careful containment, practitioners of third-sophistic feminist rhetoric would not treat the detail of the picket-line-defending grandmother as a bit of staticky noise that must be filtered out so that the clear message of women's pacifism can sound. "[T]hird sophistic ears," writes Diane Davis (who indebts her work to rhetorician Victor Vitanza, postmodern philosophers such as Jean-François Lyotard, and gender theorist Judith Butler), "are posthermeneutic *noise freaks*" (2001, 130; Davis' emphasis). Calling for a "rhetoric of exposition" that treats a thesis as a point of "naked vulnerability," third-sophistic rhetoricians argue for discursive practices that expose foundational principles, even those that allow women to gather under the (shaky) sign of feminism, to "various encounters, interruptions, contradictions" (Davis 2001, 141). Here is the promise of a stance that would open up earlier claims about feminism, women, and peacemaking to debate, introducing, as Judith Butler puts it, a "moment of political hesitation" (1997, 5).

Too frequently, however, this moment of hesitation tends toward a *permanent* indecision and disinvolvement with third-sophistic rhetoricians, joining Gary Olson in calling for a rhetoric of nonassertion (e.g., Davis 2001, 141) and claiming a feminism that is a "way of being" unfettered by any oppositional agenda (Ballif, Davis, and Mountford 2000, 938). Echoing Žižek's appeal for "critical distance toward every reigning Master-Signifier" (1993, 2), Davis champions an "all-out attack on metanarratives" as "an attack on the politics of horror that has led us around by the nose since way before the Third Reich and has not let go of us since" (2000, 104). Here, third-sophistic rhetoric joins maternalist rhetoric both in a proclaimed distrust of all platforms and principles and in a failure to recognize its own excision of potentially challenging historical detail. For example, although much of the story of the twentieth century can be written under the heading "the politics of horror," we need also to account for the persistent politics of hope: the 1917 International Women's Day revolt against Russian czarism; the Warsaw Ghetto uprising against the Nazis; the opposition at home and within army ranks that turned the tide against the U.S. war in Vietnam; the recent fights in Bolivia against water privatization. Just as maternalist rhetoric might turn us away from such moments with the judgment "too much arguing here," third-sophistic rhetoric would dismiss such disruptions through its foundational story that "missions are stupid."

For both strands of feminist rhetoric, I think, this distrust of programs and assertions, including (for third-sophistic rhetoric especially) those linked to emancipatory desires, arises not so much from the work of academics such as Gilligan as from a disillusioning experience shared by many women involved in the New Left movements of the 1960s and early 1970s. Sheila Rowbotham, for example, describes in that period the internecine warfare among a variety of small, competing Marxist-Leninist (read: Stalinist) groups: "They prefaced every statement with 'The correct Marxist position is'" which one was to learn "by rote from pamphlets and articles" (1973, 18; 19). It's in the problems, particularly with sexist chauvinism, that women experienced within such groups (see also Eschle 2001, especially 94–95) that we can locate both the move toward feminist separatism that marks maternalist rhetoric and the disillusionment with organization and activism that marks the third sophistics. That disillusionment—which intensified as many Left activists clung to the unsustainable belief that the totalitarian regimes of the Soviet Union, Cuba, or China represented socialism and not another version of (state) capitalism—continues to be expressed in postmodern denouncements of "oppositional logic and rude calculation" (Ronell 1994, 297) as well as in postmodern celebrations of our release from Cold War binaries. In an exuberant reading of Žižek's poetic account of the fall of Romanian communism, for example, Davis writes, "We are interested here in that postmodern moment, after the deterritorialization (no 'community') but before reterritorialization (new 'community'), when, in the flux of exploded identities, in the excess before re-distinction, the multiplicitous, splintered subject attempts to respond to her/his non- or rather poly-foundational multiverse" (Davis 2000, 46).

Unexpected openings and multiplications of possibility are indeed worth theorizing, pursuing, and celebrating, but a period of radical flux *does not at all* describe the historical moment in which we live. The opening created by the collapse of communism across Eastern Europe has quickly been filled by the United States as the current unrivaled economic and political superpower, so that what we now witness is the consolidation, not diffusion, of global capital and an escalation, not easing, of a genocidal politics of horror. (Recall Stephen Peter Rosen's writing *calmly* in the pages of *Harvard Magazine* about the need for the United States to be ready to deploy "unconventional weapons" and "maximum amount of force" to trounce all challenges to its global "empire" (2002, 31).) Even as former activists languish between what Arundhati Roy calls "the failed revolution and the shabby deal" (2001, 32), and even as postmodernists attempt to salvage reason to rejoice in theoretical absence and semantic instability, the Right revels in its narrative of real resurgence.

Or maybe it would be more accurate, and much less despairing, to say that with the apparent triumph of free-market capitalism backed by U.S. military supremacy (news of the death of the state proving to be premature), there have emerged in binary opposition two new sides in intense struggle: (1) the champions of neoliberal globalization who claim that "transnational companies are bringing the promise of a better life with increased security and prosperity" (summarized in Tickner 2001, 70) and (2) its ardent discontents, from the Teamsters and "turtles" (students) who joined for the historic battle in Seattle to the masses of unemployed and underemployed Argentine workers who rose up against IMF austerity measures, toppling a rapid succession of governments in 2001–2002. Such struggle marks the persistence of emancipatory projects that did not die with the fall of the Paris Commune, the rise of the Third Reich, the reversals of victories hard-won by labor, civil rights, and women's rights activists. They are struggles that, instead of being dismissed as alarmingly aggressive or hopelessly naive, should claim the attention of rhetoricians who understand that we do not have, and should not desire, the luxury of distance from this world.

Lessons from Activism School

This critique of maternalist and third-sophistic rhetoric nothwithstanding, I do find within both of these feminist rhetorical positions much that could aid me and others as we continue through "activism school." From maternalist rhetoric, *if* I can undo the gendered assignments of argument and receptivity, I take clues as to how one can make arguments, within a commitment to continuing relationship, that are necessary to sustain diverse coalitions in the midst of difficult debates. From third-sophistic rhetoric, *if* I can push past its fears of involvement with contextual demands for "rude calculation," I see the means for resisting too quick of a settlement on problematic arguments. Imagine, for instance, that activists in 1990 had taken the slogan "Sanctions, Not Bombs" as a "naked point of vulnerability" and claimed a "moment of political hesitation" so that we could inquire into the future consequences of such an assertion. *If* the insights of third-sophistic rhetoric can be relocated within a *dialectic* between the twin responsibilities of assertion and exposition, it offers powerful tools indeed.

But to claim these lessons we need to reorient both strands of feminist rhetoric toward what I believe is the fundamental question at hand: What are the full range of rhetorical practices and analytic insights we need to fight women's oppression? A full analysis and recognition of the need for inquiry beyond cultural representations is what Susan George, like many prominent feminists and global economic justice activists in the midst of the U.S. war against Afghanistan, fell short of when she announced that the glossy media images of burka-less Afghan women had led her to "rethink" her position against the U.S. war (2001a). A full range of rhetorical practices is what I failed to offer the student who, despite three semesters of work in composition and rhetoric, could not find a sentence to support her feeling that this war was wrong. We fall short of teaching the full problems and responsibilities, all that's needed to go up against systems of oppression, when we remove the tension between exposition *and* assertion, inquiry *and* argument, unsettling *and* concluding.

This isn't to say, however, that I agree with Andrea Greenbaum's contention in "Bitch Pedagogy" that we must introduce women students especially to the "robust character of what has traditionally been considered masculine discourse" to "fortify a woman's ability to succeed in the academy" (2001, 164). Traditional lessons in "strategies of rhetorical combat" (154) focus on the individual rhetor who—in keeping with and serving to perpetuate traditional social/academic structures and rewards—seeks to rise, lead, and succeed *alone*. Such lessons benefit only the small minority of students going on to jobs defined by autonomy and control. In fact—as I realized the other day when the majority of students in my literacy politics class said they expect to go on to service-sector (and, increasingly, union) jobs in education, health care, and social services—most students' futures will depend on what they learn now about collective, not individual, rhetorical strategies. How do we work in relationship with others and build democratic organizations through a valuing of agitation as much as affinity? On what basis can we question top-down expertise and assert the authority of our on-the-ground positions and knowledge? How do we unpack euphemism, get the facts, dissent from a (corporate media-produced) status quo while being mindful of and sensitive to our own and others' vulnerabilities?

Such are the key questions, and for possible answers to these questions, I bring into the classroom rhetors like Arundhati Roy, who lays out in "The Ladies Have Feelings . . . Shall We Leave It to the Experts?" (2001) the tenets of a rhetoric from below and June Jordan whose "Civil Wars" (1989) highlights the fundamental issues—about organization and leadership, spontaneity and planning—faced in any mass social movement. I also turn to examples of fighting rhetorics generated by women and men who speak through shop-floor newsletters (Teamster rank-and-filer Dawn Stanger's *UPS Yours* (n.d.) is one example) and at public rallies. In these places we find not rhetoric from and to policymakers but rhetoric from and to those who feel the daily effects of official policy, a rhetoric my students are largely unfamiliar with or have learned, as Roy puts it in her critique of academic detachment, to disdain as "a crude, simple-minded, one-sided understanding of things" (2001, 23). There *are* problems with activist rhetorics to unpack: the problem that the slogan "Sanctions, Not Bombs" perpetuates warfare in another guise; the problem that a "Hey-Hey/Ho-Ho" chant has become so familiar, it's no longer heard.[3] And language in social use, in social action—precisely what rhetoricians are dedicated to working on—is at the center of these problems.

Language is also at the center of the opposition with which this essay began, between the academy and activism school. That opposition, as Roy points out, would lead us not only to disparage the language of the activist as "crude, simple-minded, [and] one-sided" but also to disparage the language of the academic as lacking the "passion, the grit, the audacity, and, if necessary, the vulgarity to publicly take a political position" (2001, 23–24). But this is an opposition that doesn't hold steady if we look, for example, to the issue of *College Composition and Communication* in which Diane Davis' explication of third-sophistic rhetoric, "Finitude's Clamor," appeared. In that same issue (though segregated in the special section for non-tenure-track faculty) is an article by Mike Evces called "Public Rhetoric for Academic Workers: Tips from the Front Lines." Here Evces offers "rhetorical strategies from the academic labor movement" (2001, A3) including advice for building coalitions with student and labor groups and creating public events with "catchy chants" and presentations such as a "Grade-In" to evaluate a university administration's performance in such areas as health benefits and child care for workers (2001, A3–A5). Between Davis' call for a "rhetoric of exposition" that leads to an "*unsettling* of certitude" (2001, 141; Davis' emphasis) and Evces' examples of concrete provocations by the growing ranks of contingent faculty asserting their rights to more certainty, there is a keen and potentially productive tension. It's a tension I want my graduate students to ponder as they look ahead to their futures as members of the academic labor force, but more, it's a tension I believe that we all, regardless of the (increasingly dubious) privileges of rank, must attend to as we explore our full responsibilities as rhetoricians and as we consider the daily antagonisms (including bosses, bills, layoffs) from which a life in school is no escape. What might such a tension teach us? That activism school is where we need to be.

Notes

1. This isn't to say that until recently my words and actions had never tended toward confrontation. In the late 1970s at the Lorain County (Ohio) Vocational Center, I was suspended twice for fighting and once for throwing a notebook in the direction of a teacher. (I wasn't trying to hit him but to make a point that I thought his grading policy unfair.) Later, when I quit a secretarial job after not receiving a promised raise, I made sure I'd erased every Lotus 1-2-3 file I'd created. Yet, since nothing in my education had introduced me to the concept of collective confrontation and workers' power, I could only conclude from these experiences, which resulted in setbacks rather than gains, that my impulses toward confrontation and sabotage were a problem to be corrected, not to mention an aberration to hide from other feminists.

2. See also Susan Jarratt's "The Case for Conflict," which appeared in 1991 just as the "New World Order," with its low-intensity resource wars fought under the guise of humanitarian intervention, was taking shape.

3. There is also an art to finding the right words for a moment, as a colleague of mine discovered when—shortly after the collapse of Enron and amid increasing local concern about administrative spending and accountability at the University of Vermont—she coined what has turned out to be our faculty union's rallying cry: "Money for the classroom/Not the boardroom."

10

Gender, Rhetorics, and Globalization

Rethinking the Spaces and Locations of Feminist Rhetorics and Women's Rhetorics in Our Field

Eileen E. Schell

In August 1995 labor inspectors from the California Department of Industrial Relations and the U.S. Department of Labor stormed an innocuous-looking apartment complex in El Monte, California, a city near Los Angeles. Labor inspectors were shocked by what they encountered in the confines of the building. Seventy-two Thai workers, most undocumented immigrant women, were laboring there in a garment factory under conditions that rivaled the worst of global sweatshops. Workers sewed garments up to twenty hours a day, seven days a week, at wages of seventy cents an hour. Razor wire, locked gates, physical threats, intimidation, and their undocumented status kept these workers virtually enslaved ("Sweatshops in America").[1] Brought to the United States by promises of a better life and better working conditions, Rojana "Na" Cheunchujit, a Thai woman, now a labor activist, describes the conditions under which she and others were forced to work at El Monte:

> There were over 70 Thai workers at the shop. We worked 20 hours a day for the whole one year and four months I was there—until the day I was liberated. I cooked for myself. We ordered food from the owners, but they charged us really high prices, at least twice the amount.
>
> After paying the $5,000 to get here, they told me that I had to pay an additional $4,800. The said they would keep me as long as it took to pay off the $4,800 debt. It didn't matter to them how long they kept you; no specific amount of time was calculated. . . .
>
> The owners threatened to set the homes of our families on fire if we dared to escape because they knew where all of us were from, about our villages back in Thailand. Some people actually got punished. One person tried to escape, but was unsuccessful; they beat him up pretty badly. They took a

picture of him and showed it to all the other workers, to tell us what would happen if we tried to escape. (qtd. in Louie 2001, 236–37)

After liberation from the sweatshop, El Monte workers like Cheunchujit faced further injustices and trauma. Detained by the Immigration and Naturalization Service (the INS), El Monte workers were told to "go home" by the Thai Consul General. In Cheunchujit's words: "He said it was our fault that we put ourselves in this situation. He said that we were just fighting against a brick wall by staying here, and we were being a burden on the US government!" (qtd. in Louie 2001, 238). In addition, El Monte workers received mixed messages about their status in the United States from INS agents who, purportedly "helping" the workers, kept them from contact with community and labor organizers who were trying to assist them in their efforts to remain in the United States. Also, inaccurate accounts that the El Monte workers had disappeared reached the local Thai newspapers in the U.S. and were carried to Thailand, thus frightening the workers' relatives. Eventually, though, assisted by the Thai Community Development Center (CDC) and the Korean Immigrant Workers' Advocates (KIWA), Cheunchujit and others were released and began to negotiate life outside El Monte. Some, like Cheunchujit, have become activists against labor exploitation, participating in campaigns like the "Retailers Accountability Campaign [initiated by KIWA and Sweatshop Watch]" (Louie 2001, 241). Says Cheunchujit:

> We have picketed, leafleted, and visited different department stores. We try to go into the department store, meet with the management, and educate the consumers to support the boycott for accountability. We get promises from consumers not to shop at the department store again unless they change their policy. After meeting us, some consumers told us they felt bad about what happened to us and promised they wouldn't go back and shop there anymore. (qtd. in Louie 2001, 242)

Cheunchujit's interview narrative appears in Miriam Ching Yoon Louie's *Sweatshop Warriors: Immigrant Women Workers Take on the Global Factory*, a book that highlights the activist work of immigrant women workers, or "sweatshop warriors," as Louie calls them, who practice organizing strategies and activist rhetorics via Worker Centers, "independent groups where workers gather and organize themselves to carry out their fights and meet their needs" (Louie 2001, 14). Louie focuses on five Worker Centers, which "develop strategies, tactics, methodologies, and organizational forms appropriate to specific niches of workers in the new economy" (14). Where the traditional labor movement has failed, these centers are succeeding, forging new activist rhetorics, many of them feminist in orientation, that allow workers to negotiate the intersections of gender, class, race/ethnicity, and labor in the "new" or globalized economy. Also, such groups provide spaces for cultural translation for activist work, allowing immigrant women workers to "translate what was being said to them and what they wanted to say within the primarily English-speaking, US institutional and cultural environment" (14).

Representing the experiences and activism of women workers like Che-unchujit means challenging traditional narratives about exploitation that tend to portray women at the bottom of the sweatshop pyramid as "victims." Interview narratives with women activists who are sweatshop laborers reveal a different story, one in which workers do not accept victim status but are actively engaged in crafting and deploying the available means of persuasion to fight back against exploitation. As Wendy S. Hesford and Theresa A. Kulbaga point out, *Sweatshop Warriors* positions "readers as cross-cultural and transnational witnesses" and "makes visible the action that victims have taken to confront injustice, and imagines—indeed requires—a similar commitment from its readers" (2003, 93). Louie's analysis, part of the growing discourse of the antisweatshop movement and part of the larger resistance movements against globalization and the "new economy," challenges those of us in feminist rhetorical studies to adopt a transnational perspective on feminist rhetoric, one that acknowledges what Inderpal Grewal and Caren Kaplan call "transnational cultural flows." Grewal and Kaplan argue that such an understanding of transnational cultural flows allows oppositional movements to emerge:

> If feminist political practices do not acknowledge transnational cultural flows, feminist movements will fail to understand the material conditions that structure women's lives in diverse locations. If feminist movements cannot understand the dynamics of these material conditions, they will be unable to construct an effective opposition to current economic and cultural hegemonies that are taking new global forms. Without an analysis of transnational scattered hegemonies that reveal themselves in gender relations, feminist movements will remain isolated and prone to reproducing the universalizing gestures of dominant Western cultures. (1994a, 17)

Grewal and Kaplan's call for feminists to "acknowledge transnational cultural flows" participates in what Susan Stanford Friedman calls a geopolitical feminist rhetoric, a rhetoric that involves "an examination of power relations as they are embedded in the earth, in a given location, as they migrant [sic] around the earth locally, regionally, nationally, and transnationally (2001, 25). In her article "Locational Feminism: Gender, Cultural Geographies, and Geopolitical Literacies," Friedman examines how the rhetorics of U.S. feminisms utilize spatial metaphors that perpetuate particular cultural epistemologies, "underlying categories of thought that impact on feminist agencies in the world" (17). Friedman argues that feminist rhetoric has shifted from a "prevailing temporal rhetoric of awakening revelation, and rebirth" common to a second-wave generation of feminist discourse "to a partial rhetoric of location, multipositionality, and migration" that is more responsive to the contexts of third-wave feminism: the rise of postmodern discourses, the impact of multiculturalism and critical race theories, and the rise of a global economy that has impacted women in particular ways (18).

Third-wave feminist discourses draw on a "spatial rhetoric of location" that "emphasizes the interaction of gender with other forms of power relations based on such cultural categories as race, ethnicity, class, sexuality, religion, national origin, age, and so forth" (S. Friedman 2001, 20). Yet, as the processes of globalization have intensified, feminist discourses have come to reflect a geopolitical orientation in which feminism takes shape in a local and global context—local in the sense that it "emerges everywhere in indigenous forms that take shape through interactions with other feminisms and with its own local conditions. It is also global in the sense that any local formation is shaped in part by the presence of global forces within it" (26). Friedman argues that a geopolitical feminist rhetoric utilizes a transnational grammar that draws on five metaphorics: nation, border, migration, glocation, and conjuncturalism. The metaphorics of the nation draws on the discourse of nation and nationalism, which is realized through state-to-state relations in international contexts. The metaphorics of borders refers to actual geographic borders between nations and to "material conditions as they impact on gender formations but also their figural function to describe psychological, spiritual, and cultural borderlands" (27). Drawing on the "metaphorics of nation and borders," the discourse of migration reflects "on the meanings of immigration, constant travel back and forth, and diaspora for spatial modes of thinking about identity" (28). "Glocation" refers to "how the local and global are co-complicit, each implicated in the other" (30). The metaphorics of conjuncturalism allows for "the juxtaposition of different cultural formations for the light this epistemological juncture sheds on each and for the way in which each discursive system interrupts the other" (31).

Elsewhere Wendy Hesford and Theresa Kulbaga have examined the implications of Friedman's formulation of geopolitical rhetoric—the metaphorics of migration, glocation, and conjuncture—for their analysis of realist genres of Asian American and Asian (im)migrant women workers' testimonials, autobiographies, and documentaries. Hesford and Kulbaga's insightful treatment of realist genres addressing transnational contexts of labor leads them to argue for "the emergence of a methodological imperative that brings together gender, the political economy, and global/local labor practices in examining the production and consumption of realist forms and their activist potential" (100). They further call for a "feminist geopolitical rhetoric that creates spaces of intersubjectivity and that bears witness to the cultural and (trans)national circulation of bodies of evidence, bodies of (dis)identification, and bodies at risk in feminist (autobiography) and rhetorical studies" (100). Enacting a feminist geopolitical analysis of women's rhetorics and feminist rhetorics, their article provides a model for those of us seeking to widen our feminist rhetorical analyses and pedagogies to encompass transnational texts and contexts.

As a way of responding to Grewal and Kaplan's challenge to consider transnational cultural flows in feminist scholarship and activism and Hesford and Kulbaga's call for a "geopolitical rhetoric," I examine how theories of transnational feminisms and, in a related vein, gender and globalization can help feminist teachers and scholars address the geopolitics of our feminist rhetorical theories and practices. In particular, I discuss how the processes of globalization challenge us to develop multinational and multilocational approaches to feminist rhetorics given the fact that "[t]ransnational linkages influence every level of social existence" (Grewal and Kaplan 1994a, 13). Before I begin a discussion of transnational feminisms and rhetorics, I utilize Friedman's analysis of the spatial rhetorics of U.S. feminisms to provide an overview and mapping of the spatial and metaphoric locations of feminist scholarship in rhetoric and composition (Friedman 2001, 17).

Remapping Feminist Rhetorics: Women's Rhetorics in a Globalized World

If the 1960s and 1970s heralded the "canon recovery" movement for women's literature, the 1980s and 1990s were the decades for remapping women's rhetorics and feminist rhetorics. U.S. feminist rhetorical scholars have worked against the absence and erasure of women's voices in the ancient and medieval worlds, reconsidering classical rhetorical traditions, which typically have not addressed women's rhetorical action in antiquity (see Glenn 1997; Jarratt and Orig 1995). In addition, challenging histories of writing that omit women's specific experiences with acquiring and defining literate practice, Catherine Hobbs, editor of the groundbreaking edited anthology *Nineteenth-Century Women Learn to Write* (1995), has drawn together key texts and redefined the sites for women's literate practices. Working from nineteenth- and early twentieth-century contexts, Karlyn Kohrs Campbell's two-volume series on early feminist rhetoric, *Man Cannot Speak for Her* (1989), and Shirley Wilson Logan's collection of African American women's rhetorical texts, *With Pen and Voice* (1995), form a core set of women's rhetorical texts. Joy Ritchie and Kate Ronald's anthology *Available Means* (2001) provides feminist scholars and teachers of women's rhetorics with ample rhetorical texts and analytic frameworks to draw on. Scholars of African American women's rhetorics, notably Jacqueline Royster and Shirley Logan, and Native American women's rhetorics, notably Amanda Cobb and Malea Powell, are working to address the rhetorical action of women of color. Feminist rhetoricians also have fostered a healthy discourse of debate and contention over rhetorical methods and methodologies. A special issue on feminist historiography in *Rhetoric Society Quarterly* guest-edited by Patricia Bizzell usefully frames many of the major debates about how to conduct feminist rhetorical scholarship (see Bizzell 2002).

These redefinitions and relocations of feminist rhetorics have relied, in large part, on the persistent spatial metaphor of "remapping." As Cheryl Glenn puts it succinctly in her 1995 article "Remapping Rhetorical Territory," scholars in rhetoric, especially feminist scholars, are relying less on our neatly folded rhetorical maps, full of "aristocratic blue lines" and patriarchal "master narratives," and concentrating more on examining the "borders of our map, the shadowy regions" (287). We are, Glenn notes, constructing new maps "that reflect and coordinate our current institutional, intellectual, political, and personal values, all of which have become markedly more diverse and elastic in terms of gender, race, and class" (287). Glenn's metaphor of the map corresponds to what Susan Stanford Friedman refers to as the feminist rhetoric of multipositionality, which relies on the "position one occupies, the standpoint from which one speaks, and the location within which one's agency negotiates" (2001, 22). Multipositional feminist rhetorical analysis takes into account analyses of gender, race, sexuality, and class, yet the question of geopolitical orientation—what Friedman calls the "regional/national/transnational nexus" (S. Friedman 2001, 34)—remains largely unexamined in many of our studies of feminist rhetorics and women's rhetorics, The majority of analyses of women's rhetorics/feminist rhetorics have typically centered around North American and European figures, rhetorical texts, and contexts. Most historians of nineteenth- and twentieth-century rhetorics, including feminist scholars studying women's rhetorics and feminist rhetorics, and I include myself in this number, tend to focus on North American and European rhetorical figures, groups, movements, and educational institutions. Studies of women's rhetoric in antiquity are mostly focused on the Greco-Roman world, although Martin Bernal's *Black Athena* (1989) and Carol Lipson and Roberta Binkley's edited collection *Rhetoric Before and Beyond the Greek*s (2004) introduce other geographic and cultural spaces for historical study.

There are signs that feminist rhetorical theorists are beginning to consider the geopolitics of feminist rhetoric. In addition to Hesford and Kulbaga's *JAC* article calling for a "feminist geopolitical rhetoric," the fourth biennial Feminism(s) and Rhetoric(s) Conference held in 2003 at Ohio State University included the category "geopolitical and public policy" in its call for papers, and the conference sponsored a good-sized number of panels featuring feminist rhetorics in transnational contexts. The 2005 conference also featured a number of transnational panels. A growing number of feminist graduate students, whose work has not yet been published in the major journals and anthologies of our field, are also considering feminist geopolitical rhetorics. Mary Queen, a graduate student at Syracuse University, my home institution, addresses how a website authored by the Women's Affairs Technical Committee, a Palestinian women's organization, serves as a "field of rhetorical action for women activists working from within geopolitical sites of conflict to create and mediate their own representations" (2005, 2–3). Queen analyzes and interrogates how these websites create "continually changing relationships among representation, rhetorical action, and web-based technology that a/effect particular subjectivities and political alliances with Western feminists" (2–3). Although a subtle shift toward feminist geopolitical rhetoric is under way, more work needs to be done to fully engage the challenge of theorizing and practicing feminist rhetorics in an increasingly globalized world. At a time when there are calls in higher education to "internationalize" and "globalize" curricula, and calls for interdisciplinary feminist studies to engage transnational feminisms, how do we begin to enact such calls in feminist rhetorical theory and practice? When we teach courses in feminist rhetorics and women's rhetorics at the graduate and undergraduate levels, how do we account for the fact that those engaged in feminist rhetoric(s) and women's rhetorics are women across the globe, not only women in North America and Europe? How do we reinterpret and assess our histories to account for the realities of women's material bodies as they are shaped by political, social, and economic forces such as reproductive choices, marriage, work and professional life, labor migration (forced and chosen), violence, colonization, war, disease and health issues famine, and genocide? Moreover, how are transnational feminist theories and practices entering into our discussions and theorizations of women's rhetorics and feminist rhetorics? What happens to our study, theorization, and teaching of feminist rhetorics/ women's rhetorics if we begin with transnational feminisms as a starting point rather than "adding" or "grafting" on that approach, making it yet another feminism among other feminisms?

By asking these questions, I am not dismissing or devaluing North American– and European-centered women's rhetorics/feminist rhetorics. Like many feminist rhetorical scholars in the field, I have benefited from the newly drawn maps of North American and European feminist rhetorics—maps that have reshaped my understanding of feminist rhetorical theories and practices. Nor do I wish to advocate that those of us who teach feminist and women's rhetorics should simply "add" the rhetorical texts and contexts of women from other parts of the globe to our existing anthologies of women's rhetorics and feminist rhetorics. The "add and stir" approach did not work when white U.S. feminists, without shifting larger conceptualizations, simply added the works of U.S. women of color; nor will this approach work any better in the case of transnational feminisms and geopolitical rhetorics. Broader questions of theoretical, political, economic, and geographic orientation must be addressed in tandem with questions of representation. If those of us who work in feminist rhetorics wish to truly engage transnational feminisms and feminist geopolitical rhetorics, we must "develop a multinational and multilocational approach to questions of gender" (Grewal and Kaplan 1994a, 3). We must address transnational linkages, which "challenge the older, conventional boundaries of national economies, identities, and cultures" (9). These shifts in "national economies, identities, and cultures" have been popularly referred to as "globalization," a catch-all word that carries multiple, contested meanings.

Gender and Globalization

One of the most widely read and glowing popular press accounts of globalization, *The Lexus and the Olive Tree*, authored by *New York Times* foreign correspondent Thomas Friedman, an unabashed cheerleader for globalization, defines globalization as the "the inexorable integration of markets, nation-states, and technologies" that allows "individuals, corporations and nation-states to reach around the world farther, faster, deeper, and cheaper than ever before (2000, 9). This definition conflates the idea of *globalizing*, "the compression of the world and the intensification of consciousness of the world as a whole" (Robertson qtd. in Currie 1998, 1) with *globalization*, a "concept that combines a market ideology with a corresponding material set of practices drawn from the world of business" (1). No matter how one defines globalization, the process is hardly an abstract one for women, as it has "highly varied and often even opposite consequences for women," bringing "new forms of work, multiple strategies of social protection, different lifestyles and value-orientations" (Wichterich 2000, vii), all of which mean change to women's lives. Christa Wichterich dramatically illustrates the features of the globalized female work force in her insightful book *The Globalized Woman*:

> Female textile-workers from Upper Lusatia in Eastern Germany are losing their jobs to women in Bangladesh; Filipinas clean vegetables and kitchens in Kuwait; Brazilian prostitutes offer their services around Frankfurt's main railway station; and Polish women look after old people at rock bottom prices in various parts of Germany. Women in the Caribbean key in commercial entries for North American banks. (2000, viii)

This pattern of labor, migration, and immigration brought on by the integration of world economic markets has brought the "feminization of employment" to a whole new level. Working-class women in countries with the highest exports "have paid a high price for this in the shape of appalling working conditions, few rights, meagre pay, and no social security or sustainable livelihood. They are subject to exhausting and monotonous work routines that are often injurious to their health, for an hourly wage of between 16 and 60 US cents" (Wichterich 2000, 2).

Meanwhile, those of us who work as academics in the United States directly and indirectly benefit from that exploitation through the purchase of cheap goods manufactured elsewhere (often manufactured in the sweatshop pyramid and sold at retail outlets like Wal-Mart) and "cheap" global food grown and harvested in the developing world. Our consumption, along with that of our fellow Americans, grossly outpaces that of any other industrialized nation. As Grewal and Kaplan remind us, "white, Western feminists or elite women in other world locations" must acknowledge "that one's privileges in the world-system are always linked to another woman's oppression or exploitation" (1994a, 19). Thus, economic disparities and asymmetrical power relations between women in different locations and different sets of circumstances make feminist rhetorics and women's rhetorics both a challenging and a promising arena of scholarly and political practice. To truly engage feminist rhetorics in transnational contexts, we need to rethink several concepts that have been foundational to rhetorical study both inside and

outside of feminist rhetorical studies and women's rhetorical studies: the
concepts of rhetorical location, rhetorical action, and rhetorical education
for citizenship.

First, the issue of rhetorical location. Pivotal to rhetorical study is the
notion that a rhetor speaks or writes from a particular location in time and
space to a particular audience. This is a helpful concept and seemingly universal, but it is more tenuous when applied to the nation-state. Our contemporary notions of the "rhetor" often are dependent on the idea of the citizen-
rhetor of the nation-state who makes appeals to equality, freedom, rights, or to
specific interests that reflect her connection to a specific national identity.
What this particular formulation often does not account for is how national
interests and appeals are tied up in complex international and transnational
flows of capital and people. Understanding rhetorical location in a system of
global capitalism means that we have to think across borders toward an integrated analysis that accounts for transnational linkages. The transnationaliza-
tion of capitalism, as feminist scholar Chela Sandoval reminds us, means that
"elected officials are no longer leaders of singular nation-states but nexuses
for multinational interests" (2000, 183). In other words, understanding rhetorical location in a globalized world means understanding flows of capital and people across national borders. To understand how these transnational flows work,
we need to practice an integrated global analysis. As Naomi Klein argues in
*Fences and Windows: Dispatches from the Front Lines of the Globalization
Debate*, understanding transnational linkages is "about recognizing that every
piece of our high-gloss consumer culture comes from somewhere. It's about following the webs of contracted factories, shell-game subsidiaries, and outsourced
labor to find out where all the pieces are manufactured, under what conditions,
which lobby groups wrote the rules of the game and which politicians were
bought off along the way" (2002, 30). This integrated, global cultural analysis,
then, is about understanding how the products, services, and people with whom
we interact are part and parcel of a transnational system of capitalism with
complex networks of power relations, discourses, and materialities that combine
and recombine to form particular chains of connection and power.

Theories and practices of rhetoric that account for transnationalism also
must address how communication technologies shape contemporary rhetorical
action. Although rhetors still mount platforms and deliver public addresses
and pen or word-process speeches, manifestos, books, and treatises, it is also
the case that communication technologies like email, webwriting, weblogs or
blogs, and cell phones are becoming instruments of rhetorical action. For
instance, groups linked around what can loosely be called alternative globalization movements have mobilized through initial Internet communications
(email, websites, and now blogs) and physically appeared in large numbers in
Seattle, in Washington, DC, Los Angeles, Ottawa, Prague, and Genoa to protest
the policies of the World Bank and the International Monetary Fund (IMF).
These mass mobilizations achieved through Internet communication and

informal information swapping stunned those who are used to more central-ized manifesto-led political organizing. As Klein points out, the communica-tion technologies that shaped these campaigns have shaped the movements "in [their] own Web-like image" (2002, 17). "Thanks to the Net," writes Klein, "mobilizations occur with spare bureaucracy and minimal hierarchy; forced consensus and labour manifestos are fading into the background, replaced instead by a culture of constant, loosely structured and sometimes compulsive information swapping" (17). We need to account for the influence of technol-ogy and the new media in our studies of contemporary feminist rhetorics and women's rhetorics.

Finally, the goals of rhetorical education, too, must be broadened and expanded to account for global citizenship rather than simply allegiance to the values of the nation-state one resides in. We need to work with students in women's rhetorics and feminist rhetorics courses to develop an "oppositional consciousness," one that allows for them to become "citizen-subjects" aware of and responsive to the global context. (Sandoval 2000, 183). Global citizen-ship, according to Julie Andrzejewski and John Alessio, consists of three main objectives: (1) developing an "understanding of a citizen's responsibilities to others, to society, and to the environment"; (2) developing an "understanding of ethical behavior in personal, professional, and public life," and (3) develop-ing "knowledge and skills for involved responsible citizenship at the local, state, national, and global level." All three of these objectives must be accom-plished in an atmosphere of debate where what it means to be a citizen is accountable to understanding differences, whether they are differences of nationality, race, creed, gender, religion, abilities, or sexual orientation. Also, rhetorical education, as part of global citizenship, is crucial to this process of global citizenship, as it helps students work on specific information literacies such as locating "information from a variety of sources, identify[ing] underly-ing values, and investigat[ing] the veracity of information," "composing argu-ments and identify[ing] appropriate forums for taking actions," and practicing critical citizenship skills such as producing advocacy documents, evaluating political candidates, and participating in social action projects (Andrzejewski and Alessio 1999).

Keeping in mind the revision of the concepts of rhetorical location, rhetor-ical action, and rhetorical education for citizenship, what might our courses in feminist rhetorics and women's rhetorics do to address feminist geopolitical rhetorics?

Think Globally, Teach Locally: The Case Study of Sweatshop Labor

Over the past three years, in my undergraduate writing and rhetoric courses, I have taken up the issue of sweatshop labor as a dramatic and telling example of the gendered disparities and inequities to be found in the processes of globalization and to address how advocacy rhetorics, many of them feminist in orientation, have been formed to fight against such inequities. As Miriam Louie argues, "The sweatshop system takes advantage of the 'exceptional,' the 'different,' to relegate certain strata of the population into super-exploited positions and others to more privileged buffer positions—all to the benefit of the super-privileged minority sitting at the top of the power pyramid" (2001, 7). In particular, women of color pay the price in the global sweatshop. Consider that price in its real sense: "Garment workers in Los Angeles [the majority of whom are immigrant women of color], for example, each produce about $100,000 worth of goods a year, but are paid less than 2 percent of the total value. For a dress that retails for $100, $1.72 goes to the sewer, $15 to the contractor, and $50 goes to the manufacturer" (5).

Introducing students to the rhetorics behind the sweatshop labor pyramid and its connection to other local labor practices is best done concretely, by considering what Andrzejewski and Alessio call the impact of "daily consumption on the lives of other people and places in the world" (1999). I introduce my students to the issue of sweatshop labor by the simple exercise of asking them to read the labels on class members' clothing and to record where their garments were manufactured. A discussion of this activity then leads to students' investigating where and under what conditions such clothing is produced. Inevitably, our discussion leads to free trade zones and to the global and gendered work force in the garment industry. To illustrate the issues and concerns of garment workers worldwide, I show the documentary *Free Trade Slaves,* a Belgian-made film, which narrates the establishment of free trade zones throughout the world. Such trade zones allow multinational corporations to be exempted from taxes or to pay extremely low ones, and it allows them to subcontract the work and pay cheap wages to workers, namely, young women and children. Filmed on location in Sri Lanka, El Salvador, Mexico, and Morocco, *Free Trade Slaves* helps students visualize who works in garment factories worldwide. It is narrated by women and men who speak of their working conditions, their personal lives, and the impact that garment factories have on their families, their local communities, and on the environment. Focusing a course on an issue that cuts across national borders also challenges us to look beyond United States–centric scholarly print articles or books, which may not be up to date on transnational issues and may not offer graphic or pictorial representations that portray the sweatshop pyramid. In my course I encourage my students to critically analyze photographs, documentaries, Web writing, alternative media pieces, memoirs/autobiographies, historical accounts, political journalism, and organizing discourses.

In addition, in my classes we examine other public controversies regarding sweatshop labor, both domestic and global, such as the El Monte situation mentioned at the start of this chapter, the rhetorics of the controversy over Kathie Lee's brand-name Kmart clothing line, Nike's egregious labor abuses and public disinformation campaign, and Wal-Mart's "Buy American" campaign. I then ask my classes to consider how advocacy rhetorics are being deployed to fight against global sweatshops. Together my students and I analyze the advocacy rhetorics of the antisweatshop movements led by students, by sweatshop workers, by unions, and by other nongovernmental and human rights organizations who seek a just and equitable global workplace. In particular, the United Students Against Sweatshops website (www.studentsagainstsweatshops.org/) provides an interesting case study and model for students seeking to understand the role that informed citizen-students can play in organizing against sweatshops. I also ask my students to study the rhetorical advocacy work of local antisweatshop organizers such as the Student Coalition on Organized Labor at Syracuse University (SCOOL, http://students.syr.edu/scool/). In 2001, SCOOL waged a successful campaign to pressure Syracuse University to join the Worker Rights Consortium (WRC), an independent grouping composed of human rights groups, clergy, students, and others who monitor the working conditions of university apparel manufacturers across the world (see www.workersrights.org/).[2]

Syracuse University's implication in sweatshop labor via a Nike factory in Mexico, which was the site of numerous labor violations, became the basis of a local campaign to urge the university to join the WRC. Students from SCOOL camped on the quad of the university, staged guerrilla theater demonstrations, and passed out leaflets calling for the university to join the WRC. The students made it clear in their dispatches and position papers that they understood the sweatshop pyramid and the university's place within it (see The Student Coalition on Organized Labor). After months of hard work, meetings, and strategic actions on the part of SCOOL, Syracuse University finally agreed to join the Worker Rights Consortium ("Chancellor" 2001).

For students analyzing and encountering the sweatshop pyramid for the first time, the details are often startling and stand in stark contrast with the glowing rhetorics of globalization touted by many—if not most—of the colleges and universities they attend—colleges and universities that often emblazon their sports team jerseys and school sweatshirts with the telltale Nike swoosh. Through study of an issue like sweatshop labor, students discover that the universities they attend are no strangers to "sweating workers through subcontracting" (Louie 2001, 5). As Louie argues, the global factory where garments, electronics, toys, shoes, plastics, and auto parts are manufactured is complemented by the local sectors of the economy where subcontracting is utilized: "healthcare, food processing, restaurant, hotel, custodial, construction, landscaping, information processing, clerical, customer service, and other industries" (5). Universities are prime utilizers of subcontracted labor, often subcontracting cleaning services, gardening/lawn keeping services, food services, and parking services: "The workers do the same work, or more, but for lower pay and fewer benefits, while the university gets to redirect their spending, in some cases, toward higher salaries for chief administrators" (5). Many of these workers are women, and many are men and women of color.

Meanwhile, among the faculty ranks, we find increasing use of "contract" faculty, part-time and non-tenure-track faculty, who work on short-term contracts for lower salaries (Schell and Stock 2001, 5). Many of these part-time college teachers are women, especially in the humanities. In her introduction to *Universities and Globalization: Critical Perspectives*, Jan Currie further elucidates this trend: "Another concept taken from the business world, labor flexibility, has infiltrated the universities, creating a small core group of academics who receive pay and benefits and, in turn, a much larger peripheral group of contract workers (more often women) who receive lower pay and have insecure appointments with no benefits" (1998, 5). Universities, therefore, are operating their own versions of the global labor system on their local campuses.

My point in raising the issue of sweatshop labor in my classes and, by connection, subcontracting on university campuses, whether I am teaching a course on women's rhetorics, feminist rhetorics, or first-year writing for that matter, is to provide students with a case study of globalization that highlights "transnational linkages" and multinational and multilocational approaches to the question of gender and feminisms. I urge my students to investigate sweatshop labor from multiple angles and to assess the rhetorical strategies of the various stakeholders: corporate retailers and manufacturing perspectives, activist and advocacy perspectives, unionist perspectives, worker perspectives, consumer perspectives, and student perspectives among others. Gender and feminist perspectives are interlaced throughout these analyses, as many of the activists and organizers around this issue articulate openly feminist perspectives, and most of the workers are women. I conclude the unit on sweatshop labor by asking students to give formal presentations on their research and their essays. The presentation session, which extends for several class periods, allows students to discuss and debate positions taken by different stakeholders, assess their rhetorical strategies, and consider the sorts of rhetorical and material action that they believe government leaders, manufacturers, retailers, human rights organizations, labor unions, student activists, and consumers should take to address the inequities of the sweatshop pyramid.

This unit on sweatshop labor, more than any other I have attempted in my seventeen years of teaching college writing and rhetoric, has galvanized student interest and passion, as it provides them with the opportunity to think critically about the rhetorics of everyday life, about the clothing they wear, the brands they love, and the systems of production and distribution that lie behind them. In addition, the unit challenges students to think critically and creatively about how they, as college students and global citizens, imagine alternatives to the current sweatshop labor pyramid. Some students have gone on to become active in antisweatshop activities on campus, and others have extended work begun in my class into other classes. Most students comment that investigating the rhetoric of the sweatshop pyramid has made them think critically about their role in it and has helped them understand how globalization works "on the ground" in their daily lives and in the lives of the women and men who work to support that pyramid.

Those of us who teach women's rhetorics, feminist rhetorics, and first-year writing have an opportunity and a challenge, now more than ever, to write, teach, engage, and enact rhetorical theories and practices that account for transnational texts and contexts, for multinational and multilocational approaches to gender and feminisms, and for the responsibilities of global citizenship. There is no right way to enact this sort of rhetorical practice and teaching, no common textbook or syllabus, but there is an ethics and politics to this teaching that asks that our rhetorical classrooms serve as spaces that provide us and our students "with the information and tools to understand what is happening in the world, how it affects our lives, the lives of others, and the planet itself" (Andrezejewski and Alessio 1999). Rhetorical education for global citizenship is an important and necessary component of our students' educational experiences, and feminist scholars who study women's rhetorics and feminist rhetorics can be at the forefront of such educational efforts for global citizenship.

Notes

1. The National Retail Federation provides a useful mini-history of sweatshops, "Sweatshops in America: From the Jungle to El Monte," from which I have drawn this overview. Despite the usefulness of this portion of the website, it should be noted, however, that the National Retail Federation foundation protects the interests of retailers, although it claims to be proactive in preventing sweatshops. Other aspects of the National Retail Federation contain open propaganda supporting "free trade" and boasting of the U.S. economy's dominance. Therefore, I cite a portion of this website with a caution to readers that the remainder of the website is largely taken up by propaganda for American retailers.

2. January 2001 attacks against workers at a Korean-owned factory in Atlixco, Puebla, Mexico, that manufactured college sweatshirts for Nike brought the issue of sweatshop labor to the forefront at Syracuse University and a number of other college campuses nationwide. As a news dispatch authored by E. Brakken indicated, "800 workers producing Nike sweatshirts for export to U.S. colleges and universities" went on strike "against a company paying 75 cents per hour, demanding that their rights be respected. They have called on Nike to send a fully authorized representative to the scene to publicly ratify a resolution to the conflict that recognizes their newly-formed Kukdong Workers' Coalition." Unfortunately the labor actions brought violence: "police and thugs from the 'company union' attacked the occupation, sending over 15 workers to the hospital," and this incident brought international attention to their struggles (2001).

Works Cited

AAUP Professional Liability/Marsh Affinity Group Services. 2002. "You could be sued for simply doing your job." Mailing. Seabury and Smith. (June).

Acker, Kathy. 1972. *Politics*. New York: Papyrus.

————. 1984. *Don Quixote: Which Was a Dream*. New York: Grove.

————. 1989. *Great Expectations*. New York: Grove.

————. 1990. "Humility." In *The Seven Cardinal Virtues*, ed. Alison Fell. London: Serpent's Tail.

————. 1996. *Pussy, King of the Pirates*. New York: Grove.

————. 1997. *Bodies of Work: Essays*. London: Serpent's Tail.

Acosta, Teresa Palomo. n.d. "Home Altars." In *The Handbook of Texas Online*. www.tsha.utexas.edu/handbook/online/articles/view/HH/izh1.html. (accessed March 19, 2003).

Ain't I a Woman? A Midwest Newspaper of Women's Liberation. 1970. Editorial. June 26.

Alexander, M. Jacqui, Lisa Albrecht, Sharon Day, and Mab Segrest, eds. 2003. *Sing, Whisper, Shout, Pray: Feminist Visions for a Just World*. Berkeley, CA: Edge Work Books.

Allen, Beverly. 1996. *Rape Warfare: The Hidden Genocide in Bosnia-Herzegovina and Croatia*. Minneapolis: University of Minnesota Press.

Allen, Pamela. 1970. *Free Space: A Perspective on the Small Group in Women's Liberation*. New York: Times Change.

Allison, Dorothy. 1995. *Two or Three Things I Know for Sure*. New York: Penguin Putnam.

Amnesty International. 1999. *Amnesty International Report*. www.amnesty.org/ailib/aireport/index.html (accessed October 11, 2005).

————. 2003a. *Amnesty International Report*. www.amnesty.org/ailib/aireport/index.html (accessed October 11, 2005).

————. 2003b. "Bosnia-Herzegovina: Justice Cannot Be Achieved on the Cheap." News release. November 12, 2003. http://amnesty-news.c.tep1.com/maabEDuaa14LobcPvizb'.

————. n.d. "Key figures of ICTY Cases." News release. http://157.150.195.46/icty/glance/index.htm. (accessed October 11, 2005).

Andrezejewski, Julie, and John Alessio. 1999. "Education for Global Citizenship and Social Responsibility." *Progressive Perspectives*. 1, no. 2 (Spring): 1–23. www.uvm.edu/~dewey/monographs/glomono.html#Education%20for%20Global%20Citizenship%20and%20Social (accessed June 20, 2005).

"Anna Deavere Smith." 1994. In *Current Biography Yearbook,* ed. Judith Graham, 544–47. New York: H. W. Wilson.

Anzaldúa, Gloria. 1987. *Borderlands/La Frontera: The New Mestiza.* San Francisco: Aunt Lute Books.

Aristotle. 1991. *The Rhetoric: A Theory of Civic Discourse.* Trans. George Kennedy. New York: Oxford University Press.

Aronowitz, Stanley, and Henry A. Giroux. 1991. *Postmodern Education; Politics, Culture, and Social Criticism.* Minneapolis: Minnesota University Press.

Atkins, G. Douglas. 2000a. "Art and Anger—Upon Taking Up the Pen Again: On Self(e)- Expression." *JAC: A Journal of Composition Theory* 20:414–26.

———. 2000b. "On Writing Well: Or, Springing the Genie from the Inkpot." *JAC: A Journal of Composition Theory* 20:73–85.

Bachelard, Gaston. 1964. *The Psychoanalysis of Fire.* Trans. Alan C. M. Ross. New York: Beacon.

———. 1994. *The Poetics of Space.* New York: Beacon.

Baer, Ulrich. 2002. *Spectral Evidence: The Photography of Trauma.* Cambridge: MIT Press.

Bailiff, Michelle. 2001. *Seduction, Sophistry, and the Woman with the Rhetorical Figure.* Pittsburgh: University of Pittsburgh Press.

Bakhtin, Mikhail. 1990. *The Dialogic Imagination: Four Essays.* Trans. Michael Holquist and Caryl Emerson. Austin: University of Texas Press.

Baldwin, James. 1985. "Notes for a Hypothetical Novel." In *The Price of the Ticket*: *Collected Non-Fiction, 1948–1985.* London: M. Joseph.

Ballif, Michelle, Diane Davis, and Roxanne Mountford. 2000. "Toward an Ethics of Listening." *JAC: A Journal of Composition Theory* 20, no. 4 (Fall): 931–42.

Bambara, Toni Cade. 1970. *The Black Woman: An Anthology.* New York: New American Library.

Barthes, Roland. 1994. *The Semiotic Challenge.* Trans. Richard Howard. Berkeley: University of California Press.

Benderly, Jill. 1997. "Rape, Feminism, and Nationalism in the War in Yugoslav Successor States." In *Feminist Nationalism,* ed. Lois West, 59–72. New York: Routledge.

Benedict, Kimberley Michelle. 2002. "Authorial Alliances: Collaboration Between Religious Women and Scribes in the Middle Ages." PhD diss., Stanford University.

Berlin, James A. 1992. "Poststructuralism, Cultural Studies, and the Composition Classroom." *Rhetoric Review* 11 (Fall): 16–33.

Berlin, James A., and Michael J. Vivion, eds. 1992. *Cultural Studies in the English Classroom.* Portsmouth, NH: Heinemann-Boynton/Cook.

Bernal, Martin. 1989. *Black Athena: The Afroasiatic Roots of Classical Civilization.* New Brunswick: Rutgers University Press.

Bernard, Cheryl. 1994. "Rape as Terror: The Case of Bosnia." *Terrorism and Political Violence* 6 (Spring): 29–43.

Berthoff, Ann E. 1984. "Is Teaching Still Possible?" *College English* 46:743–55.

————. 1987. Preface to *Literacy: Reading the Word and the World*, by Paulo Freire and Donaldo Macedo. South Hadley: Bergin and Garvey.

Beverley, John. 1992. "The Margin at the Center: On *Testimonio* (Testimonial Narrative)." In *De/Colonizing the Subject: The Politics of Gender in Women's Autobiography*, ed. Smith and Watson, 91–114. Minneapolis: University of Minneapolis Press.

Bizzell, Patricia. 2002. Preface to "Special issue: Feminist historiography in rhetoric." *Rhetoric Society Quarterly* 32, no. 1 (Winter): 7–10.

Bizzell, Patricia, and Bruce Herzberg. 1990. *The Rhetorical Tradition: Readings from Classical Times to the Present*. Boston: Bedford.

Blair, Carole. 1999. "Contemporary U. S. Memorial Sites as Exemplars of Rhetoric's Materiality." In *Rhetorical Bodies*, ed. Jack Selzer and Sharon Crowley, 16–57. Madison: University of Wisconsin.

Boler, Megan. 1997. "The Risks of Empathy: Interrogating Multiculturalism's Gaze." *Cultural Studies* 11 (2): 253–73.

Boltanski, Luc. 1999. *Distant Suffering: Morality, Media, and Politics*. Cambridge: Cambridge University Press.

Boose, Lynda E. 2002. "Crossing the River Drina: Bosnian Rape Camps, Turkish Impalement, and Serb Cultural Memory." *Signs* 28, no. 1 (Autumn): 71–96.

Bordo, Susan. 1993. *Unbearable Weight: Feminism, Western Culture, and the Body*. Berkeley: University of California Press.

Bose, Purnima, and Linta Varghese. 2001. "Mississippi Masala, South Asian Activism, and Agency." In Hesford and Kozol 2001, 137–68.

Boston Women's Health Course Collective. 1971. *Our Bodies Our Selves: A Course by and for Women*. Boston: New England Free Press.

Bow, Leslie. 2001. "Third-World Testimony in the Era of Globalization: Vietnam, Sexual trauma, and Le Ly Hayslip's Art of Neutrality." In Hesford and Kozol 2001, 169–94.

Boxer, Marilyn Jacoby. 1998. *When Women Ask the Questions: Creating Women's Studies in America*. Baltimore: Johns Hopkins University Press.

Brakken, E. 2001. "Police Raid Strike at Nike Factory in Mexico." www.globalexchange. org/economy/corporations/nike/kukdong011401.html (accessed June 20, 2005).

Brannon, Lil. 1993. "M[other]: Life on the Outside." *Written Communication* 10, no. 3 (July): 457–465.

Bridwell-Bowles, Lillian. 1992. "Discourse and Diversity: Experimental Writing Within the Academy." *College Composition and Communication*. 43 (3): 349–68.

Brodkey, Linda, and Michelle Fine. 1996. "Presence of Mind in the Absence of Body." In *Writing Permitted in Designated Areas Only*, by Linda Brodkey, 114–29. Minneapolis: Minnesota University Press.

Brody, Michal, ed. 1985. *Are We There Yet? A Continuing History of Lavender Woman, A Chicago Lesbian Newspaper, 1971–1976*. Iowa City: Aunt Lute Books.

Brown, Bill. 1999. "The Secret Life of Things (Virginia Woolf and the Matter of Modernism)." *Modernism/Modernity* 6 (2): 1–28.

Brown, Michael Barratt. 1997a. The role of economic factors in social crisis: The Case of Yugoslavia." *New Political Economy* 2 (July): 299–316.

———. 1997b. "Restating My Case: A Reply to Magas and Kearns." *New Political Economy* 2 (November): 473–75.

Brown, Wendy. 1995. *States of Injury: Power and Freedom in Late Modernity.* Princeton: Princeton University Press.

Brownmiller, Susan. 2000. *In Our Time: Memoir of a Revolution.* New York: Delta.

Bruffee, Kenneth. 1972–73. "Collaborative Learning: Some Practical Models." *College English* 34:634–43.

Buchanan, Lindal. 2005. *Regendering Delivery: The Fifth Canon and Antebellum Women Rhetors.* Carbondale: Southern Illinois University Press.

Burke, Kenneth. 1950. From *A Rhetoric of Motives.* In Bizzell and Herzberg, 1990, 1018–34.

———. 1966. From *Language as Symbolic Action.* In Bizzell and Herzberg 1990, 1034–41.

Butler, Johnnella E. 1985. "Toward a Pedagogy of Everywoman's Studies." In *Gendered Subjects: The Dynamics of Feminist Teaching,* ed. Margo Culley and Catherine Portuges, 230–39. New York: Routledge.

Butler, Judith. 1997. *Gender Trouble: Feminism and the Subversion of identity.* New York: Routledge.

Calling the Ghosts: A Story about Rape, War, and Women. 1996. Produced by Bowery Productions. Directed by Mandy Jacobson and Karmen Jelincic. 63 minutes. Women Make Movies. Film.

Campbell, David. 1998. *National Deconstruction: Violence, Identity, and Justice in Bosnia.* Minneapolis: University of Minnesota Press.

Campbell, JoAnn, ed. 1996. *Toward a Feminist Rhetoric: The Writing of Gertrude Buck.* Pittsburgh: University of Pittsburgh Press.

Campbell, Karlyn Kohrs. 1989. *Man Cannot Speak for Her: A Critical Study of Early Feminist Rhetoric.* 2 vols. New York: Greenwood.

Cannon, Katie Geneva. 1996. *Katie's Canon: Womanism and the Soul of the Black Community.* New York: Continuum.

Carr, Robert. 1994. "Crossing the First World/Third World Divides: Testimonial, Transnational Feminisms, and the Postmodern Condition." In Grewal and Kaplan 1994b, 153–72.

Cash, Marie Romero. 1998. *Living Shrines: Home Altars of New Mexico.* Santa Fe: Museum of New Mexico Press.

Castro, Fidel. 1970/1982. "The new role for women in Cuban society." In *Women and the Cuban revolution,* ed. Elizabeth Stone. New York: Pathfinder Press.

"Chancellor Q & A: Sweatshops." 2001. *Syracuse University News.* (March 31). www.google.com/u/syracuse?q=cache:5njZZjPnGXIJ:sunews.syr.edu/print.asp %3Fid%3D3270114+Chancellor+Shaw+and+sweatshops&hl=en&ie=UTF-8 (archived November 25, 2004, and accessed June 20, 2005).

Chandler, Katherine, and Melissa Goldthwaite. 2004. *Surveying the Literary Landscapes of Terry Tempest Williams.* Salt Lake City: University of Utah Press.

Chomsky, Noam. 1999. "Crisis in the Balkans." *Z Magazine.* (May). www.zmag.org/ZMag/articles/may99chomsky.htm (accessed December 3, 2003).

Chow, Rey. 1993. *Writing Diaspora: Tactics of Intervention in Contemporary Cultural Studies.* Bloomington: Indiana University Press.

Chun, Wendy Hui Kyong. 2002. "Unbearable Witness: Toward a Politics of Listening." In *Extremities: Trauma, Testimony, and Community*, ed. Nancy K. Miller and Jason Tougaw, 143–65. Urbana: University of Illinois Press.

Cixous, Helene. 1975/1986 "Sorties." In *The Newly Born Woman*, 91–100. Trans. Betsy Wing. Minneapolis: University of Minnesota Press.

———. 1981. "Castration or Decapitation?" *Signs* 7 (1): 41–55.

Cobb, Amanda. 2000. *Listening to our Grandmother's Stories: The Bloomfield Academy for Chickasaw Females, 1852–1949.* Lincoln and London: University of Nebraska Press.

Collins, Patricia Hill. 1991. *Black Feminist Thought: Knowledge, Consciousness, and the Politics of Empowerment.* New York: Routledge.

———. 1999. "What's in a Name? Womanism, Black Feminism, and Beyond." In *Race, Identity, and Citizenship: A Reader*, ed. Jonathan Xavier Inda, Louis F. Miron, and Rodolfo D. Torres, 126–37. Malden: Blackwell.

Condit, Celeste. 1999. "The Materiality of Coding: Rhetoric, Genetics, and the Matter of Life." In Selzer and Crowley 1999, 326–56.

Connors, Robert J. 1996a. "Comment and Response." *College English* 58:968–74.

———. 1996b. "Teaching and Learning as a Man." *College English* 58:137–57.

Copelon, Rhonda. 1988. "Surfacing Gender: Reconceptualizing Crimes against Women in Times of War." In *The Women and War Reader*, ed. Lois Ann Lorentzen and Jennifer Turpin, 63–79. New York: New York University Press.

Cullens, Chris. 1999. Gimme shelter: At home with the millennium. *differences: A Journal of Feminist Cultural Studies* 11 (2): 204–27.

Currie, Jan. 1998. Introd. to *Universities and globalization: Critical perspectives*, ed. Jan Currie and Angela Newson, 1–14. Thousand Oaks, CA: Sage Publications.

Daniell, Beth. 2003. *A Communion of Friendship: Literacy, Spiritual Practice, and Women in Recovery.* Carbondale: Southern Illinois University Press.

Davidson, Cathy N. 1986. *Revolution and the Word: The Rise of the Novel in America.* Oxford: Oxford University Press.

Davidson, Neil. 1999. "The trouble with 'ethnicity.'" *International Socialism Journal* 84 (Autumn). http://pubs.socialstreviewindex.org.uk/isj84/davidson.htm (accessed December 3, 2003).

Davis, D. Diane. 2000. *Breaking up [at] totality: A rhetoric of laughter.* Carbondale: Southern Illinois University Press.

———. 2001. "Finitude's Clamor; or, Notes toward a Communitarian Literacy." *College Composition and Communication* 53:119–45.

Day, Kami, and Michele Eodice. 2001. *(First person)2: A study of co-authoring in the academy.* Logan: Utah State University Press.

Dear sisters. 1970. *off our backs: the feminist news journal.* 1, no. 1 (February 27): 2.

Dell'Olio, Anselma. 1970. "The Founding of Feminist Theatre." In *Notes from the Second Year: Women's Liberation,* ed. Shulamith Firestone and Anne Koedt, 101–2. New York: Notes.

Derrida, Jacques. 1987. *The Post Card: From Socrates to Freud and Beyond.* Trans. Eric Prenowitz. Chicago: University of Chicago Press.

Dewey, John. 1925/1984. "The Development of American Pragmatism." In *The Later Works, 1925–1953.* Vol. 2., ed. Jo Ann Boydston, 3–21. Carbondale: Southern Illinois University Press, 1984.

Dickson, Barbara. 1999. "Reading Maternity Materially: The Case of Demi Moore." In Selzer and Crowley 1999, 297–13.

Dissoi Logoi, or Dialexeis. 1972. In *The Older Sophists: A Complete Translation by Many Hands of the Fragments in Die Fragmente der Vorsokratiker,* trans. and ed. Rosamund Kent Sprague, 279–93. Columbia: University of South Carolina Press.

Donawerth, Jane, ed. 2002. *Rhetorical Theory by Women Before 1900.* Lanham: Rowman & Littlefield.

Drakulic, Slavenka. 2001a. "Bosnian Women Witness." *Nation* (March 19): 5–6.

———. 2001b. *S: A Novel About the Balkans.* New York: Penguin Books.

Durie, Jane. 1996. "Emancipatory Education and Classroom Practice: A Feminist Post-structuralist Perspective." *Studies in Continuing Education.* 18 (2): 135–46.

"Earth Onion Theatre Group Scrapbook." 1971. *off our backs* 2:2 (October): 1–5.

Ede, Lisa. 2004. *Situating Composition.* Carbondale: Southern Illinois University Press.

Ede, Lisa, Cheryl Glenn, and Andrea Lunsford. 1995. "Border Crossings: Intersections of Rhetoric and Feminism." *Rhetorica* 13 (Autumn): 401–41.

Ede, Lisa, and Andrea A. Lunsford. 1991. *Singular Texts/Plural Authors: Perspectives on Collaborative Writing.* Carbondale: Southern Illinois University Press.

Editorial. 1976. *Big Mama Rag.* 4:6 (June): 2.

Egan, Susanna. 1999. *Mirror Talk: Genres of Crisis in Contemporary Autobiography.* Chapel Hill: University of North Carolina Press.

Ehrenreich, Barbara, and Deirdre English. 1977. *Complaints and Disorders: The Sexual Politics of Sickness (Glass Mountain Pamphlet #2).* Old Westbury: The Feminist Press.

Elbow, Peter. 1981. *Writing with Power: Techniques for Mastering the Writing Process.* New York: Oxford University Press.

Ellsworth, Elizabeth. 1992. "Why Doesn't this Feel Empowering? Working Through the Repressive Myths of Critical Pedagogy." In ed. Luke and Gore 1992, 90–119.

Enloe, Cynthia. 2000. *Maneuvers: The International Politics of Militarizing Women's Lives.* Berkeley: University of California Press.

Enos, Richard. 2002. "The Archaeology of Women in Rhetoric: Rhetorical Sequencing as a Research Method for Historical Scholarship. *Rhetoric Society Quarterly* 32 (1): 65–79.

Eschle, Catherine. 2001. *Global Democracy, Social Movements, and Feminism.* Boulder: Westview.

Evces, Mike. 2001. "Public Rhetoric for Academic Workers: Tips from the Front Lines." *Forum: A Newsletter of the Non-Tenure-Track Faculty Special Interest Group* 5.1. *College Composition and Communication* 53: A3–A5.

Faigley, Lester. 1992. *Fragments of Rationality: Postmodernity and the Subject of Composition.* Pittsburgh: University of Pittsburgh Press.

Felman, Shoshana, and Dori Laub. 1992. *Testimony: Crises of Witnessing in Literature, Psychoanalysis, and History.* New York: Routledge.

"Feminism(s) and Rhetoric(s): Call for Papers." 2003. *Fourth Biennial Feminisms and Rhetorics Conference, Ohio State University, October 23–25, 2003.* www.inform. umd.edu/EdRes/Topic/Diversity/General/Conferences/rhet102503.html (accessed June 20, 2005).

Fernandes, Leela. 2001. "Reading 'India's Bandit Queen': A Trans/National Feminist Perspective on the Discrepancies of Representation." In Hesford and Kozol, 47–75.

Firestone, Shulamith, and Anne Koedt. 1970. Editorial. *Notes from the Second Year: Women's Liberation.* 2.

Fiske, John. 1992. "Cultural Studies and the Culture of Everyday Life." In Grossberg et al., 154–73.

Flannery, Kathryn T. 2001. "Anonymity, Pseudonymity, and Collective Authorship: Rethinking Ethos and the Politics of Discourse." In *Professing Rhetoric: Selected Papers from the 2000 Rhetoric Society of America Conference,* ed. Frederick J. Antczak. New York: Erlbaum.

———. 2005. *Feminist Literacies, 1968–75.* Urbana: University of Illinois Press.

Fleckenstein, Kristie S. 1997. "Creating a Center that Holds: Spirituality Through Exploratory Pedagogy. In *The Spiritual Side of Writing: Releasing the Learner's Whole* Potential, ed. Regina Paxton Foehr and Susan Schiller, 25–33. Portsmouth, NH: Boynton/Cook.

———. 1998. "Resistance, Women, and Dismissing the 'I'." *Rhetoric Review* 17 (1): 107–25.

Flynn, Elizabeth A. 1988. "Composing as a Woman." *College Composition and Communication* 39:423–35.

———. 2002. *Feminism Beyond Modernism.* Carbondale: Southern Illinois University Press.

Foss, Karen, and Sonja Foss, eds. 1991. *Women Speak: The Eloquence of Women's Lives.* Prospect Heights, IL: Waveland.

Foss, Karen, Sonja Foss, and Cyndy L. Griffin. 1999. *Feminist rhetorical theories.* Thousand Oaks, CA: Sage.

Foucault, Michel. 1971/1990. From *The Order of Discourse.* In Bizzell and Herzberg, 1154–64.

———. 1972. *The Archaeology of Knowledge.* New York: Routledge.

Fredrick, Christine Ann Nguyen. 2004. *Feminist Rhetoric in Cyberspace.* New York: Routledge.

Free Trade Slaves. 1998. A report by Joan Salvat, Stef Soetewey, and Peter Breuls. Produced by Films for the Humanities and Sciences. 56 minutes. TV Catalunya. Kanakna Productions. Videorecording.

Freeman, Marsha. 1999. "International Institutions and Gendered Justice." *Journal of International Affairs* 52, no. 2 (Spring): 513–33.

Friedman, Susan Stanford. 2001. "Locational Feminism: Gender, Cultural Geographies, and Geopolitical Literacy." In *Feminist Locations: Global and Local, Theory and Practice*, ed. Marianne DeKoven. New Brunswick, NJ: Rutgers University Press.

Friedman, Thomas. 2000. *The Lexus and the Olive Tree*. New York: Anchor Books.

Gallagher, Chris W. 2002. *Radical Departures: Composition and Progressive Pedagogy*. Urbana, IL: National Council of Teachers of English.

Garver, Paul. 1971. Who We Are. In *The Counter-Culture Joins the Faculty,* 22–28. Cambridge, MA: Church Society for College Work.

Geertz, Clifford. 2000. *The Interpretation of Cultures*. New York: Basic Books.

George, Susan. 2001a. "Neo-liberalism and the New World Order." Paper read at The Graduate Center City University of New York's *Globalization and Resistance Conference,* November 16–17, 2001, New York.

———. 2001b. "Clusters of Crisis and Planetary Contract." *Sand in the Wheels* 105 (21 November): 1–4.

Gere, Anne Ruggles. 1994. "Common Properties of Pleasure: Texts in Nineteenth Century Women's Clubs." In *The Construction of Authorship: Textual Appropriation in Law and Literature*, ed. Martha Woodmansee and Peter Jaszi, 383–99. Durham, NC: Duke University Press.

———. 1997. *Intimate Practices: Literacy and Cultural Work in U.S. Women's Clubs: 1880–1920*. Urbana: University of Illinois Press.

Gilligan, Carol. 1982. *In a Different Voice: Psychological Theory and Women's Development*. Cambridge, MA: Harvard University Press.

Gilmore, Leigh. 1994. *Autobiographics: A Feminist Theory of Women's Self-Representation*. Ithaca, NY: Cornell University Press.

Giroux, Henry. 1983. *Theory and Resistance in Education*. South Hadley, MA: Bergin and Garvey.

———. 1988. *Schooling and the Struggle for Public Life: Critical Pedagogy in the Modern Age*. Minneapolis: University of Minnesota Press.

Giroux, Henry A., and P. McLaren. 1986. "Teacher Education and the Politics of Engagement." *Harvard Educational Review* 6 (3): 213–38.

Glenn, Cheryl. 1995. "Remapping Rhetorical Territory." *Rhetoric Review* 13, no. 2 (Spring): 287–303.

———. 1997. *Rhetoric Retold: Regendering the Tradition from Antiquity Through the Renaissance*. Carbondale: Southern Illinois University Press.

———. 2002. "Silence: A Rhetorical Art for Resisting Discipline(s)." *JAC: A Journal of Composition Theory* 22.2: 261–91.

———. 2004. *Unspoken: The Rhetoric of Silence*. Carbondale: Southern Illinois University Press.

Goggin, Maureen Daly. 2002. "An *Essamplaire Essai* on the Rhetoricity of Needlework Sampler Making: A Contribution to Theorizing and Historicizing Rhetorical Praxis." *Rhetoric Review* 21 (4): 309–38.

———. 2004. "Visual Rhetoric in Pens of Steel and Inks of Silk: Challenging the Great Visual/Verbal Divide." In *Defining Visual Rhetorics*, ed. Charles A. Hill and Marguerite Helmers, 87–110. Mahway, NJ: Erlbaum.

Gonzales, Jennifer A. 1999. "Archaeological Devotion." In *With Other Eyes: Looking at Race and Gender in Visual Culture*, ed. Lisa Bloom, 184–212. Minneapolis: University of Minnesota Press.

Gore, Jennifer. 1993. *The Struggle for Pedagogies: Critical and Feminist Discourses as Regimes of Truth*. New York: Routledge.

Gore, Jennifer, and Carmen Luke, eds. 1992. *Feminisms and Critical Pedagogy*. New York: Routledge.

Gorgias. 1990. *Encomium of Helen*. In Bizzell and Herzberg 1990, 44–46.

Greenbaum, Andrea, ed. 2001. "Bitch Pedagogy: Agonistic Discourse and the Politics of Resistance." In *Insurrections: Approaches to Resistance in Composition Studies*, 151–68. Albany: State University of New York Press.

Grewal, Inderpal. 1998. "On the New Global Feminism and the Family of Nations: Dilemmas of Transnational Feminist Practice." In Shohat 1998, 501–30.

Grewal, Inderpal, and Caren Kaplan. 1994a. "Introduction: Transnational Feminist Practices and Questions of Postmodernity." In Grewal and Kaplan 1994b, 1–33.

———. eds. 1994b. *Scattered Hegemonies: Postmodernity and Transnational Feminist Practices*. Minneapolis: University of Minnesota Press.

———. 2001. "Global Identities: Theorizing Transnational Studies of Sexuality." *GLQ* 7 (4): 663–79.

Grimstad, Kirsten, and Susan Rennie, eds. 1973. *The New Woman's Survival Catalog: A Woman-Made Book*. New York: Coward.

Gross, Louise, and Phyllis MacEwan. 1970. "On Day Care." Boston: New England Free Press. Pamphlet reprint.

Grossberg, Lawrence, Cary Nelson, and Paula Treichler, eds. 1992. *Cultural Studies*. New York: Routledge.

Guy-Sheftall, Beverly. 1998. "Sisters in Struggle: A Belated Response." In *The Feminist Memoir Project*, edited by Rachel Blau DuPlessis and Ann Snitow, 485–92. New York: Three Rivers.

Hall, Stuart. 1992. "Cultural Studies and Its Theoretical Legacies." In Grossberg, Nelson, and Traichler 1992, 277–94.

Hardt, Michael, and Antonio Negri. 2000. *Empire*. Cambridge, MA: Harvard University Press.

Harris, Joseph. 1989. "The Idea of Community in the Study of Writing." *College Composition and Communication* 40:11–22.

Hartman, Joan, and Ellen Messer-Davidow, eds. 1991. *(En)Gendering Knowledge: Feminists in Academe*. Knoxville: University of Tennessee Press.

Hass, Kristin Ann. 1998. *Carried to the Wall*. Berkeley: University of California Press.

Haynes, Mike. 1993. "Theses on the Balkan War." *International Socialism Journal* 83 (Summer). www.isj1text.ble.org.uk/pubs/isj83/haynes.htm (accessed December 3, 2003).

Helmers, Marguerite. 2001. "Media, Discourse, and the Public Sphere." *College English* 63, no. 4 (March): 429–48.

———. 2002. "Popular Icons and Contemporary Memory: An Apology, Year 2001." *Enculturation: A Journal for Rhetoric, Writing, and Culture* 3, no. 2 (Fall). http://enculturation.gmu.edu/3_2/helmers/index.html.

Hennessy, Rosemary. 1992. *Materialist Feminism and the Politics of Discourse.* New York: Routledge.

Hesford, Wendy S. 2001. "Reading Rape Stories: Material Rhetoric and the Trauma of Representation." In Hesford and Kozol 2001, 13–46.

Hesford, Wendy S., and Wendy Kozol, eds. 2001. *Haunting Violations: Feminist Criticism and the Crisis of the "Real."* Urbana: University of Illinois Press.

Hesford, Wendy S., and Theresa A. Kulbaga. 2003. "Labored Realisms: Geopolitical Rhetoric and Asian American (Im)migrant Women's (Auto)biography." *JAC: A Journal of Composition Theory* 23 (1): 77–108.

Hobbs, Catherine. 1995. *Nineteenth-Century Women Learn to Write.* Charlottesville: University Press of Virginia.

Hobbs, June Hadden. 1997. *"I Sing for I Cannot be Silent": The Feminization of American Hymnody, 1879–1920.* Pittsburgh: University of Pittsburgh Press.

Hollis, Karyn L. 2004. *Liberating Voices: Writing at Bryn Mawr Summer School for Women Workers.* Carbondale: Southern Illinois University Press.

hooks, bell. 1984. "Black Women: Shaping Feminist Theory." In *Feminist Theory: From Margin to Center,* 1–17. Boston: South End.

———. 1989. *Talking Back: Thinking Feminist, Thinking Black.* Boston: Southend Press.

———. 1994a. *Teaching to Transgress: Education as the Practice of Freedom.* New York: Routledge.

———. 1994b. "Toward a Revolutionary Feminist Pedagogy." In *Falling into Theory,* ed. David Richter, 74–79. Boston: Bedford.

———. 2003. *Teaching Community: A Pedagogy of Hope.* New York: Routledge.

Hopper, Peggy, and Steve Foldz. n.d. "I Don't Want to Change My Lifestyle—I Want to Change My Life." In *Hysteria.* Boston: New England Free Press.

Hozic, Aida. 2000. "Making of the Unwanted Colonies: (Un)imagining Desire." In *Cultural Studies and Political Theory,* ed. Jodi Dean, 228–40. Ithaca, NY: Cornell University Press.

Hudson-Weems, Clenora. 1993. *Africana Womanism: Reclaiming Ourselves.* Troy, MI: Bedford.

Huse, Donna. 1971. "Women's Liberation and the Politics of Evolution." In *The Counter-Culture Joins the Faculty,* 44–53. Cambridge, MA: Church Society for College Work.

Ignatieff, Michael. 1997. *The Warrior's Honor: Ethnic War and the Modern Conscience.* New York: Henry Holt.

———. 2002. "How to Keep Afghanistan from Falling Apart: The Case for a Committed American Imperialism." *New York Times Magazine,* July 28, 26.

Jackson, Sue. 1997. "Crossing Borders and Changing Pedagogies: From Giroux and Freire to Feminist Theories of Education." *Gender and Education* 9, no. 4 (December): 457–67.

Jacobson, Mandy. 2003. Interview by Katherine Lewis. *Film Nation.* December 3. http://homearts.com/depts/pl/movie/10jacobs.htm'.

James, William. 1898/1978. "The Pragmatic Method." In *Essays in Philosophy: The Works of William James,* ed. Fredson Bowers, Frederick Burkhardt, and Ignas K. Skrupskelis, 123–39. Cambridge, MA: Harvard University Press.

———. 1975. *Pragmatism and the Meaning of Truth.* Cambridge, MA: Harvard University Press.

Jarratt, Susan. 1991a. "Feminism and Composition: The Case for Conflict." In *Contending with Words: Composition and Rhetoric in a Postmodern Age,* ed. Patricia Harkin and John Schilb, 105–24. New York: Modern Language Association.

———. 1991b. *Rereading the Sophists: Classical Rhetoric Refigured.* Carbondale: Southern Illinois University Press.

———. 1998. "As We Were Saying." In Jarratt and Worsham, 1–18.

———. 2000. "Beside Ourselves: Rhetoric and Representation in Postcolonial Feminist Writing." In *The Kinneavy Papers: Theory and the Study of Discourse,* ed. Lynn Worsham, Sidney I. Dobrin, and Gary A. Olsen, 327–52. Albany: State University of New York Press, 2000.

———. 2002. "Sappho's Memory." *Rhetoric Society Quarterly* 32 (1): 11–43.

Jarratt, Susan C. and Rory Org. 1995. "Aspasia: Rhetoric, Gender, and Colonial Ideology." In Lunsford, 9–24.

Jarratt, Susan C., and Lynn Worsham, eds. 1998. *Feminism and Composition Studies: In Other Words.* New York: Modern Language Association.

Jay, Paul. 2001. "Beyond Discipline? Globalization and the Future of English." *Publications of the Modern Language Association of America* 116:32–47.

Johnson, Cheryl. 1994. "Participatory Rhetoric and the Teacher as Racial/Gendered Subject." *College English* 56:411–419.

Johnson, Nan. 2002. *Gender and Rhetorical Space in American Life, 1866–1910.* Carbondale: Southern Illinois University Press.

Johnson, Paul. 2001. "The Answer to Terrorism? Colonialism." *Wall Street Journal.* October 6, 2001. www.opinionjournal.com/extra/?id=95001283.

Jones, Ellen. 2001. "Empty Shoes." In *Footnotes: On Shoes,* ed. Shari Benstock and Suzanne Ferriss, 197–232. New Brunswick, NJ: Rutgers.

Jordan, Joan. 1968. "The Place of American Women: Economic Exploitation of Women." *Revolutionary Age* 1:3. Pamphlet reprint. Detroit: Radical Education Project.

Jordan, June. 1989. "Civil Wars." In *Moving Towards Home: Political Essays.* London: Virago.

———. 1993. "Where Is the Love?" In *Windows: Exploring Personal Values Through Reading and Writing,* ed. Olivia Bertagnolli and Jeff Rackham, 335–40. New York: Harper Collins.

Kaplan, Caren. 1992. "Resisting Autobiography: Out-Law Genres and Transnational Feminist Subjects." In *De/Colonizing the Subject: Politics and Gender in Women's Autobiographical Practice*, ed. Julia Watson and Sidonie Smith, 115–38. Minneapolis: University of Minnesota Press.

———. 1994. "The Politics of Location as Transnational Feminist Critical Practice." In Grewal and Kaplan, 1994b.

Kates, Susan. 1999. *Activist Rhetorics and American Higher Education: 1885–1937.* Carbondale: Southern Illinois University Press.

Kennedy, Rosanne. 2004. "The Affective Work of Stolen Generations Testimony: From the Archives to the Classroom." *Biography* 27 (1): 48–77.

Kincaid, Jamaica. 2000. *A Small Place.* New York: Farrar Straus & Giroux.

King, Martin Luther, Jr. 1963/1999. "Letter from Birmingham Jail." In *The American Values Reader,* ed. Harvey Wiener and Nora Eisenberg, 411–27. Boston: Allyn and Bacon.

Kirin Jambresic, Renata. 1996. "Narrating War and Exile Experiences." In *War, Exile, Everyday Life: Cultural Perspective*, ed. Renata Jambresic Kirin and Maja Povrzanovic, 63–82. Zagreb: Institute of Ethnology and Folklore Research.

Kirsch, Gesa. 1996. "Comment and Response." *College English* 58:966–68.

Kirsch, Gesa E., Faye Spencer Maor, Lance Massey, Lee Mickoson-Massey, and Mary P. Sheridan-Rabideau, eds. 2003. *Feminism and Composition: A Critical Sourcebook.* Boston: Bedford/St. Martin's.

Klein, Naomi. 2002. *Fences and Windows: Dispatches from the Front Lines of the Anti-Globalization Debate.* New York: Picador.

Knight, Janice. 2001. "The Word Made Flesh: Reading the Body in Puritan America." Paper read at *The Emergence of the Female Reader, 1500–1800 Conference*, Oregon State University. Corvallis, May 19.

Kolbert, Elizabeth. 2003. "The Student." *New Yorker*, October 13, 62–74.

Kroll, Jack. 1993. "Fire in the City of Angels." *Newsweek* June 28, 62–63.

Kundera, Milan. 1984. *The Unbearable Lightness of Being.* Trans. Michael Henry Heim. New York: Harper.

LaCapra, Dominick. 1999. "Trauma, Absence, Loss." *Critical Inquiry* 25 (Summer): 696–727.

———. 2001. *Writing History, Writing Trauma.* Baltimore: Johns Hopkins University Press.

Lahr, John. 1993. "Under the Skin. *New Yorker*, June 28, 90–94.

Lamb, Catherine. 1991. "Beyond Argument in Feminist Composition." *College Composition and Communication* 42:11–24.

LeClair, Tom. 1986. "The Lord of La Mancha and Her Abortion." Review of *Don Quixote: Which Was a Dream,* by Kathy Acker. *New York Times Book Review*, November 30, sec. 7:10.

Lee, Amy. 2000. *Composing Critical Pedagogies: Teaching Writing as Revision.* Urbana, IL: National Council of Teachers of English.

Leverenz, Carrie Shively. 1994. "Peer Response in the Multicultural Composition Classroom: Dissensus—A Dream (Deferred)." *Journal of Advanced Composition* 14:167–86.

Lewis, Suzanne. 1999. *The Rhetoric of Power in the Bayeux Tapestry.* Cambridge: Cambridge University Press.

Linenthal, Edward. 2001. *The Unfinished Bombing: Oklahoma City in American History.* New York: Oxford.

Lipson, Carol, and Roberta Binkley, eds. 2004. *Rhetoric Before and Beyond the Greeks.* Albany: State University of New York Press.

Liss, Andrea. 1998. *Trespassing Through Shadows: Memory, Photography, and the Holocaust.* Minneapolis: University of Minnesota Press.

Lloyd, Carol. 1998. "Voice of America." *Salon, December 8,* www.salon.com/bc/1998/12/cov_08bc.html.

Logan, Shirley Wilson, ed. 1995. *With Pen and Voice: A Critical Anthology of Nineteenth-Century African American Women.* Carbondale: Southern Illinois University Press.

———. 1998. "'When and Where I Enter': Race, Gender, and Composition Studies." In Jarrat and Worsham 1998, 45–57.

———. 1999. *"We Are Coming": The Persuasive Discourse of Nineteenth-Century Black Women.* Carbondale: Southern Illinois University Press.

Logie, John. 1999. "The Author('s) Proper(ty): Rhetoric, Literature, and Constructions of Authorship." PhD diss. Pennsylvania State University.

Lorde, Audre. 1984. *Sister Outsider.* Freedom, CA: Crossing.

Louie, Miriam Ching Yoon. 2001. *Sweatshop Warriors: Immigrant Women Workers Take on the Global Factory.* Boston: South End.

Lovibond, Sabina. 1994. "Maternalist Ethics: A Feminist Assessment." *South Atlantic Quarterly* 93:779–902.

Lugones, Maria. 1990. "Playfulness, 'World'-Traveling, and Loving Perception." In *Making Face, Making Soul: Haciendo Caras*, ed. Gloria Anzaldúa, 390–402. San Francisco: Aunt Lute.

Luke, Carmen. 1992. "Feminist Politics in Radical Pedagogy." In Luke and Gore 1992, 25–53.

———. 1996. Introd. to *Feminisms and Pedagogies of Everyday Life,* ed. Carmen Luke, 1–27. Albany: State University of New York Press.

Luke, Carmen, and Jennifer Gore. 1992. *Feminisms and Critical Pedagogy.* New York: Routledge.

Lunsford, Andrea, ed. 1995. *Reclaiming Rhetorica: Women in the History of Rhetoric.* Pittsburgh: University of Pittsburgh Press.

Lynch, Dennis A., Diana George, and Marilyn M. Cooper. 1997. "Moments of Argument: Agonistic Inquiry and Confrontational Cooperation." *College Composition and Communication* 48:61–85.

MacKinnon, Catherine. 1993. "Turning Rape into Pornography: Postmodern Genocide." *Ms.* (July/August): 24–30.

————. 1998. "Rape Genocide, and Women's Human Rights." In *Violence Against Women: Philosophical Perspectives*, ed. Stanley G. French, Wanda Teays, and Laura M. Purdy, 43–54. Ithaca, NY: Cornell University Press.

Magas, Branka. 1997. "Unforgettable Yugoslavia: A Reply to Barratt Brown." *New Political Economy* (November): 465–69.

Manchevski, Milcho. 1994. *Before The Rain.* Grammercy Pictures.

Manguel, Alberto. 1997. *A History of Reading.* New York: Penguin.

Martin, Jane Roland. 2000. *Coming of Age in Academe: Rekindling Women's Hopes and Reforming the Academy.* New York: Routledge.

Martin, Neil. 1994. On Race, Riots, and National Recognition: Stanford's Anna Deavere Smith Looks Back at Two Frantic, Fabulous Years. *Palo Alto Online,* March 18. www.paloaltoonline.com/weekly/morgue/cover/1994_Mar_18.QAAR18.html.

Marx, Karl. 1845/1941. *Theses on Feuerbach. Ludwig Feuerbach and the Outcome of Classical German Philosophy* (1886), ed. C. P. Dutt. New York: International Publishers, 1941.

Mather, Anne. 1974. "A History of Feminist Periodicals, Part I." *Journalism History* 1 (3): 82–83.

————. 1975. "A History of Feminist Periodicals, Part III." *Journalism History* 2 (1): 19–23.

Mattingly, Carol. 1999. *Well-Tempered Women: Nineteenth-Century Temperance Rhetoric.* Carbondale: Southern Illinois University Press.

————. 2002. *Appropriate(ing) Dress: Women's Rhetorical Style in Nineteenth Century America.* Carbondale: Southern Illinois University Press.

Mauss, Marcel. 2000. *The Gift: The Form and Reason for Exchange in Archaic Societies.* Trans. W. E. Halls. New York: Norton.

McAfee, Kathy, and Myrna Wood. 1969. "What is the Revolutionary Potential of Women's Liberation?" *Leviathan* 1 (June).

McCaffery, Larry. 1996. "The Path of Abjection: An Interview with Kathy Acker." In *Some Other Frequency: Interviews with Innovative American Authors,* 14–35. Philadelphia: University of Pennsylvania Press.

McCrary, Donald. 2001. "Womanist Theology and Its Efficacy for the Writing Classroom. *College Composition and Communication* 52 (4): 521–50.

McCrobbie, Angela. 1992. "Post-Marxism and Cultural Studies: A Post-script." In Grossberg, Nelson, and Treichler 1992, 719–30.

McGee, Michael Calvin. 1982. "A Materialist's Conception of Rhetoric." In *Explorations in Rhetoric: Studies in Honor of Douglas Ehninger,* ed. Ray E. McKerrow, 24–45. Glenview, IL: Scott, Foresman.

McLaren, Peter. 1988. "Schooling the Postmodern Body: Critical Pedagogy and the Politics of Enfleshment." *Journal of Education* 170 (3): 53–83.

————. 1989. *Life in Schools: An Introduction to Critical Pedagogy in the Foundations of Education.* New York: Longman.

McWilliam, Erica. 1997. "Beyond the Missionary Position: Teacher Desire and Radical Pedagogy." In *Learning Desire: Perspectives on Pedagogy, Culture, and the Unsaid,* ed. Sharon Todd, 217–36. New York: Routledge.

Miller, Daniel. 1987. *Material Culture and Mass Consumption*. Oxford: Blackwell.

Miller, Jean Baker, and Irene Pearce Stiver. 1997. *The Healing Connection: How Women Form Relationships in Therapy and in Life*. Boston: Beacon.

Miller, Susan. 1991. *Textual Carnivals: The Politics of Composition*. Carbondale: Southern Illinois University Press.

Morrison, Toni. 1993/1999. *The Nobel Lecture in Literature, 1993*. New York: Alfred A. Knopf, 1999.

Mountford, Roxanne. 2003. *The Gendered Pulpit: Preaching in American Protestant Spaces*. Carbondale: Southern Illinois University Press.

Mullin, Molly. 2001. *Culture in the Marketplace: Gender, Art, and Value and the American Southwest*. Durham, NC: Duke University Press.

Munday, Mildred Brand. 1975. "Women, Literature, and the Dynamics of the Classroom." In Schramm 1975, 68–85.

Nafisi, Azar. 2003. *Reading* Lolita *in Tehran*. New York: Random House.

Nikolic-Ristanovic, Vesna. 1999. "Living Without Democracy and Peace: Violence Against Women in the Former Yugoslavia." *Violence Against Women* 51, no. 1 (January): 63–81.

Nilsen, Alleen Pace. 2002. "Sexism in English: A 1990s Update." In Ratcliffe, *Critical Literacies*. 209–218.

Olsen, Lance. 1994. "Introduction to Kathy Acker." *The Artist in Society Conference*. Chicago (October). www.uidaho.edu/LS/Eng/Fugue/fugue10.html.

Olson, Gary. 1999. "Toward a Post-Process Composition: Abandoning the Rhetoric of Assertion." In *Beyond the Writing Process Paradigm: Post-Process Theory*, ed. Thomas Kent, 7–15. Carbondale: Southern Illinois University Press.

Omalade, Barbara. 1987. "A Black Feminist Pedagogy." *Women's Studies Quarterly* 15:33–39.

Orner, Mimi. 1992. "Interrupting the Calls for Student Voice in 'Liberatory' Education: A Feminist Poststructuralist Perspective." In Luke and Gore 1992, 74–89.

Orner, Mimi, Janet Miller, Elizabeth Ellsworth. 1995. "Excessive Moments and Educational Discourses that Try to Contain Them." *Educational Theory* 45 (4): 71–91.

Paine, Charles. 1999. *The Resistant Writer: Rhetoric as Immunity, 1850 to the Present*. Albany: State University of New York Press.

Payne, Michelle. 1994. "Rend(er)ing Women's Authority in the Writing Classroom." In *Taking Stock: The Writing Process Movement in the '90s*, ed. Lad Tobin and Thomas Newkirk, 97–114. Portsmouth, NH: Boynton/Cook.

Penezic, Vida. 1995. "Women in Yugoslavia." In *Postcommunism and the Body Politic*, ed. Ellen E. Berry, 57–77. New York: New York University Press.

Pennebaker, James W. 1991. "Self-Expressive Writing: Implications for Health, Education, and Welfare." In *Nothing Begins with N: New Investigations of Freewriting*, ed. Pat Belanoff, Peter Elbow, and Sheryl Fontaine, 157–69. Carbondale: Southern Illinois University Press.

Perelman, Chaim. 1958/1990. "From *The New Rhetoric: A Theory of Practical Reasoning*." In Bizzell and Herzberg 1990, 1077–103.

PM3: The Women's Movement, Where It's At. 1971. Tallahassee: Florida Free Press.

Pough, Gwendolyn D. 2004. *Check It While I Wreck it: Black Womanhood, Hip-Hop Culture, and The Public Sphere.* Boston: Northeastern University Press.

Powell, Malea. 2002. "Native (Un)Doings: Stories for Revising Rhetorics of Empire." Lecture, Syracuse University, Syracuse, New York, November 13. Abstract available at http://wrt.syr.edu/newsarchive/powell/powell.html.

Power, Samantha. 2002. *"A Problem from Hell": America and the Age of Genocide.* New York: HarperCollins.

Qualley, Donna. 1997. *Turns of Thought: Teaching Composition as Reflexive Inquiry.* Portsmouth, NH: Boynton/Cook.

Queen, Mary. 2005. "Technologies of Representations: Fields of Rhetorical Action in Transnational Feminism." PhD diss. in progress. Syracuse University.

Radway, Janice. 2001. 1984. *Reading the Romance: Women, Patriarchy, and Popular Literature.* Chapel Hill: University of North Carolina Press.

———. "On the Sociability of Reading: Books, Self-fashioning and the Creation of Communities." Keynote address, *The Emergence of the Female Reader, 1500–1800* conference, Oregon State University Corvallis, May 18.

Ramet, Sabrina P., ed. 1999. *Gender Politics in the Western Balkans: Women and Society in Yugoslavia and the Yugoslavia Successor States.* University Park: Pennsylvania State University Press.

Ratcliffe, Krista. 1996. *Anglo-American Feminist Challenges to the Rhetorical Traditions: Virginia Woolf, Mary Daly, Adrienne Rich.* Carbondale: Southern Illinois University Press.

———. 1999. "Rhetorical Listening: A Trope for Interpretive Invention and a 'Code of Cross-Cultural Conduct.'" *College Composition and Communication* 51 (2): 195–224.

———. ed. 2002a. *Critical Literacies: A Reader for Marquette University's First-Year English Program.* Boston: Pearson.

———. 2002b. "Marquette University's First-Year English Program: Critical Literacies." Marquette University Department of English, August. http://academic.mu.edu/engl/firstyear/ (accessed January 17, 2003).

———. 2005. *Rhetorical Listening: Identification, Gender, Whiteness.* Carbondale: Southern Illinois University Press.

Reed, Christopher, ed. 1996. *Not at Home: The Suppression of Domesticity in Modern Art and Architecture.* London: Thames and Hudson.

Rejali, Darius M. 1998. "After Feminist Analyses of Bosnian Violence." In *The Women and War Reader,* ed. Lois Ann Lorentzen and Jennifer Turpin, 26–32. New York: New York University Press.

Reynolds, Nedra. 1998. "Interrupting Our Way to Agency: Feminist Cultural Studies and Composition." In Jarratt and Worsham 1998, 58–73.

Rhodes, Jacqueline. 2005. *Radical Feminism, Writing, and Critical Agency: From Manifesto to Modem.* Albany: State University of New York Press.

Rich, Adrienne. 1973. *The Dream of a Common Language: Poems 1974–77.* New York: Norton.

———. 1975. *Adrienne Rich's Poetry,* ed. Babara Charlesworth Gelpi and Albert Gelpi. New York: Norton.

———. 1979. *On Lies, Secrets, & Silence: Selected Prose 1966–78.* New York: Norton.

———. 1986. *Blood, Bread, and Poetry: Selected Prose 1979–1985.* New York: Norton.

———. 1993. *What is Found There: Notebooks on Poetry and Politics.* New York: Norton.

Richards, I. A. 1936. *The Philosophy of Rhetoric.* London: Oxford University Press.

Ritchie, Joy, and Kate Ronald. 1998. "Riding Long Coattails, Subverting Tradition: The Tricky Business of Feminists Teaching Rhetoric(s)." In Jarratt and Worsham 1998, 217–38.

———. eds. 2001. *Available Means: An anthology of Women's Rhetoric(s).* Pittsburgh: University of Pittsburgh Press.

Roberts, Joan I. 1975. "A Multi-faceted Approach to a Women's Studies Course: Using a Little to Accomplish a Lot." In Schram 1975, 86–106.

Robbins, Sarah. 2004. *Managing Literacy, Mothering America: Women's Narratives on Reading and Writing in the Nineteenth Century.* Pittsburgh: University of Pittsburgh Press.

Ronald, Kate, and Joy Ritchie. 2005. "Pedagogy and Public Engagement: The Uses of Women's Rhetorics." In *Rhetorical Woman: Roles and Representations*, ed. Hildy Miller and Lillian Bridwell-Bowles, 206–28. Tuscaloosa: University of Alabama Press.

Ronell, Avital. 1994. *Finitude's score: Essays for the End of the Millennium.* Lincoln: University of Nebraska Press.

Roof, Judith, and Robyn Wiegman. 1995. *Who Can Speak? Authority and Critical Identity.* Urbana: University of Illinois Press.

Rosen, Stephen Peter. 2002. "The Future of War and the American Military." *Harvard Magazine* 104 (May–June): 29–31.

Rothberg, Michael. 2000. *Traumatic realism: The Demands of Holocaust Representation.* Minneapolis: University of Minnesota Press.

Rowbotham, Sheila. 1973. *Woman's Consciousness, Man's World.* London: Penguin.

Roy, Arundhati. 2001. "The Ladies Have Feelings, So. . . Shall We Leave It to the Experts?" *Power Politics.* Cambridge: South End Press.

Royster, Jacqueline Jones, ed. 1994. "When the First Voice You Hear Is Not Your Own." *College Composition and Communication* 47:29–40.

———. 1997. *Southern Horrors and Other Writings: The Anti-Lynching Campaign of Ida B. Wells, 1892–1900.* Boston: Bedford/St. Martin's.

———. 2000. *Traces of a Stream: Literacy and Social Change Among African American Women.* Pittsburgh: University of Pittsburgh Press.

Ruddick, Sara. 1989. *Maternal Thinking: Towards a Politics of Peace.* Boston: Beacon.

Rush, Florence. 1971. "Woman in the Middle." In *Notes from the Third Year: Women's Liberation*, ed. Shulamith Firestone and Anne Koedt, 18–21. New York: Notes.

Russo, Mary. 1997. *The Female Grotesques: Carnival and Theory*. New York: Columbia University Press.

San Francisco Women's Street Theatre. 1973. "This is a Cranky." In *Guerilla Street Theater Handbook*, ed. Henry Lesnick. New York: Bard, 317–55.

Sánchez-Casal, Susan. 2001. "I Am [Not] Like You: Ideologies of Selfhood in *I, Rigoberta Menchú: An Indian woman in Guatemala*." In Hesford and Kozol 2001, 76–110.

Sandoval, Chela. 2000. *Methodology of the Oppressed*. Minneapolis: University of Minnesota.

Sante, Luc. 1992. *Evidence*. New York: Noonday Press.

Scarry, Elaine. 1987. *The Body in Pain: The Making and Unmaking of the World*. New York: Oxford University Press.

Schell, Eileen E., and Patricia Lambert Stock. 2001. "Working Contingent Faculty in[to] Higher Education." In *Moving a Mountain: Transforming the Role of Contingent Faculty in Composition Studies and Higher Education*, ed. Eileen E. Schell and Patricia Lambert Stock, 1–44. Urbana, IL: National Council of Teachers of English.

Schramm, Sarah Slavin, ed. 1975. *Do-It-Yourself: Women's Studies, Female Studies VIII*. Pittsburgh: KNOW.

Selfe, Cynthia L. 2000. "To His Nibs, G. Douglas Atkins—Just in Case You're Serious About Your Not-So-Modest Proposal." *JAC: A Journal of Composition Theory* 20: 405–13.

Selzer, Jack, and Sharon Crowley. 1999. *Rhetorical Bodies*. Madison: University of Wisconsin.

Sharer, Wendy B. 2004. *Vote and Voice: Women's Organizations and Political Literacy, 1915–30*. Carbondale: Southern Illinois University Press.

Shaughnessy, Mina P. 1977. *Errors and Expectations: A Guide for the Teacher of Basic Writing*. New York: Oxford University Press.

Sheldrake, Philip. 2001. "Human Identity and the Particularity of Place." *Spiritus* 1:43–54.

Shohat, Ella. 1998. Introd. to *Talking Visions: Multicultural Feminism in a Transnational Age*, ed. Ella Shohat, 1–62. New York: New Museum of Contemporary Art and MIT Press.

Shohat, Ella, and Robert Stam. 1994. *Unthinking Eurocentrism: Multiculturalism and the Media*. New York: Routledge.

Shome, Raka. 1999. "Postcolonial Interventions in the Rhetorical Canon: An 'Other' View." In *Contemporary Rhetorical Theory: A Reader*. New York: Guilford.

Shor, Ira. 1980. *Critical Teaching and Everyday life*. Boston: South End.

Shor, Ira, and Paulo Freire. 1987. *A Pedagogy for Liberation: Dialogues on Transforming Education*. New York: Bergin and Garvey.

Simon, Roger, Sharon Rosenberg, and Claudia Eppert, eds. 2000. *Between Hope and Despair: Pedagogy and the Remembrance of Historical Trauma*. Lanham, MD: Rowman and Littlefield.

The Sky: A Silent Witness. 1995. Produced by Amnesty International Film. Directed by Midge Mackenzie. 27 minutes. Women Make Movies. Film.

Smith, Anna Deavere. 1992. *Fires in the Mirror: Crown Heights, Brooklyn, and Other Identities.* New York: Doubleday.

———. 1994. *Twilight Los Angeles, 1992.* New York: Doubleday.

Smith, John E. 1986. "Time and Qualitative Time." *Review of Metaphysics* 40:3–16.

Smitherman, Geneva. 1973. "White English in Blackface, or Who Do I Be?" *Black Scholar.* (May–June): 3–15.

———. 1977. *Talkin' and Testifyin': The Language of Black America.* Boston: Houghton Mifflin.

———. 1999. "CCCC's Role in the Struggle for Language Rights." *College Composition and Communication* 50:349–76.

Smyth, Laura. 2001. *Preaching with Their Hands: The Role of the Carthusians in the Transmission of Women's Texts in Late Medieval England.* PhD diss. Stanford University.

Solnit, Rebecca. 2001. *Wanderlust: A History of Walking.* New York: Penguin.

Sommer, Doris. 1988. "'Not Just a Personal Story': Women's Testimonios and the Plural Self." In *Life/Lines: Theorizing Women's Autobiography,* ed. Bella Brodzki and Celeste Schenck, 107–30. Ithaca, NY: Cornell University Press.

Sommers, Nancy. 1992. "Between the Drafts." *College Composition and Communication* 43:23–31.

Spivak, Gayatri Chakravorty. 1988. "Can the Subaltern Speak?" In *Marxism and the Interpretation of Culture,* ed. Cary Nelson and Lawrence Grossberg, 271–313. Urbana: University of Illinois Press.

Stanger, Dawn. n.d. *UPS Yours.* Underhill, VT: Self-published monthly newsletter.

Starhawk. 2001. "Only Poetry Can Address Grief: Moving Forward after 911." *Sand in the Wheels* 101 (24 October): 6–12.

Stepanek, Marcia. n.d. "Creative Reality: Anna Deavere Smith." *Women in Communications.* www.awic-dc.org/text/womennews_Deavere-Smith.html.

Stewart, Susan. 1991. *Crimes of Writing: Problems in the Containment of Representation.* New York: Oxford University Press.

Stiglmayer, Alexandra, ed. 1994. *Mass Rape: The War Against Women in Bosnia-Herzegovina.* Lincoln: University of Nebraska Press.

The Student Coalition on Organized Labor of Syracuse University. n.d. http://students.syr.edu/scool/ (accessed June 20, 2005).

Sturken, Marita. 1997. *Tangled Memories: The Vietnam War, the AIDS Epidemic, and the Politics of Remembering.* Berkeley: University of California Press.

Sutherland, Christine Mason, and Rebecca Sutcliffe, eds. 1999. *The Changing Tradition: Women in the History of Rhetoric.* Calgary: University of Calgary Press.

Swearingen, C. Jan. 1991. *Rhetoric and Irony: Western Literacy and Western Lies.* New York: Oxford University Press.

"Sweatshops in America: From *The Jungle* to El Monte." n.d. The National Retail Federation. www.sweatshops-retail.org/nrf%20website/history.htm.

"Theater In Search of the American Character." n.d. Ford Foundation. www.forfound.org/publications//ff_report/view_ff_report_detail.cfm?report_index=111.

Tickner, J. Ann. 2001. *Gendering World Politics: Issues and Approaches in the Post–Cold War Era.* New York: Columbia University Press.

Tobin, Jacqueline, Raymond Dobard, Maude Southwell Wahlman, and Cuesta Benberry. 2000. *Hidden in Plain View: A Secret Story of Quilts and the Underground Railroad.* New York: Bantam.

Tompkins, Jane. 1987. "Me and My Shadow." *New Literary History* 19:169–78.

Tong, Rosemarie Putnam. 1998. *Feminist Thought: A More Comprehensive Introduction.* Boulder, CO: Westview Press.

Tonkovich, Nicole. 1993. "Rhetorical Power in the Victorian Parlor: *Godey's Ladies Book* and the Gendering of Nineteenth-Century Rhetoric." In *Oratorical Culture in Nineteenth-Century America,* ed. Gregory Clark and S. Michael Halloran, 158–83. Carbondale: Southern Illinois University Press.

Travis, Trysh. 2003. "Divine Secrets of the Cultural Studies Sisterhood: Women Reading Rebecca Wells." *American Literary History* 15, no. 1 (Spring): 134–61.

Trimbur, John. 1989. "Consensus and Difference in Collaborative Learning." *College English* 51:602–16.

"Tropico" 2002. *MacAddict* 66 (February 2002). Demonstration CD-ROM.

Turner, Kay. 1999. *Beautiful Necessity: The Art and Meaning of Women's Altars.* New York: Thames and Hudson.

United Students Against Sweatshops (USAS). n.d. www.studentsagainstsweatshops.org/ (accessed June 20, 2005).

Upchurch, Gail. 2003. "The Blurred Boundaries of Gender: Alice Walker's Womanist Vision." *Warpland: A Journal of Black Literature and Ideas* 9 (2): 123–30.

Vranic, Seada. 1996. *Breaking the Wall of Silence: The Voices of Raped Bosnia.* Zagreb: Isdanja Antibarbarus.

Walker, Alice. 1982. *The Color Purple.* New York: Pocket Books.

———. 1984a. "Each One, Pull One: Thinking of Lorraine Hansberry." In *Horses Make a Landscape Look More Beautiful*, 50–53. New York: Harcourt, Brace, Jovanovich.

———. 1984b. Womanist. In *In Search of Our Mother's Gardens: Womanist Prose*, xi–xii. New York: Harcourt, Brace, Jovanovich.

———. 1992. *Possessing the Secret of Joy.* New York: Pocket Books.

———. 1997. *Anything We Love Can Be Saved: A Writer's Activism.* New York: Random House.

Walker, Alice, and Pratibha Parmar. 1993. *Warrior Marks: Female Genital Mutilation and the Sexual Blinding of Women.* New York: Harcourt Brace & Company.

Walker, Margaret. 1972. "For My People." In *Black Writers of America: A Comprehensive Anthology*, ed. Richard Barksdale and Kenneth Kinnamon. New York: Macmillan.

Warnock, Tilly. 1996. "Kenneth Burke." In *Encyclopedia of Rhetoric and Composition*, ed. Theresa Enos, 90–92. New York. Garland.

Webb, Marilyn. 1980. Untitled. *off our backs* 10, no. 2 (February): 5, 33.

Weine, Stevan. 1999. *When History Is a Nightmare: Lives and Memories of Ethnic Cleansing in Bosnia-Herzegovina.* New Brunswick, NJ: Rutgers University Press.

Welch, Kathleen. 1990. *The Contemporary Reception of Classical Rhetoric.* Hillsdale, NJ: Erlbaum.

Welch, Nancy. 1997. *Getting Restless: Rethinking Revision in Writing Instruction.* Portsmouth, NH: Boynton/Cook.

———. 1998. "Sideshadowing Teacher Response." *College English* 60:374–39.

———. 1999. Playing with Reality: Writing Centers After the Mirror Stage. *College Composition and Communication* 51:51–69.

Wells, Susan. 1996. "Rogue Cops and Health Care: What Do We Want from Public Writing?" *College Composition and Communication* 47:325–41.

———. 1999. "Legible Bodies: Nineteenth-Century Women Physicians and the Rhetoric of Dissection." In *Rhetorical Bodies*, ed. Jack Selzer and Sharon Crowley, 58–74. Madison: University of Wisconsin.

Wertheimer, Molly Meijer, ed. 1999. *Listening to Their Voices: The Rhetorical Activities of Historical Women.* Columbia: University of South Carolina Press.

Wichterich, Christa. 2000. *The Globalized Woman: Report from a Future of Inequality.* Trans. Patrick Camiller. Melbourne: Spinifex Press.

Williamson, Joseph. 1971. "Recruiting Joshua." In *The Counter-Culture Joins the Faculty,* 39–43. Cambridge, MA: Church Society for College Work.

Willis, Ellen. 2001. "The U.S., Islam, and Terrorism." Paper read at The Graduate Center City University of New York's *Globalization and Resistance Conference,* November 16–17, New York.

Wilson, Ruth. n.d. "Teaching as a Sacred Activity." *Paths of Learning*, July 14, 2004. www.pathsoflearning.org/library/teaching-sacred.cfm.

"Women for a Better Society." n.d. *Womankind: A Newspaper for Women* 1 (1): 1.

"Women Must Control Our Own Medical Destiny." 1974. *Big Mama Rag* 2, no. 7 (May): 7, 11.

Woodward, Susan L. 2000. "Violence-Prone Area or International Transition? Addressing the Role of Outsiders in Balkan Violence." In *Violence and Subjectivity,* ed. Veena Das, Arthur Kleinman, Mamphela Ramphele, and Pamela Reynolds, 19–45. Berkeley: University of California Press.

Wooldridge, Susan Goldsmith. 1996. *Poemcrazy: Freeing Your Life with Words.* New York: Three Rivers.

The Worker Rights Consortium. n.d. www.workersrights.org/ (accessed June 20, 2005).

Worsham, Lynn. 1991. "Writing Against Writing: The Predicament of *Ecriture Féminine* in Composition Studies." In *Contending with Words: Composition Studies in a Postmodern Age*, ed. Patricia Harkin and John Schilb, 82–104. New York: Modern Language Association.

———. 1998. Going Postal: Pedagogic Violence and the Schooling of Emotion. *Journal of Advanced Composition* 18 (2): 213–45.

Yudice, George. 1991. "*Testimonio* and Postmodernism: Whom Does Testimonial Writing Represent?" Special issue: "Voices and the Voiceless in Testimonial Literature." *Latin American Perspectives,* ed. Georg Gugelberger and Michael Kearney. 18 (70):15–31.

Zaeske, Susan. 2003. *Signatures of Citizenship: Petitioning, Antislavery, and Women's Political Identity.* chapel Hill: University of North Carolina Press.

Zboray, Ronald J., and Mary Saracino Zboray. 1996. "Books, Reading, and the World of Goods in Antebellum New England." *American Quarterly* 48 (4): 587–622.

Zimmermann, Patricia Rodden. 2000. *States of Emergency: Documentaries, Wars, Democracies.* Minneapolis: University of Minnesota Press.

Žižek, Slovoj. 1993. *Tarrying with the Negative: Kant, Hegel, and the Critique of Ideology.* Durham, NC: Duke University Press.

———. 2002. "Shadows of the Real: Why the 20th Century Is Worth Fighting For." Lecture, University of Vermont—Burlington, April 8.